RUSSIAN PHRASEBOOK AND DICTIONARY

(Revised)

For my parents,
Karl and Olena Haber

RUSSIAN PHRASEBOOK AND DICTIONARY

(Revised)

Erika Haber

HIPPOCRENE BOOKS
New York

For information, contact:
HIPPOCRENE BOOKS, INC.
171 Madison Avenue
New York, NY 10016

ISBN 0-7818-0190-7

ACKNOWLEDGMENTS

I would like to thank my friends and colleagues for their advice and support on this project. I am particularly grateful to Stephen J. Fields for his concrete suggestions, continued encouragement and boundless friendship.

HOW TO USE THIS BOOK

In order to use this book most effectively, it is essential to read through the first chapter on the Russian language. This chapter provides charts for pronunciation of the English transcription, which allows you to "speak" Russian without knowing the Cyrillic alphabet. Once you are familiar with the pronunciation, look over chapter two, which lists everyday expressions. Each successive chapter covers basic words, phrases and concepts most often encountered by travellers to the Soviet Union in typical daily situations. Chapter fourteen helps you make sense of the Russian number system and provides you with frequently used time expressions. Finally, chapter fifteen gives reference information such as holidays and commonly encountered abbreviations.

A unique feature of this phrase book, the Russian-English, English-Russian Dictionary provides over 4,000 useful words, defined and listed with handy transliteration for easy, on-the-spot pronunciation.

A NOTE ON THE LAYOUT

A slash separates alternative Russian phrases for the same English word.
Russian nouns have gender: they can be masculine, feminine or neuter. Past tense verb forms in Russian also show gender and number. When both the masculine and feminine nominal and verbal forms are given, the masculine is presented first, usually followed by a slash and the feminine form.

TABLE OF CONTENTS

I. THE LANGUAGE

The Cyrillic Alphabet

The Russian language is written in Cyrillic, an alphabet developed from ancient Greek.

Russian letter	English sound	Russian letter	English sound
А/а	ah	Р/р	ehr
Б/б	beh	С/с	ehs
В/в	veh	Т/т	teh
Г/г	geh	У/у	oo
Д/д	deh	Ф/ф	ehf
Е/е	yeh	Х/х	kha
Ё/ё	yoh	Ц/ц	tseh
Ж/ж	zheh	Ч/ч	chah
З/з	zeh	Ш/ш	shah
И/и	ee	Щ/щ	shchah
Й/й	y	Ъ/ъ	hard sign
К/к	kah	Ь/ь	soft sign
Л/л	ehl	Ы/ы	ih
М/м	ehm	Э/э	eh
Н/н	ehn	Ю/ю	yoo
О/о	oh	Я/я	yah
П/п	peh		

Pronunciation

Like English, Russian spelling is not strictly phonetic. One letter may have more than one sound value. That is why we use a system of transcription in which each symbol is assigned a constant value. The English transcription in this book will show you how to pronounce the Russian words even if you do not know the Cyrillic alphabet. The transcription only *approximates* the Russian sounds, however, since no sound is exactly like its Russian counterpart.

1

Vowels

Russian vowels are shorter and purer than the English vowel sounds they resemble. Depending on where the stress falls in a word, the sound value of some Russian vowels may change. The following chart provides the approximate sounds of stressed vowels.

Russian vowel	English approximation	English transcription
а	like the a in 'father'	ah
я	like ya in 'yard'	yah
э	like e in 'bet'	eh
е	like ye in 'yet'	yeh
о	like o in 'note'	oh
ё	like yo in 'yore'	yoh
и	like ee in 'beet'	ee
ы	like i in 'pit'	ih
у	like oo in 'shoot'	oo
ю	like ew in 'pew'	yoo

Consonants

Russian consonants can be pronounced as either 'soft' or 'hard', voiced or voiceless. 'Softening' (or palatalization) occurs when the letter is pronounced closer to the front of the mouth or hard palate. In Russian this occurs when consonants are followed by the vowels я, е, ё, и, ю or the 'soft sign' (ь). Sometimes the palatalization of a letter can change the meaning of a word. For instance, брат (braht) means 'brother', whereas брать (braht') means 'to take'. Voiced consonants, those that make the vocal cords vibrate, become voiceless when they occur at the end of a word or before a voiceless consonant. For instance, 'город' is phonetically represented as 'gohraht', not 'gohrahd' and 'вчера' becomes 'fchehrah', not 'vchehrah'. Likewise, voiceless consonants become voiced before voiced consonants. Fortunately, you do not have to learn the rules for this; all of these distinctions will be made for you in the English transcriptions provided.

2

Russian consonant	English approximation	English transcription
б	like the **b** in 'book'	b
в	like the **v** in 'vote'	v
г	like the **g** in 'goat'	g
д	like the **d** in 'dad'	d
ж	like the **s** in 'leisure'	z h
з	like the **z** in 'zebra'	z
к	like the **k** in 'cake'	k
л	like the **l** in 'lake'	l
м	like the **m** in 'mom'	m
н	like the **n** in 'nap'	n
п	like the **p** in 'pit'	p
р	like the **r** in 'red'	r
с	like the **s** in 'sail'	s
т	like the **t** in 'tail'	t
ф	like the **f** in 'fish'	f
х	like the **ch** in 'Bach'	k h
ц	like the **ts** in 'hats'	t s
ч	like the **ch** in 'chip'	c h
ш	like the **sh** in 'ship'	s h
щ	like **sh** followed by **ch**	shch

Diphthongs

When two vowels occur together in Russian, they are both pronounced. The only diphthongs in Russian are formed by a combination of a vowel and an ee-kratkoe (й).

Russian diphthong	English approximation	English transcription
ой	like the **oy** in 'toy'	o y
ей	like the **ey** in 'hey'	e y
ай	like **ye** in 'bye'	a y
яй	like the above sound with the **y** of 'yet' preceding it	y a y
ый	like the **i** in 'pit' followed by the **y** of 'yet'	i h y
ий	like the long **e** in 'maybe'	e e y
уй	like the **ooey** in 'phooey'	o o y
юй	like the above sound with the **y** of 'yet' preceding it	y o o y

3

Other Letters

separative signs	English transcription	explanation
ь	'	The 'soft sign' is not pronounced. It simply shows that the preceding consonant is soft.
ъ	"	The 'hard sign' is also not pronounced. It separates a prefix ending in a consonant from a stem beginning in a vowel.

semi-vowel		
й	y	The 'ee-kratkoe' is a semi-vowel and always occurs with a full vowel as in diphthongs.

Stress

Stress is very important in Russian. Only one syllable in each word is stressed. Secondary stresses, commonly found in English pronunciation, should be avoided. The location of the stress in a word determines the pronunciation of certain vowels. Unstressed vowels are less distinct and slightly shorter than their stressed counterparts.

unstressed vowel	pronounced like Russian vowel		example
о	a	окно́	- ahknoh, not ohknoh
e	и	еда́	- yeedah, not yehdah
я	и	язы́к	- yeezihk, not yahzihk

Normally stress is not marked in Russian texts. In this book the stressed syllable will be printed in capital letters (ie: пустя́к - poostYAK).
Commonly, in phrases of several short words, only one word will be stressed in the phrase (ie: как вас зову́т?/kahk vahz zahVOOT?).

4

Declension

Unlike English, Russian expresses the relations between words in a sentence by inflection. Nouns and adjectives take different endings depending on their function in a sentence. In Russian these functions are grouped into six different categories called cases. Each case has its own endings. This explains why the same word may have different endings depending on its usage in a sentence.

II. ESSENTIAL EXPRESSIONS

The Basics

Yes./No.	Да./Нет.	dah/nyeht
Maybe.	Мо́жет быть.	MOHzheht biht'
Please.	Пожа́луйста.	pahZHAHLstah
Thank you.	Спаси́бо.	spahSEEbah
Thank you very much.	Большо́е спаси́бо.	bahl'SHOHyeh spahSEEbah
Thank you for the help/information.	Спаси́бо за по́мощь/за информа́цию.	spahSEEbah zah POHmahshch/zah eenfahrMAHtsee-yoo
You're welcome.	Не́ за что./ Пожа́луйста.	NYEHzahshtah/ pahZHAHLstah
Ok.	Ла́дно.	LAHDnah
I beg your pardon.	Прости́те.	prahsTEEtyeh
Excuse me.	Извини́те.	eezveeNEEtyeh
Why?	Почему́?	pahcheeMOO
Because.	Потому́ что.	pahtahMOOshtah
That's the way it is.	Про́сто так.	PROHStah tahk
Good.	Хорошо́.	khahrahSHOH
Bad.	Пло́хо.	PLOHkhah
Can you tell me, please..	Скажи́те, пожа́луйста...	skahZHEEtyeh pahZHAHLstah
Help me.	Помоги́те мне.	pahmahGEEtyeh mnyeh
Is that right?	Пра́вильно?	PRAHveel'nah
Be so kind...	Бу́дьте добры́.	BOOT'tyeh dahbRIH
What?	Что?	shtoh
What's that?	Что э́то?	shtoh EHtah
What does that mean?	Что э́то зна́чит?	shtoh EHtah ZNAHcheet
Where?	Где?	gdyeh
Where to?	Куда́?	kooDAH
How?	Как?	kahk
How far?	Как далеко́?	kahk dahleeKOH
How long?	Как до́лго?	kahk DOHLgah
When?	Когда́?	kahgDAH
Who?	Кто?	ktoh

Who is that?	Кто э́то?	ktoh EHtah
I can't.	Я не могу́.	yah nee mahGOO
I want to	Я хочу́	yah khahCHOO
rest/	отдохну́ть/	ahddahkhNOOT'/
eat/	есть/	yehst'/
drink/	пить/	peet'/
sleep.	спать.	spaht'

Greetings

Hello.	Здра́вствуйте.	ZDRAHSTvooytyeh
Hi.	Приве́т.	preevYEHT
Good	До́брое	DOHbrahyeh
morning.	у́тро.	OOtrah
Good	До́брый	DOHbrihy
afternoon.	день.	dyehn'
Good	До́брый	DOHbrihy
evening.	ве́чер.	VYEHchehr
Good	Споко́йной	spahKOYnoy
night.	но́чи.	NOHchee
Goodbye.	До свида́ния.	dahsveeDAHneeyah
See you	До ско́рой	dahSKOHray
later.	встре́чи.	VSTRYEHchee
Bye.	До ско́рого./	dahSKOHrahvah/
	Пока́.	pahKAH
All the	Всего́	vseeVOH
best!	до́брого.	DOHbrahvah

Introductions

In Russia, people usually address one another by their first name and patronymic. To form the patronymic they add a suffix--usually '-ovich' for men and '-ovna' for women--to their father's first name. For example, if Ivan's father's name is Boris, he would be called 'Ivan Borisovich'. Likewise, if Anna's father's name is Mikhail, her patronymic would be 'Anna Mikhailovna'. If they know one another well or if they are talking to a child, Russians may use a diminutive form like Styopa or Svyeta.

When their names and patronymics are unknown, you may hear men addressed as господи́н

(gahspahDEEN) and women as госпожа́
(gahspahZHAH). These are roughly equivalent to
'Mr.' and 'Mrs.'

What's your name?	Как вас зову́т?	kahk vahz zahVOOT
My name is...	Меня́ зову́т...	meenYAH zahVOOT
Pleased to meet you.	О́чень прия́тно.	OHcheen' preeYAHTnah
It's a pleasure to meet you.	О́чень рад с ва́ми познако́миться.	OHcheen' raht SVAHmee pahznahKOHmeetsah
May I introduce you to...	Разреши́те познако́мить вас...	rahzreeSHEEtyeh pahznahKOHmeet' vahs
my husband.	с мои́м му́жем.	smahEEM MOOzhehm
my wife.	с мое́й жено́й.	smahEY zhehNOY
How are you?	Как вы пожива́ете?	kahk vih pahzheh-VAHeetyeh
I'm fine, thanks.	Прекра́сно, спаси́бо.	preeKRAHSnah spahSEEbah
And you?	А вы́?	ah VIH
I'm ok.	Так себе́./ Ничего́.	tahk seeBYEH/ neecheeVOH
I'm not well.	Мне пло́хо.	mnyeh PLOHkhah
How're things?	Как дела́?	kahk deeLAH

Personal Information

Where are you from?	Отку́да вы?	ahtKOOdah vih
I am from...	Я из...	yah ees
America.	Аме́рики.	ahMYEHreekee
Canada.	Кана́ды.	kahNAHdih
England.	А́нглии.	AHNgleeee
What's your nationality?	Кто вы по- национа́льности?	ktoh vih pah nahtseeahNAHL'-nahstee
I am...	Я...	yah

American. (m/f)	америка́нец/ америка́нка.*	ahmeereeKAHN-eets/ahmeeree-KAHNkah
Canadian. (m/f)	кана́дец/ кана́дка.	kahNAHdeets/ kahNAHTkah
British. (m/f)	англича́нин/ англича́нка.	ahngleeCHAHN-een/ahnglee-CHAHNkah
What are you doing here?	Что вы здесь де́лаете?	shtoh vih zdyehs' DYEHlaheetyeh
I am a tourist. (f)	Я тури́ст/ тури́стка.	yah tooREEST/ tooREESTkah
I'm stuyding.	Я учу́сь.	yah oochOOS'
I'm here on business.	Я здесь по дела́м.	yah zdyehs' pah deeLAHM
What's your profession?	Кто вы по профе́ссии?	ktoh vih pahprahf-YEHSseeee
I am a(n)...	Я...	yah
student. (m/f)	студе́нт/ студе́нтка.	stoodYEHNT/ stoodYEHNTkah
teacher. (m/f)	учи́тель/ учи́тельница.	ooCHEEtyehl'/ -neetsah
professor.	профе́ссор.**	prahfYEHSsahr
businessman.	бизнесме́н.**	beezneesMYEHN
journalist. (m/f)	журнали́ст/ журнали́стка.	zhoornahlEEST/ -kah
nurse.	медсестра́.	meedseesTRAH
housewife.	хозя́йка.	khahzYAYkah
doctor.	врач.	vrahch
lawyer.	адвока́т.	ahdvahKAHT
engineer.	инжене́р.	eenzhehnYEHR
chemist.	хи́мик.	KHEEmeek

---

*Russian does not have articles (a, the), nor does it have a present tense form of the verb "to be."
When there is a different word used for the masculine and feminine forms, both forms will be given, with the masculine form first, followed by the feminine (f) form.
** Not all professions have a masculine and feminine form. Some use one word for both male and female members of their profession.

9

How long have you been here already?	Ско́лько вре́мени вы уже́ здесь?	SKOHL'kah VRYEHmeenee vih oozhEH zdyehs'
I have been here...	Я уже́ здесь...	yah oozhEH zdyehs'
a day.	день.	dyehn'
a week.	неде́лю.	neeDYEHlyoo
a month.	ме́сяц.	MYEHseets
Do you like it here?	Вам тут нра́вится?	vahm toot NRAHveetsah
Yes, very much.	Да, мне о́чень нра́вится.	dah mnyeh OHcheen' NRAHveetsah
No, not at all.	Нет, мне совсе́м не нра́вится.	nyeht mnyeh sahfSYEHM nee NRAHveetsah
We're having a good time.	Мы хорошо́ прово́дим вре́мя.	mih kharahSHOH prahVOHdeem VRYEHmyah
I'm having a wonderful time.	Я здесь прекра́сно провожу́ вре́мя.	yah zdyehs' preeKRAHSnah prahvahZHOO VRYEHmyah
Where are you staying?	Где вы останови́лись?	gdyeh vih ahstahnahVEElees'
At the hotel...	В гости́нице...	vgahsTEEneetseh
Are you married? (m/f)	Вы жена́ты?/ Вы за́мужем?	vih zhehNAHtih/ vih ZAHmoozhehm
Yes, I am/No, I am not. (men)	Да, жена́т./ Нет, не жена́т.	dah zhehNAHT/ nyeht nee zhehNAHT
Yes, I am/No, I am not. (women)	Да, за́мужем./ Нет, не за́мужем.	dah ZAHmoozh-ehm/nyeht nee ZAHmoozhehm
Do you have children?	У вас есть де́ти?	oo vahs yehst' DYEHtee

10

Making Oneself Understood

Do you speak...	Вы говори́те...	vih gahvahREEtyeh
English?	по-англи́йски?	pahahngLEEskee
Russian?	по-ру́сски?	pahROOSskee
German?	по-неме́цки?	pahneeMYEHtskee
French?	по-францу́зски?	pahfrahnTSOOskee
Spanish?	по-испа́нски?	paheesPAHNskee
Only a little.	То́лько немно́го.	TOHL'kah neemNOHgah
None at all.	Нет, совсе́м нет.	nyeht sahfSYEHM nyeht
I understand Russian, but I don't speak well.	Я понима́ю по-ру́сски, но пло́хо говорю́.	yah pahneeMAHyoo pahROOSskee noh PLOHkhah gahvahRYOO
Do you under-stand?	Вы понима́ете?	vih pahnee-MAHeetyeh
No, I don't under-stand.	Нет, не понима́ю.	nyeht nee pahneeMAHyoo
Please speak more slowly.	Пожа́луйста, говори́те ме́дленее.	pahZHAHLstah gahvahREEtyeh MYEHdleenyehyeh
Please repeat that.	Пожа́луйста, повтори́те.	pahZHAHLstah pahftahREEtyeh
Please write it down.	Пожа́луйста, напиши́те э́то.	pahZHAHLstah nahpeeSHEEtyeh EHtah
Translate this for me, please.	Переведи́те, пожа́луйста.	peereeveeDEEtyeh pahZHAHLstah
What does this/that mean?	Что э́то зна́чит?	shtoh EHtah ZNAHcheet
What did he/she say?	Что он/она́ сказа́л(а)? *	shtoh ohn/ahNAH skahzAHL(ah)

*Past tense verb forms for women subjects end in the letter "a."

11

III. AT THE AIRPORT

Passport Control

When you arrive in Russia you will have to go
through "Passport control" (Па́спортный
контро́ль/ PAHSpahrtnihy kahnTROHL') where
they will check your passport and visa. Here they
may ask you several questions to verify your
identity. This is not the place to impress them with
your knowledge of Russian. The less you seem to
know, the sooner they will finish with you.

Your passport, please.	Ваш па́спорт, пожа́луйста.	vahsh PAHSpahrt pahZHAHLstah
Here it is.	Во́т он.	voht ohn
How long are you staying?	На ско́лько вре́мени вы здесь?	nah SKOHL'kah VRYEHmeenee vih zdyehs'
A few days.	Не́сколько дней.	NYEHskahl'kah dnyey
A week.	Неде́лю.	neeDYEHlyoo
Two weeks.	Две неде́ли.	dvyeh neeDYEHlee
A month.	Ме́сяц.	MYEHseets
Two months.	Два ме́сяца.	dvah MYEHseetsah
I'm here...	Я зде́сь...	yah zdyehs'
on vacation.	в о́тпуске.	VOHTpooskyeh
on business.	по дела́м.	pahdeelAHM
to study.	учу́сь.	ooCHOOS'
I don't under-stand.	Я не понима́ю.	yah nee pahneeMAHyoo
I don't know.	Я не зна́ю.	yah nee ZNAHyoo

Customs

You will have to fill out customs declarations upon
entering and leaving the country. Be sure to declare
all jewelry, photographic equipment and other
valuables, so that you do not have to pay duty fees on
them when you leave.

12

English	Russian	Pronunciation
Customs.	Таможня.	tahMOHZHnyah
To pass through customs.	Проходить таможенный досмотр.	prahkhahDEET' tahMOHZHehnnihy dahsMOHTR
Customs Official.	Таможенник.	tahMOHZHehnneek
Have you anything to declare?	Вы хотите что-нибудь объявить?	vih khahTEEtyeh shtohneeboot' ahb"yeeVEET'
Open this suitcase.	Откройте этот чемодан.	ahtKROYtyeh EHtaht chehmahDAHN
What is this?	Что это?	shtoh EHtah
You'll have to pay duty on this.	Вам надо заплатить за это пошлину.	vahm NAHdah zah-plahTEET' zah EH-tah POHSHleenoo
It's for my personal use.	Это для личного пользования.	EHtah dlyah LEESH-nahvah POHL'-zahvahneeyah
It's a gift.	Это подарок.	EHtah pahDAHrahk
May I bring this in?	Можно это провезти?	MOHZHnah EHtah prahveezTEE
It's not new.	Это не новый.	EHtah nee NOHvihy
Do you have any more luggage?	Есть у вас ещё багаж?	yehst' oo vahs yeeSHCHOH bahgAHSH
Is that all?	Это всё?	EHtah vsyoh
I have...	У меня...	oo meenYAH
a carton of cigarettes.	блок сигарет.	blohk seegahrYEHT
a bottle of wine/ whiskey.	бутылка вина / виски.	bootlHLkah veeNAH/ VEEskee
I don't understand.	Я не понимаю.	yah nee pahneeMAHyoo
Does anyone here speak English?	Говорит здесь кто-нибудь по-английски?	gahvahREET zdyehs' KTOHneeboot' pahahngLEEskee

Baggage

English	Russian	Pronunciation
Luggage claim.	Выдача багажа.	VIHdahchah bahgahZHAH

13

Porter.	Носи́льщик.	nahSEEL'shchehk
Are there any luggage carts?	Теле́жки е́сть?	teelYEHSHkee yehst'
Please carry this...	Пожа́луйста, возьми́те...	pahZHAHLstah vahz'MEEtyeh
luggage.	бага́ж.	bahgAHSH
suitcase.	чемода́н.	chehmahDAHN
That's mine, (too).	Это мое́, (то́же).	EHtah mahYOH (TOHzheh)
There's a suitcase missing.	Одного́ чемода́на не хвата́ет.	ahdnahVOH chehmahDAHnah nee khvahTAHeet
Take these things to the...	Отнеси́те э́ти ве́щи к...	ahtneeSEEtyeh EHtee VYEHshchee k
bus.	авто́бусу	ahfTOHboosoo
taxi.	такси́.	tahkSEE
customs.	тамо́жне.	tahMOHZHneh
baggage room.	ка́мере хране́ния.	KAHmeeryeh khrahNYEHneeyah
How much do I owe you? (f)	Ско́лько я вам до́лжен/ должна́?	SKOHL'kah yah vahm DOHLzhehn/ dahlzhNAH
My luggage is lost.	Багажа́ не́т.	bahgahZHAH nyeht

Currency Exchange

It is best to change money at the airport or in your hotel. Hours of operation are often irregular, however, so you should plan ahead. Try not to exchange more than you need because the re-exchange rate is less than the exchange rate and you will lose money. You will have to present your passport and currency declaration form each time you change money. You may bring in as much foreign currency as you like, but Russian money is not allowed out of the country.

Currency exchange.	Обме́н валю́ты.	ahbMYEHN vahLYOOtih

Where can I change some money?	Где можно обменять валюту?	gdyeh MOHZHnah ahbmeenYAHT' vahLYOOtoo
I'd like to change some dollars.	Я хотéл(а) бы обменять дóллары.	yah khahtYEHL(ah) bih ahbmeenYAHT' DOHLlahrih
Can you cash these traveler's checks?	Мóжете вы обменять эти дорóжные чéки?	MOHZHehtyeh vih ahbmeenYAHT' EHtee dahrOHZH- nihyeh CHEHkee
Can you change this for rubles?	Мóжете вы обменять это на рублú?	MOHZHehtyeh vih ahbmeenYAHT' EHtah nah rooBLEE
What's the exchange rate?	Какóй валютный курс?	kahKOY vahLYOOtnihy koors
Can you give me smaller bills?	Мóжете вы дать мне мéлкими купюрами?	MOHZHehtyeh vih daht' mnyeh MYEHLkeemee kooPYOOrahmee

Car Rental

Driving in Russia is only for the very brave at heart. Gas stations are scarce and gas is very expensive. Road regulations are complex and strictly enforced, even on foreigners, who are subject to the full severity of Russian law. You can rent cars at the airport or through some Intourist hotels, but you must have an international driver's license. Insurance premiums are usually included in the rental fee and gas is bought with coupons sold by Intourist, the Russian tourism agency.

Car rental.	Прокáт машин.	prahKAHT mahSHEEN
I'd like to rent a car.	Я хотéл(а) бы взять напрокáт машину.	yah khahtYEHL(ah) bih vzyaht' nahprahKAHT mahSHEEnoo

15

What's the rate...	Сколько это стоит...	SKOHL'kah EHtah STOHeet
per day?	в день?	vdyehn'
per week?	в неделю?	vneeDYEHlyoo
What's the charge per kilometer?	Сколько стоит километр?	SKOHL'kah STOHeet keelahMYEHtr
Are the price of gas and oil included?	Бензин и масло включены в цену?	beenZEEN ee MAHSlah vklyoochehNIH VTSEHnoo
I need it for...	Она мне нужна...	ahNAH mnyeh noozhNAH
a day.	на день.	nah dyehn'
3 days.	на три дня.	nah tree dnyah
a week.	на неделю.	nah neeDYEHlyoo
2 weeks.	на две недели.	nah dvyeh neeDYEHlee
Here's my (international driver's) license.	Вот мои (международные водительские) права.	voht mahEE (meezhdoonah- ROHDnihyeh vah- DEEteel'skeeyeh) prahVAH
Here's my credit card.	Вот моя кредитная карточка.	voht mahYAH kreeDEETnahyah KAHRtahchkah
I am not familiar with this car.	Я не знаком(а) с этой машиной.	yah nee znahKOHM- (ah) SEHtay mahSHEEnay
What is this?	Что это?	shtoh EHtah
Explain this to me.	Объясните это.	ahb"yeeSNEEtyeh EHtah
Show me how this mechanism works.	Покажите мне, как этот механизм работает.	pahkahZHEEtyeh mnyeh kahk EHtaht meekhah- NEEzm rahBOH- taheet
Where can I buy gas?	Где мне купить бензин?	gdyeh mnyeh kooPEET' beenZEEN

16

Where can I buy gas coupons?	Где можно купить талоны на бензин?	gdyeh MOHZHnah kooPEET' tah-LYOHnih nah beenZEEN
Gas pump.	Бензоколо́нка.	beenzahkahlOHNkah
Service station.	Автозапра́ -вочная ста́нция.	ahftahzahPRAH-vahchnahyah STAHNtseeyah
Parking lot.	Стоя́нка (для автомоби́ля).	stahYAHNkah (dlyah ahftahmahBEE-lyah)

IV. AT THE HOTEL

Hotel arrangements must be made before you arrive in Russia and payment is expected in advance. Most Russian hotels open to foreign tourists are run by Intourist. Although you may select an Intourist hotel you would like to stay in, the Intourist agency makes the final decision. A variety of services are usually available at your hotel, depending on its size. The larger ones will have a post office, currency exchange office, gift shop, restaurant, bar, dry cleaner, laundry, hair dresser and barbershop. Intourist hotels also usually have an information or service office (бюро́ обслу́ж-ивание /byooROH ahpSLOOzhehvahneeyeh), where the staff knows some English and can answer your questions, give advice and sometimes book tours.

Check In

Upon checking in at your hotel, you will be given something resembling a temporary visa, called a про́пуск (PROHpoosk), which you will be expected to show at the door to gain entry to the hotel and again to the hall moniter to get your keys each time you return to your room.

Do you speak English?	Вы говори́те по-англи́йски?	vih gahvahREEtyeh pahahngLEEskee
My name is...	Моя́ фами́лия...	mahYAH fahMEEleeyah
I have a reser-vation.	Я заказа́л(а) зара́нее.	yah zahkahZAHL(ah) zahRAHNeeyeh
Here are my documents.	Вот мои́ докуме́нты.	voht mahEE dahkoomYEHNtih
I'd like a single/ double room.	Я хоте́л(а) бы но́мер на одного́/ на двои́х.	yah khahtYEHL(ah) bih NOHmeer nah ahdnahVOH/nah dvahEEKH

18

I'd like a room with...	Я хоте́л(а) бы но́мер с...	yah khahtYEHL(ah) bih NOHmeer s
a double bed.	двуспа́льной крова́тью.	dvooSPAHL'nay krahVAHt'yoo
two twin beds.	двумя́ крова́тями.	dvoomYAH krahVAHteemee
a bath.	ва́нной.	VAHNnay
a shower.	ду́шем.	DOOSHehm
a private toilet.	туале́том./ убо́рной.	tooahlYEHTahm/ oobOHRnay
a telephone.	телефо́ном.	teeleeFOHnahm
a television.	телеви́зором.	teeleeVEEzahrahm
a balcony.	балко́ном.	bahlKOHnahm
a nice view.	хоро́шим ви́дом.	khahROHSHeem VEEDahm
Is there...	Есть...	yehst'
room service?	обслу́живание в но́мере?	ahpSLOOzheevahnee-yeh VNOHmeeryeh
a dining room?	столо́вая?	stahLOHvahyah
a restaurant?	рестора́н?	reestahRAHN
air conditioning?	кондиционе́р?	kahndeetsehah-NYEHR
heating?	отопле́ние?	ahtahpLYEHneeyeh
hot water?	горя́чая вода́?	gahRYAHcheeyah vahDAH
a garage?	гара́ж?	gahrAHSH
May I see the room?	Мо́жно посмотре́ть но́мер?	MOHZHnah pahsmahtRYEHT' NOHmeer
Yes, I'll take it.	Да, э́то подойдёт.	dah EHtah pahdahdYOHT
No, I don't like it.	Нет, мне не нра́вится.	nyeht mnyeh nee NRAHveetsah
Do you have anything else?	Есть ли у вас друго́й но́мер?	yehst' lee oo vas droogOY NOHmeer
I asked for a room with a bath.	Я проси́л(а) но́мер с ва́нной.	yah prahSEEL(ah) NOHmeer SVAHNnay

Registration

Once your reservation has been confirmed, you will be asked to present your passport and fill out a registration form. Your passport may be kept over night for processing, but you should be able to pick it up the next day. If you plan to exchange money, be sure you do it before you register, since you'll need your passport to carry out the transaction.

English	Russian	Pronunciation
Registration.	Регистра́ция.	reegeeSTRAHtseeyah
Registration form.	Анке́та для приезжа́ющих.	ahnKYEHtah dlyah preeeeZHAHyooshcheekh
Fill out this form.	Запо́лните анке́ту.	zahPOHLneetyeh ahnKYEHtoo
Sign here.	Подпиши́тесь тут.	pahtpeeSHEEtyehs' toot
Your passport, please.	Ваш па́спорт, пожа́луйста.	vash PAHSpahrt pahZHAHLstah
How long will you be here?	Как до́лго вы здесь пробу́дете?	kahk DOHLgah vih zdyehs' prah-BOOtyehtyeh
What does this mean?	Что э́то зна́чит?	shtoh EHtah ZNAHcheet
What's my room number?	Како́й у меня́ но́мер?	kahKOY oo meenYAH NOHmeer
My key, please.	Мой ключ, пожа́луйста.	moy klyooch pahZHAHLstah
Take my luggage to my room, please.	Доста́вьте, пожа́луйста, мой бага́ж в но́мер.	dahSTAHF'tyeh pahZHAHLstah moy bahgAHSH VNOHmeer
Is there an elevator?	Есть лифт?	yehst' leeft

The Staff

You will find that the most important person at your hotel will be the hall moniter. It is a good idea to be polite and friendly to her, because she can make your stay much more pleasant. If she likes you, she may miraculously produce hard to find items like lightbulbs and extra hangers.

Hall/Floor moniter.	Дежу́рная.	deeZHOORnahyah
Doorman.	Швейца́р.	shvayTSAHR
Porter.	Носи́льщик.	nahSEEL'shcheek
Maid.	Го́рничная.	GOHRneechnahyah
Receptionist.	Секрета́рша.	seekreeTAHRshah
Switchboard operator.	Телефони́стка.	teeleefahnEESTkah
Waiter.	Официа́нт.	ahfeetseeAHNT
Waitress.	Официа́нтка.	ahfeetseeAHNTkah
Manager.	Дире́ктор.	deeRYEHKtahr

Questions

The voltage in Russia is 220 A.C.. The plugs and sockets are like those used in Europe, so Americans should bring electrical adaptors and converters for their electrical appliances like hair dryers and electric razors.

Can you please bring me...	Прошу́ принеси́те мне...	prahSHOO preeneeSEEtyeh mnyeh
a towel.	полоте́нце.	pahlahTYEHNtseh
a blanket.	одея́ло.	ahdeeYAHlah
a pillow.	поду́шку.	pahDOOSHkoo
a pillowcase.	на́волочку.	NAHvahlahchkoo
an ashtray.	пе́пельницу.	PYEHpeel'neetsoo
some hangers.	не́сколько ве́шалок.	NYEHskahl'kah VYEHshahlahk
some soap.	мы́ло.	MIHlah
Where are the toilets?	Где убо́рная?	gdyeh oobOHRnahyah
Where is the...	Где...	gdyeh
restaurant?	рестора́н?	reestahRAHN
bar?	бар?	bahr
post office?	по́чта?	POHCHtah

information office?	бюро́ обслу́живания?	byooROH ahpSLOO-zhehvahneeyah
hair dresser/ barber?	парик-ма́херская?	pahreek-MAHKHeerskahyah
currency exchange office?	мо́жно обменя́ть валю́ту?	MOHZHnah ahbmeenYAHT' vahLYOOtoo
light switch?	вы́ключатель?	VIHklyoocheeteel'
electrical outlet?	розе́тка?	rahzYEHTkah

Problems

You should be aware that hot water is routinely shut off for several weeks at a time in Russia during the summer for annual repairs.

The ...	... не	... nee
doesn't work.	рабо́тает.	rahBOHtaheet
shower.	душ.	doosh
faucet.	кран.	krahn
toilet.	туале́т.	tooahlYEHT
heating.	отопле́ние.	ahtahpLYEHneeyeh
air condi- tioning.	кондиционе́р.	kahndeetsehah-NYEHR
light.	свет.	svyeht
radio.	ра́дио.	RAHdeeoh
television.	телеви́зор.	teeleeVEEzahr
telephone.	телефо́н.	teeleeFOHN
electrical socket.	розе́тка.	rahzYEHTkah
There is no...	Нет...	nyeht
(hot) water.	(горя́чей) воды́.	(gahRYAHchey) vahDIH
lamp.	ла́мпы.	LAHMpih
light.	све́та.	SVYEHtah
fan.	вентиля́тора.	veenteeLYAH-tahrah
The sink is clogged.	Ра́ковина засорена́.	RAHkahveenah zahsahreeNAH

The door/ window is jammed.	Дверь/окно́ не закрыва́ется.	dvyehr'/ahkNOH nee zahkrihVAH-eetsah
The door doesn't lock.	Замо́к в двери́ не рабо́тает.	zahmOHK vdveeREE nee rahBOHtaheet
Can it be repaired?	Мо́жно почини́ть э́то?	MOHZHnah pahchee-NEET' EHtah

Check Out

I'm leaving today/ tomorrow morning.	Я уезжа́ю сего́дня/ за́втра у́тром.	yah ooyeeZHAHyoo seeVOHdnyah/ ZAHFtrah OOtrahm
Please prepare my bill.	Пригото́вьте мне счёт, пожа́луйста.	preegahTOHF'tyeh mnyeh shchoht pahZHAHLstah
Do you accept credit cards?	Мо́жно оплати́ть креди́тной ка́рточкой?	MOHZHnah ahplahTEET' kreeDEETnay KAHRtahchkay
I think there's a mistake.	Мне ка́жется, что вы ошиблись.	mnyeh KAZHehtsah shtoh vih ahshEEBlees'
Could you please send someone to get my bags?	Пришли́те, пожа́луйста, кого́-нибудь вы́нести мой бага́ж.	preeSHLEEtyeh pahZHAHLstah kahVOHneeboot' VIHneestee moy bahgAHSH
Where can I get a cab?	Где мо́жно пойма́ть такси́?	gdyeh MOHZHnah payMAHT' tahkSEE

If you feel daring, ask your travel agent about the possibility of staying in a Russian Bed and Breakfast--a rapidly growing and very popular alternative to Russian hotels.

23

V. AT THE RESTAURANT

Eating out in Russia can be fun and interesting, but do not expect it to be like at home. Restaurants are relatively inexpensive, but with the exception of some of the regional dining establishments, the food is mediocre at best. Russian restaurant staff are not known for their eagerness to please and service can be quite slow. Do not be surprised to be seated at a table with people you don't know; it is a common practice in Eastern Europe, particularly in smaller restaurants. Dishes that don't have prices on the menu are not available. Your best bet is to ask your waiter for his suggestions and then choose accordingly.

Types of Establishments

Pecторáн (reestahRAHN)
Restaurants generally have a broad choice of dishes, as well as orchestras and dancing. Russians usually go early and make a leisurely evening of it. Reservations are strongly recommended and can usually be made through your hotel. Restaurants typically close by 11pm.

Кафé (kahfYEH)
Cafe's can vary quite a bit, but in general the better ones resemble restaurants, except for a slightly more limited menu. They usually close between 9 and 10 pm.

Кооперати́вное кафé
(kahahpeerahTEEVnahyeh kahfYEH)
Like its name suggests, cooperative cafes are privately run dining establishments. The quality of food and service should be higher due to the profit motive, but be prepared for higher prices, as well.

Столо́вая (stahLOHvahyah)
As in the U.S., cafeteria's can be found in most
institutions like universities, libraries and factories.
They are self-serve and inexpensive. Alcohol is
prohibited.

Заку́сочная/Буфе́т
(zahKOOsahchnahyah/boofYEHT)
Snack bars are found virtually everywhere in
Russia from train stations to music conservatories.
Here one can get a variety of light snacks such as
open-faced sandwiches, fruit, cookies, bottled water
and juices.

Пельме́нная (peel'MYEHNnahyah)
Small cafes specializing in пельме́ни(peel'MYEH-
nee)--small, Siberian, meat-filled dumplings. Many
of these specialty food places do not have seats;
instead, customers eat side-by-side, standing up at
counters.

Бли́нная (BLEENnahyah)
Another type of specialty cafe, the блинная,
offers paper-thin Russian pancakes filled with
caviar or fruit, called блины́ (bleenIH). Блины́
are commonly ordered as hors d'oeuvres in larger
restaurants, but can also be enjoyed as a meal onto
themselves.

Пирожко́вая (peerahshKOHvahyah)
Similar to the Пельменная and Блинная, these
small establishments specialize in пирожки́
(peerahzh-KEE)--large dumplings filled with meat,
cheese or fruit and served with a dollop of sour
cream.

Шашлы́чная (shahshLIHCHnahyah)
For those who want to try dishes from the Caucuses
and Central Asia, this type of restaurant specializes
in шашлы́к (shahshLIHK)--a shish kebob usually
made with lamb and vegetables.

Кафе́-конди́терская (kahfYEH-kahnDEEteer-skahyah)
Closer to what we normally think of as a cafe, this type of establishment serves tea, cookies, cake and other sweets.

Кафе́-моро́женое (kahfYEH-mahROHZH-ehnahyeh)
Similar to Western-style ice cream parlors, these cafes offer ice cream, cookies, and other sweets.

Ча́йная (CHAYnahyah)
This small tea shop offers a variety of teas, coffee, cookies and pastries.

Бар (bahr)
These days most bars are found in Intourist hotels. Patronage is usually limited to hotel guests and only foreign currency is accepted.

The Preliminaries

I'm hungry. (M/F)	Я го́лоден./ Я голодна́.	yah GOHlahdeen/ yah gahlahdNAH
I'd like to eat/drink.	Мне хо́чется есть/пить.	mnyeh KHOHcheht-sah yehst'/peet'
Can you recommend a good restaurant?	Мо́жете ли вы рекомендо-ва́ть хоро́ший рестора́н?	MOZHehtyeh lee vih reekahmyehndah-VAHT' khahROHshee reestahRAHN?
Do you serve breakfast/ lunch/ dinner?	Подаёте ли вы за́втрак/ обе́д/ у́жин?	pahdahYOHtyeh lee vih ZAHFtrahk/ ahbYEHT/ OOZHeen
I'd like to make a reser-vation.	Я хоте́л(а) бы заказа́ть сто́лик.	yah khahtYEHL(ah) bih zahkahZAHT' STOHleek

26

There are 2/3/4 of us.	Нас дво́е/ тро́е/ че́тверо.	nahs DVOHyeh/ TROHyeh/ CHEHtveerah
We'll come at six.	Мы бу́дем в шесть.	mih BOOdeem vshehst'
Where is the coat check?	Где гардеро́б/ раздева́лка?	gdyeh gahrdeerOHP/ rahzdeevAHLkah
Coat check number.	Номеро́к.	nahmeerOHK
Where are the bathrooms?	Где убо́рная?	gdyeh oobOHRnahyah
Is this place taken/ reserved/ free?	Это ме́сто за́нято/ зака́зано/ свобо́дно?	EHtah MYEHstah/ ZAHNeetah/ zahKAHZahnah/ svahBOHDnah
It's taken/ reserved/ free.	Оно́ за́нято/ зака́зано/ свобо́дно.	ahNOH ZAHNeetah/ zahKAHZahnah/ svahBOHDnah
Have a seat!	Сади́тесь!	sahDEEtees'
We'd prefer a table...	Мы предпочи- та́ем сто́лик...	mih preedpahchee- TAHeem STOHleek
in the corner.	в углу́.	voogLOO
by the window.	у окна́.	oo ahkNAH
outside.	на откры́том во́здухе.	nah ahtKRIHTahm VOHZdookhyeh
May we have another table?	Да́йте нам, пожа́луйста, друго́й сто́лик.	DAYtyeh nahm pahZHAHLstah droogOY STOHleek
Is smoking permitted here?	Мо́жно здесь кури́ть?	MOHZHnah zdyehs' kooREET'

Ordering

| Waiter./ Waitress. | Официа́нт./ Официа́нтка. | ahfeetseeAHNT/ ahfeetseeAHNTkah |
| This way please. | Сюда́, пожа́луйста. | sooDAH pahZHAHLstah |

27

May I have a menu, please.	Принесите, пожалуйста, меню.	preeneeSEEtyeh pahZHAHLstah meenYOO
Have you decided?	Вы уже выбрали?	vih oozhEH VIHbrahlee
What do you recommend?	Что вы посоветуете?	shtoh vih pahsah-VYEHtooyehtyeh
I recommend...	Я советую вам взять...	yah sahVYEHtooyoo vahm vzyaht'
Unfortunately, we don't have...	К сожалению, у нас нет...	ksahzhahLYEH-neeyoo oo nahs nyeht
Why not take this instead.	Лучше возьмите вот это.	LOOCHsheh vahz'MEEtyeh voht EHtah
What would you like?	Что вы хотите?	shtoh vih khahTEEtyeh
Go ahead.	Слушаю вас.	SLOOshahyoo vahs
I'll have...	Я хочу...	yah khahCHOO
for appetizers...	на закуску...	nah zahKOOskoo
for the first course...	на первое...	nah PYEHRvahyeh
for the second course...	на второе...	nah vtahROHyeh
for the third course/ desert...	на третье/ на сладкое...	nah TRYEHt'yeh/ nah SLAHTkahyeh
A small portion.	Маленькую порцию.	MAHleen'kooyoo POHRtseeyoo
What would you like to drink?	Что бы вы хотели выпить?	shtoh bih vih khahtYEHlee VIHpeet'
That's all, thank you.	Это всё, спасибо.	EHtah vsyoh spahSEEbah

The Meal

| Enjoy your meal! | Приятного аппетита! | preeYAHTnahvah ahppeeTEEtah |

28

English	Russian	Pronunciation
How is it?	Ну, как вам нра́вится?	noo kahk vahm NRAHveetsah
It's very tasty.	О́чень вку́сно.	OHcheen' VKOOSnah
Please pass me...	Переда́йте, пожа́луйста...	peereeDAYtyeh pahZHAHLstah
Please bring me...	Принеси́те мне, пожа́луйста...	preeneeSEEtyeh mnyeh pah-ZHAHLstah
a cup.	ча́шку.	CHAHSHkoo
a glass.	стака́н.	stahKAHN
a fork.	ви́лку.	VEELkoo
a knife.	нож.	nohsh
a spoon.	ло́жку.	LOHSHkoo
a plate.	таре́лку.	tahRYEHLkoo
a napkin.	салфе́тку.	sahlFYEHTkoo
an ashtray.	пе́пельницу.	PYEHpeel'neetsoo
some salt.	соль.	sohl'
some pepper.	пе́рец.	PYEHreets
sugar.	са́хар.	SAHKHahr
water.	воду́.	vahDOO
bread and butter.	хлеб и ма́сло.	khlyehp ee MAHSlah
Can I have some more of this?	Принеси́те ещё немно́го э́того.	preeneeSEEtyeh yeeSHCHOH neemNOHgah EHtahvah
Would you like anything else?	Что́-нибудь ещё?	SHTOHneeboot' yeeSHCHOH

Complaints

English	Russian	Pronunciation
I have a complaint.	У меня́ жалоба́.	oo meenYAH zhahlahBAH
This is...	Э́то...	EHtah
cold.	хо́лодное.	KHOHlahdnahyeh
hot.	горя́чее.	gahRYAHchee
too spicy.	сли́шком о́строе.	SLEESHkahm OHStrahyeh
too sweet/ salty.	сли́шком сла́дкое/ пересо́лень.	SLEESHkahm SLAHTkahyeh/pee -reeSOHleen

29

sour.	ки́слое.	KEESlahyeh
stale.	не све́жее.	nee SVYEHzhee
tough.	жёсткое.	ZHOHSTkahyeh
overdone.	пережа́рено.	peereeZHAHreenah
underdone.	недожа́рено.	needahZHAHreenah
This is	Э́то	EHtah
dirty.	гря́зное.	GRYAHZnahyeh
I don't like	Э́то мне не	EHtah mnyeh nee
this.	нра́вится.	NRAHveetsah
You can take	Мо́жно э́то	MOHZHnah EHtah
this away.	убра́ть.	oobRAHT'
There's been	Вы не	vih nee
a mistake.	ошиби́лись?	ahshEEBlees'
This isn't	Я э́того не	yah EHtahvah nee
what I	зака́зывал(а).	zahKAHzihvahl-
ordered.		(ah)
I ordered...	Я заказа́л(а)...	yah zahkahZAHL(ah)
I don't want	Я э́того	yah EHtahvah nee
it.	не хочу́.	khahCHOO

The Check

Although tipping was officially discouraged, it is becoming more prevalent now and is always appreciated. Between ten and fifteen percent is about average for waiters. More than extra rubles, Russians often welcome small gifts such as a pack of cigarettes or chewing gum, perfume, cigarette lighters or key chains.

We're	Мы	mih zahKOHN-
finished.	зако́нчили.	cheelee
I have had	Мне	mnyeh
enough.	хва́тит.	KHVAHteet
Bring me	Принеси́те	preeneeSEEtyeh
the check,	мне счёт,	mnyeh shchoht
please.	пожа́луйста.	pahZHAHLstah
There's been	Вы не	vih nee
a mistake.	ошиби́лись?	ahshEEBlees'
How did you	Что вхо́дит	shtoh FKHOHdeet
get this	в э́ту	VEHtoo
total?	су́мму?	SOOMmoo

Is a tip included?	Чаевы́е включены́ в счёт?	chaheeVIHyeh fklyoochehNIH fshchoht
Pay the cashier.	Плати́те в ка́ссу.	plahTEEtyeh FKAHSsoo
We'd like to pay separately.	Мы хоте́ли бы плати́ть отде́льно.	mih khahtYEHLee bih plahTEET' ahdDYEHL'nah
Do you accept...	Вы принима́ете...	vih preenee-MAHyehteh
traveler's checks?	доро́жные че́ки?	dahrOHZHnihyeh CHEHkee
credit cards?	креди́тные ка́рточки?	kreeDEETnihyeh KAHRtahchkee
Intourist food vouchers?	тало́ны на пита́ние Интури́ста?	tahLOHnih nah peeTAHneeyeh eentooREESTah
Thank you, this is for you.	Спаси́бо, э́то для вас.	spahSEEbah EHtah dlyah vahs

Snack Bars and Cafeterias

At Russian snack bars, just like in the U.S., you usually pick up what you want yourself or else ask someone behind the counter for it. Russian cafeteria's are a bit more complex. First, you decide what you want from a printed menu at the cashier's window. Then, you tell the cashier what you want, pay her and receive food coupons for the desired items. Next, you either take the coupons to the serving line and pick up your meal, or you take a seat and someone collects your coupons and brings you your food. Be sure to carry small bills with you because the cashiers very often will not accept large ruble notes.

What's this?	Что э́то тако́е?	shtoh EHtah tahKOHyeh
Please give me one of those.	Да́йте, пожа́луйста, оди́н тако́й.	DAYtyeh pahZHAHLstah ahDEEN tahKOY

31

I'd like (that), please.	Я хотéл(а) бы (э́то), пожáлуйста.	yah khatYEHL(ah) bih (EHtah) pahZHAHLstah
Please give me a piece of that.	Дáйте, пожáлуйста, кусóк э́того.	DAYtyeh pahZHAHLstah koosOHK EHtahvah
May I help myself?	Я могý взять сам(á)?	yah mahGOO vzyaht' sahm(AH)
Just a little.	Тóлько немнóго.	TOHL'kah neemNOHgah
A little more, please.	Побóльше, пожáлуйста.	pahBOHL'sheh pahZHAHLstah
Enough?	Достáточно?	dahsTAHTahchnah
Anything else?	Чтó-нибудь ещё?	SHTOHneeboot' yeeSHCHOH
That's all, thank you.	Э́то всё, спасúбо.	EHtah vsyoh spahSEEbah
How much is it?	Скóлько э́то стóит?	SKOHL'kah EHtah STOHeet
Is that to go?	Мóжно ли на вы́нос?	MOHZHnah lee nah VIHnahs

VI. FOOD AND DRINK

The main thing to keep in mind with regards to the various foods and drinks listed in this chapter is their limited availability. Not everything will be available everywhere you go, so be prepared to experience new foods and methods of preparation.

Breakfast

Where can I have breakfast?	Где можно позавтракать?	gdyeh MOHZHnah pahZAHFtrahkat'
What time is breakfast served?	Во сколько завтрак?	vahSKOHL'kah ZAHFtrahk
How late is breakfast served?	До которого часа можно завтракать?	dahkahTOHrahvah cheeSAH MOHZHnah ZAHFtrahkat'
I'd like...	Я хотел(а) бы...	yah khahtYEHL(ah) bih
(black) coffee.	(чёрный) кофе.	(CHOHRnihy) KOHfyeh
with milk.	с молоком.	smahlahKOHM
with sugar.	с сахаром.	SSAHkhahrahm
without sugar.	без сахара.	byehs SAHkhahrah
tea.	чай.	chay
with lemon.	с лимоном.	sleeMOHnahm
with milk.	с молоком.	smahlahKOHM
with honey.	с мёдом.	SMYOHdahm
with sugar.	с сахаром.	SSAHkhahrahm
cocoa.	какао.	kahKAHoh
milk.	молоко.	mahlahKOH
juice.	сок.	sohk
orange.	апельсиновый.	ahpeel'SEEnahvihy
grapefruit.	грейпфрутовый	greypFROOtahvihy
tomato.	томатный.	tahMAHTnihy
kefir (a yogurt drink).	кефир.	keeFEER

33

bread.	хлеб	khlyehp
toast.	поджáренный хлеб.	pahdZHAHreennihy khlyehp
a roll.	бýлочку.	BOOlahchkoo
butter.	мáсло.	MAHSlah
cheese.	сыр.	sihr
pot cheese.	творóг.	tvahrOHK
jam.	варéнье.	vahRYEHN'yeh
honey.	мёд.	myoht
hot cereal.	кáшу.	KAHshoo
hot buck-wheat cereal.	грéчневую кáшу.	GRYEHCHneevooyoo KAHshoo
hot rice cereal.	рисовую кáшу.	REEsahvooyoo KAHshoo
farina.	мáнную кáшу.	MAHNnooyoo KAHshoo
oat meal.	овсяную кáшу.	ahfSYAHnooyoo KAHshoo
eggs.	яйца.	YAYtsah
scrambled eggs.	яичницу- болтýнью.	yahEECHneetsoo-bahlTOON'yoo
a fried egg.	яичницу.	yahEECHneetsoo
a boiled egg.	варёное яйцó.	vahrYOHnahyeh yayTSOH
a hard-boiled egg.	крутóе яйцó.	krooTOHyeh yayTSOH
salt./pepper.	соль./пéрец.	sohl'/PYEHreets

Appetizers

Served in several courses beginning with a variety of hot and cold appetizers, a Russian meal can last an entire evening. Russian appetizers are quite hearty and may often seem like an entire meal onto themselves.

Appetizers.	Закýски.	zahKOOSkee
For an appetizer I want...	На закýску я хочý...	nah zahKOOSkoo yah khahCHOO

English	Russian	Pronunciation
(black/red) caviar.	(зернистую/ кетовую) икру.	zeerNEESTooyoo/ keeTOHvooyoo eekROO
cold, boiled pork with vegetables.	бужениńну с гарниńром.	boozhehNEEnoo zgahrNEERahm
cold roast beef with vegetables.	ростбиф с гарниńром.	ROHSTbeef zgahrNEERahm
assorted meat/fish plate.	ассортиń мясное/ рыбное.	ahssahrTEE meesNOHyeh/ RIHBnahyeh
smoked/ pickled herring.	копчёную/ мариноńванную селёдку.	kahpCHOHnooyoo/ mahreeNOHvahnnooyoo seeIYOHTkoo
meat/fish in aspic.	мясное/рыбное заливное or студень.	meesNOHyeh/RIHBnahyeh zahleevNOHyeh or STOOdeen'
sausage.	колбасу́.	kahlbahSOO
sturgeon.	осетри́ну.	ahseetREEnoo
lox.	сёмгу.	SYOHMgoo
pancakes with...	блины́...	bleenIH
caviar.	с икро́й.	seekROY
herring.	с се́льдью.	SSYEHL'd'yoo
sour cream.	со смета́ной.	sahsmeeTAHnay
jam.	с варе́ньем.	zvahrYEHN'yehm
small pies filled with...	пирожки́...	peerahshKEE
meat.	с мя́сом.	SMYAHsahm
cabbage.	с капу́стой.	skahPOOstay
rice.	с ри́сом.	SREEsahm
potatoes.	с карто́шкой.	skahrtOHSHkay
meat-filled dumplings.	пельме́ни.	peel'MYEHnee
marinated/ salted mushrooms	мариноńванные/ солёные грибы́.	mahreeNOHvahnnihyeh/sahlYOHnihyeh greebIH

mushrooms baked in a sour cream sauce.	жульéн из грибóв.	zhool'YEHN ees greeBOHF
chicken baked in a sour cream sauce.	жульéн из кýрицы.	zhool'YEHN ees KOOreetsih
Russian vegetable salad.	винегрéт.	veeneegRYEHT
cucumber salad.	салáт из огурцóв.	sahLAHT ees ahgoorTSOF
tomato salad.	салáт из помидóров.	sahLAHT ees pahmeeDOHrahf
cabbage salad.	салáт из капýсты.	sahLAHT ees kahPOOstih
radish salad.	салáт из редíски.	sahLAHT ees reeDEESkee
potato salad.	картóфельный салáт.	kahrTOHfeel'nihy sahLAHT
meat salad.	столíчный салáт.	stahlEECHnihy sahLAHT
saurkraut.	кíслую капýсту.	KEESlooyoo kahPOOstoo
liver pate.	паштéт из печёнки.	pashTYEHT ees peechOHNkee
olives.	маслíны.	mahsLEEnih
radishes.	редíску.	reeDEESkoo

Soups

For the first course I want...	На пéрвое я хочý...	nah PYEHRvahyeh yah khahCHOO
Please bring me some...	Принесíте мне, пожáлуйста...	preeneeSEEtyeh mnyeh pahZHAHLstah
borsch.	бóрщ.	bohrshch
boullion.	бульóн.	bool'OHN
cabbage soup.	щи.	shchee

36

English	Russian	Pronunciation
chicken soup...	кури́ный суп...	kooREEnihy soop
with noodles.	с лапшо́й.	slahpSHOY
with rice.	с ри́сом.	SREEsahm
cold kvas soup.	окро́шку.	ahkROHSHkoo
cold vegetable soup.	свеко́льник.	sveeKOHL'neek
fish soup.	уху́.	ooKHOO
mushroom soup.	грибно́й суп.	greebNOY soop
pea soup.	горо́ховый суп.	gahROHKHahvihy soop
pickled cucumber soup.	рассо́льник.	rahsSOHL'neek
potato soup.	карто́фельный суп.	kahrTOHfeel'nihy soop
spicy Georgian beef soup.	харчо́.	khahrCHOH
tart meat/ fish soup.	мясну́ю / ры́бную соля́нку.	meesNOOyoo/ RIHBnooyoo sahlYAHNkoo
vegetable soup.	овощно́й суп.	ahvahshchNOY soop

Grains and Cereals

I'd like...	Я хоте́л(а) бы...	yah khahtYEHL(ah) bih
rice.	рис.	rees
pilaf.	плов.	plohf
pasta.	макаро́ны.	mahkahROHnih
potatoes.	карто́фель.	kahrTOHfeel'
fried.	жа́реный.	ZHAHreenihy
boiled.	отварно́й.	ahtvahrNOY
mashed.	пюре́.	pyoorYEH
baked.	печёный.	peechOHNihy
buckwheat.	гре́чневую ка́шу.	GRYEHCHneevooyoo KAHshoo

Vegetables

English	Russian	Pronunciation
What kind of vegetables are available?	Какие у вас óвощи?	kahKEEyeh oo vahs OHvahshchee
Cabbage.	Капуста.	kahPOOstah
Red cabbage.	Красная капуста.	KRAHSnahyah kahPOOstah
Beets.	Свёкла.	SVYOHKlah
Tomatoes.	Помидóры.	pahmeeDOHrih
Potatoes.	Картóфель.	kahrTOHfeel'
Radishes.	Редис.	reeDEES
Cucumbers.	Огурцы.	ahgoorTSIH
Egg plant.	Баклажáны.	bahklahzhAHNih
Mushrooms.	Грибы.	greebIH
Peas.	Горóх.	gahROHKH
Green beans.	Фасóль.	fahSOHL'
Wax beans.	Жёлтая фасóль.	ZHOHLtahyah fahSOHL'
Carrots.	Моркóвь.	mahrKOHV'
Onions.	Лук.	look
Leeks.	Зелёный лук.	zeelYOHnihy look
Corn.	Кукуруза.	kookooROOzah
Green peppers.	Сладкий перец.	SLAHTkeey PYEHRehts
Red peppers.	Красный перец.	KRAHSnihy PYEHRehts
Parsley.	Петрушка.	peeTROOSHkah
Turnips.	Репа.	RYEHpah
Garlic.	Чеснóк.	cheesNOHK
Cauliflower.	Цветнáя капуста.	tsveetNAHyah kahPOOstah
Horseradish.	Хрен.	khryehn

Preparation

English	Russian	Pronunciation
How is this dish prepared?	Как приготовляют это блюдо?	kahk preegahtahvLYAHyoot EHtah BLYOOdah
It's...	Онó...	ahNOH
baked.	печёное.	peechOHNahyeh
boiled.	варёное.	vahrYOHNahyeh
braised.	тушённое.	tooshOHNnahyeh

38

breaded.	панирóванное.	pahneeROHvahn-nahyeh
chopped.	рýбленное.	ROObleennahyeh
fried.	поджáренное.	pahdZHAHreen-nahyeh
ground.	мóлотое.	MOHlahtahyeh
marinated.	маринóванное.	mahreeNOHvahn-nahyeh
poached.	отварнóе.	ahtvahrNOHyeh
raw.	сырóе.	sihrOHyeh
roasted.	жáреное.	ZHAHreenahyeh
smoked.	копчёное.	kahpCHOHNahyeh
steamed.	паровóе.	pahrahVOHyeh
stuffed.	фарширóванное.	fahrsheeROHvahn-nahyeh

Meat and Meat Dishes

What kind of meat dishes do you have?	Какúе у вас мяснýе блюда?	kahKEEyeh oo vahs meesNIHyeh BLYOOdah
What kind of meat do you have?	Какóе у вас мясо?	kahKOHyeh oo vahs MYAHsah
For the second course I want...	На вторóе я хочý...	nah ftahROHyeh yah khahCHOO
Mutton.	Барáнину.	bahRAHNeenoo
Lamb.	Молодýю барáнину.	mahlahDOOyoo bahRAHNeenoo
Lamb chop.	Барáнью отбивнýю.	bahRAHN'yoo ahtbeevNOOyoo
Beef.	Говядину.	gahvYAHDeenoo
Pork.	Свинúну.	sveeNEEnoo
Pork chop.	Свинýю отбивнýю.	sveeNOOyoo ahtbeevNOOyoo
Veal.	Телятину.	teelYAHTeenoo
Veal cutlet.	Телячью отбивнýю.	teelYAHCH'yoo ahtbeevNOOyoo
Ham.	Ветчинý.	veetcheeNOO
Roast beef.	Рóстбиф.	ROHSTbeef

Pot roast.	Тушёную говядину.	tooshOHNooyoo gahvYAHDeenoo
Meat patties.	Биточки.	beetOHCHkee
Beefsteak.	Бифштекс.	beefSHTYEHKS
Bacon.	Бекон.	beekOHN
Meat loaf.	Рулет мясной.	roolYEHT meesNOY
Meat balls.	Тефтели.	teefTYEHlee
Sausages.	Сосиски.	sahSEEskee
Shnitzel.	Шницель.	SHNEEtsehl'
Meat stew.	Рагу.	rahGOO
Liver.	Печёнку.	peechOHNkoo
Kidneys.	Почки.	POHCHkee
Cutlet.	Котлету отбивную.	kahtLYEHtoo ahtbeevNOOyoo
Tongue.	Язык.	yeezIHK
Shish kebob.	Шашлык.	shahshLIHK
Ground lamb kebob.	Люля-кебаб.	lyoolYAH-keeBAHP
Goulash.	Гуляш.	goolYAHSH
Beef casserole.	Жаркое.	ZHAHRkahyeh
Chopped meat in a sauce.	Азу.	ahZOO
Beef Stroganoff.	Бефстроганов.	beefSTROHgahnahf
Cabbage rolls with meat.	Голубцы.	gahloopTSIH

Poultry and Game

What kind of poultry/ wild game dishes do you have?	Какие у вас блюда с птицей/ дичью?	kahKEEyeh oo vahs BLOOdah spteeTSEY/ deeCH'YOO
Chicken.	Курица.	KOOreetsah
Duck.	Утка.	OOTkah
Goose.	Гусь.	goos'
Turkey.	Индейка.	eenDEYkah
Woodcock.	Вальдшнеп.	VAHL'Tshneep
Pigeon.	Голубь.	GOHloop'

40

Hazel grouse.	Ря́бчик.	RYAHPcheek
Rabbit.	Кро́лик.	KROHleek
Hare.	За́яц.	ZAHeets
Venison.	Оле́нина.	ahLYEHneenah
Chicken Kiev.	Котле́ты по-ки́евски.	kahtLYEHtih pah-KEEeefskee
Georgian fried chicken.	Цыплёнок табака́.	tsihpLYOHnahk tahbahKAH
Chicken cutlets.	Пожа́рские котле́ты.	pahZHAHRskeeyeh kahtLYEHtih

Fish and Seafood

What kind of fish do you have?	Кака́я у вас ры́ба?	kahKAHyah oo vahs RIHBah
I'll take...	Я возьму́...	yah vahz'MOO
sturgeon.	осетри́ну.	ahseetREEnoo
pike-perch.	суда́ка.	soodAHKah
trout.	форе́ль.	fahrYEHL'
pike.	щу́ку.	SHCHOOkoo
flounder.	ка́мбалу.	KAHMbahloo
carp.	ка́рпа.	KAHRPah
halibut.	па́лтус.	PAHLtoos
cod.	треску́.	treesKOO
salmon.	лососи́ну.	lahsahSEEnoo
tuna.	тунца́.	toonTSAH
herring.	се́льдь.	syehl't'
sea food.	да́ры мо́ря.	DAHrih MOHRyah
prawns.	креве́ток.	kreeVYEHTahk
crayfish.	ра́ков.	RAHKahf
oysters.	у́стрицы.	OOStreetsih

Fruit

Most restaurants do not offer fresh fruit on their menus, but you may be able to buy it at public markets, snack bars and kiosks.

| What kind of fruit do you have? | Каки́е у вас фру́кты? | kahKEEyeh oo vahs FROOKtih |

41

English	Russian	Pronunciation
Are they fresh?	Они свежие?	ahNEE SVYEHzhehyeh
Apples.	Яблоки.	YAHBlahkee
Oranges.	Апельсины.	ahpeel'SEEnih
Tangerines.	Мандарины.	mahndahREEnih
Pears.	Груши.	GROOshee
Peaches.	Персики.	PYEHRseekee
Plums.	Сливы.	SLEEvih
Melon.	Дыня.	DIHNyah
Watermelon.	Арбуз.	ahrBOOS
Bananas.	Бананы.	bahNAHNih
Apricots.	Абрикосы.	abreeKOHsih
Pineapple.	Ананас.	ahnahnAHS
Grapes.	Виноград.	veenahgRAHT
Raisins.	Изюм.	eezYOOM
Figs.	Инжир.	eenZHEER
Dates.	Финики.	FEEneekee
Lemon.	Лимон.	leemOHN
Grapefruit.	Грейпфрут.	GREYPfroot
Prunes.	Чернослива.	cheernahSLEEvih
Currants.	Смородина.	smahROHdeenah
Strawberries.	Клубника.	kloobNEEkah
Wild strawberries.	Земляника.	zeemleeNEEkah
Cherries.	Черешня.	cheerYEHSHnyah
Blackberries.	Ежевика.	yeezhehVEEkah
Cranberries.	Клюква.	KLYOOKvah
Raspberries.	Малина.	mahLEEnah
Blueberries.	Черника.	chehrNEEkah

Dessert

Russians claim that their ice cream, sold at kiosks year-round, is the best in the world. Whether you agree or not, it is certainly worth a taste.

English	Russian	Pronunciation
What do you have for dessert?	Что у вас на десерт?	shtoh oo vas nah deesYEHRT
I'd like...	Я хотел(а) бы...	yah khatYEHL(ah) bih
ice cream.	мороженое.	mahROHZHehnahyeh
a cookie.	печенье.	peechEHN'yeh

pie.	пиро́г.	peerOHK
pastry.	пиро́жное.	peerOHZHnahyeh
honey	медо́вый	meedOHvihy
cake.	пря́ник.	PRYAHneek
cake.	торт.	tohrt
stewed fruit.	компо́т.	kahmPOHT
thin	бли́нчики.	BLEENcheekee
pancakes		
with jam.		
thin fruit	кисе́ль.	keesYEHL'
jelly.		
marzipan.	марципа́н.	mahrtseePAHN
filled	по́нчики.	POHNcheekee
doughnuts.		
an eclair.	экле́р.	ehkLYEHR
chocolate.	шокола́д.	shahkahLAHT
baked	запека́нку.	zahpeeKAHNkoo
pudding.		

Drinks

Russians are a tea-drinking people. Tea is usually served pre-sweetened with honey, jam or sugar. Although coffee has gained in popularity, it is still much more expensive than tea. Bottled fruit juices and waters are also very popular, as are softdrinks. Drinking tap water, especially in St. Petersburg, is not a good idea.

What do you	Каки́е	kahKEEyeh
have to	у вас	oo vas
drink?	напи́тки?	nahPEETkee
Please bring	Пожа́луйста,	pahZHAHLstah
me...	принеси́те	preeneeSEEtyeh
	мне...	mnyeh
(black)	(чёрный)	(CHOHRnihy)
coffee.	ко́фе.	KOHfyeh
with milk.	с молоко́м.	smahlahKOHM
with sugar.	с са́харом.	SSAHkhahrahm
without	без са́хара.	byehs SAHkhahrah
sugar.		
tea.	чай.	chay
with lemon.	с лимо́ном.	sleeMOHnahm

with milk.	с молоко́м.	smahlahKOHM
with honey.	с мёдом.	SMYOHdahm
with jam.	с варе́ньем	svahrYEHN'ehm
a Pepsi.	пе́пси.	PYEHPsee
I'd like a	Я хоте́л(а)	yah khahtYEHL(ah)
glass of...	бы стака́н...	bih stahKAHN
milk.	молока́.	mahlahKAH
lemonade.	лимона́да.	leemahNAHdah
I'd like a	Я хоте́л(а) бы	yah khahtYEHL(ah)
bottle of...	буты́лку...	bih bootlHLkoo
mineral	минера́льной	meeneeRAHL'nay
water.	воды́.	vahDIH
I'd like a	Я хоте́л(а) бы	yah khahtYEHL(ah)
bottle of ...	буты́лку ...	bih bootlHLkoo
juice.	со́ка.	SOHkah
apple.	я́блочного.	YAHBlahchnahvah
cherry.	вишнёвого.	veeshNYOHvahvah
grape.	виногра́дного.	veenahgRAHDnahvah

Alcoholic Drinks

Hard liquor is now available for purchase from kiosks on the street in Russia. The most popular wines of the region come from Georgia and the Crimea. Sweet, and similar to a sparkling wine, Russian champagne is a good choice with dessert. Vodka comes in a variety of flavors and is most often served chilled in 50 gram shot glasses. It is the custom to drink the shot all at once and chase it with bread or raw vegetables.

Do you serve alcohol?	У вас есть алкого́льные напи́тки?	oo vahs yehst' ahlkahGOHL'-nihyeh nahPEET-kee
Which wine would you recom-mend?	Како́е вино́ вы рекоменду́ете?	kahKOHyeh VEEnah vih reekahmeen-DOOeetyeh
How much is a bottle of...	Ско́лько сто́ит буты́лка...	SKOHL'kah STOHeet bootlHLkah

I'd like a glass/ bottle of...	Я хоте́л(а) бы стака́н/ буты́лку...	yah khatYEHL(ah) bih stahKAHN/ bootIHLkoo
wine.	вина́.	veenAH
red wine.	кра́сного вина́.	KRAHSnahvah veenAH
white wine.	бе́лого вина́.	BYEHlahvah veenAH
dry wine.	сухо́го вина́.	sookhOHvah veenAH
sweet wine.	сла́дкого вина́.	SLAHTkahvah veenAH
Georgian wine.	грузи́нского вина́	groozEENskahvah veenAH
Russian champagne (sparkling wine).	росси́йского шампа́нского.	rahsSEEYskahvah shahmPAHNskahvah
beer.	пи́ва.	PEEvah
kvas.	ква́са.	KVAHsah
vodka.	во́дки.	VOHTkee
pepper-flavored vodka.	перцо́вки.	peertsOHFkee
lemon-flavored vodka.	лимо́нной.	leemOHNnay
cherry-flavored vodka.	вишнёвки.	veeshNYOHFkee
dark, smooth, old vodka.	ста́рки.	STAHRkee
whiskey.	ви́ски.	VEESkee
straight up.	чи́стого.	CHEEStahvah
with ice.	со льдо́м	sahl'dOHM
with soda.	с со́довой.	sahSOHdahvay
Azerbaijani/ Armenian brandy.	азербайджа́нский / армя́нский конья́к.	ahzeerbaydzhAHNskeey/ahrmYAHNskeey kahn'YAHK
a gin (and tonic).	джин (с то́ником).	dzheen (STOHneekahm)
a scotch.	шотла́ндское ви́ски.	shahtLAHNTskahyeh VEESkee

Toasts

To your health!	За ваше здоро́вье!	zah VAHsheh zdahROHV'yeh
To peace and friendship!	За мир и дру́жбу!	zah meer ee DROOSHboo
I wish you happiness/ health/ success!	Жела́ю ва́м сча́стья/ здоро́вья/ успе́ха!	ZHEHlahyoo vahm SHAHST'yah/ zdahROHV'yah/ oosPYEHkhah
Congrat-ulations!	Поздравля́ю вас!	pahzdrahvLYAHyoo vahs

VII. SERVICES

Currency Exchange

If you do not exchange your money upon arrival at the airport or in your hotel, you may also exchange it at a foreign-trade bank. Be forewarned, however, that they often keep unusual hours and you may not be able to find one when you need one. Remember that you will need your passport and customs declaration to carry out the transaction. The ruble is the equivalent of 100 kopecks, but due to inflation, kopecks are seldom used very much anymore.

English	Russian	Pronunciation
Currency exchange.	Обме́н валю́ты.	ahbMYEHN vahLYOOtih
Where can I exchange money?	Где мо́жно обменя́ть валю́ту?	gdyeh MOHZHnah ahbmeenYAHT' vahLYOOtoo
Where can I find the nearest foreign-trade bank?	Где нахо́дится ближа́йшее вне́шторг отделе́ние ба́нка?	gdyeh nahKHOHdeetsah blee-ZHAYsheyeh VNYEHSHtahrg ahtdyehlYEHN-eeyeh BAHNka
When does the bank open?	Во ско́лько открыва́ется банк?	vahSKOHL'kah aht-krihVAHeetsah bahnk
How late is the bank open?	Во ско́лько закрыва́ется банк?	vahSKOHL'kah zahkrihVAHeet-sah bahnk
The bank is open from 9:30 am to 1 pm.	Банк рабо́тает с 9.30 до 1.	bahnk rahBOHtaheet spahlahVEEnah deesYAHtahvah dah cheesAH
What is the exchange rate for dollars today?	Како́й сего́дня обме́нный курс до́ллара?	kahKOY seeVOHdnyah ahbMYEH-nihy koors DOHL-lahrah?

47

English	Russian	Pronunciation
I'd like to change some dollars.	Я хоте́л(а) бы обменя́ть до́ллары.	yah khahtYEHL(ah) bih ahbmeen-YAHT' DOHLlahrih
I'd like to cash some traveler's checks.	Я хоте́л(а) бы разменя́ть доро́жные че́ки.	yah khahtYEHL(ah) bih rahzmeen-YAHT' dahROHZH-nihyeh CHEHkee
Can I purchase an international money order here?	Мо́жно здесь доста́ть междунаро́дный почто́вый перево́д?	MOHZHnah zdyehs' dahsTAHT' meezh-doonahROHDnihy pahchTOHvihy peereeVOHT
What's the charge?	Ско́лько сто́ит?	SKOHL'kah STOHeet
I'm expecting money from America.	Для меня́ должны́ быть де́ньги из Аме́рики.	dlyah meenYAH dahlzhNIH biht' DYEHNgee ees ahMYEHreekee
Has it arrived?	Они́ уже́ пришли́?	ahNEE oozhEH preeshLEE
Go to the cashier's office.	Иди́те в ка́ссу.	eeDEEtyeh FKAHSsoo
Where is the cashier's office?	Где ка́сса?	gdyeh KAHSsah
When is the cashier open?	Когда́ ка́сса откры́та?	kahgDAH KAHSsah ahtKRIHtah
Are you the cashier?(f)	Вы касси́р(ша)?	vih kahsSEER(shah)
Here's my identification.	Вот моё удостовере́ние ли́чности.	voht mahYOH oodah-stahveerYEHNee-yeh LEECHnahstee
Here's my passport.	Вот мой па́спорт.	voht moy PAHSpahrt
Where do I sign?	Где мне подписа́ть?	gdyeh mnyeh pahtpeeSAHT'

English	Russian	Pronunciation
May I please have large bills?	Да́йте мне, пожа́луйста, кру́пными купю́рами.	DAYtyeh mnyeh pahZHAHLstah KROOPnihmee koopYOORahmee
May I please have small bills?	Да́йте мне, пожа́луйста, ме́лкими купю́рами.	DAYtyeh mnyeh pahZHAHLstah MYEHLkeemee koopYOORahmee
Can you give me small change?	Да́йте мне, пожа́луйста, ме́лкими моне́тами.	DAYtyeh mnyeh pahZHAHLstah MYEHLkeemee mahNYEHtahmee
I think you've made a mistake.	Мне ка́жется, что вы ошиблись.	mnyeh KAHZHehtsah shtoh vih ahshEEBlees'

Mail

In addition to the regular postal services, the main branch post office provides international telegram and telephone services. In both Moscow and St. Petersburg, the main post offices are open twenty-four hours. Packages to be sent out of Russia must be brought to a post office unwrapped. There they will be weighed, inspected, wrapped and stamped.

English	Russian	Pronunciation
Post office.	По́чта.	POHCHtah
Letter./ Letters.	Письмо́./ Пи́сьма.	pees'MOH/ PEEs'mah
Where's the nearest post office?	Где ближа́йшая по́чта?	gdyeh bleeZHAYshahyah POHCHtah
Where's the main post office?	Где почта́мт?	gdyeh pahchtAHMT
When does the post office open /close?	Во ско́лько открыва́ется/ закрыва́ется по́чта?	vahSKOHL'kah ahtkrihVAHeetsah /zahkrihVAHeet-sah POHCHtah

49

English	Russian	Pronunciation
The post office is open from 9 to 6.	По́чта рабо́тает с 9. до 6.	POHCHtah rahBOHtaheet sdeevyahTEE dah shehsTEE
Where can I find a mailbox?	Где мо́жно найти́ почто́вый я́щик?	gdyeh MOHZHnah nayTEE pahchTOH-vihy YAHshcheek
Can I buy ... here?	Мо́жно здесь купи́ть...	MOHZHnah zdyehs' kooPEET'
envelopes.	конве́рты.	kahnVYEHRtih
post cards.	откры́тки.	ahtKRIHTkee
stamps.	ма́рки.	MAHRkee.
Please give me ten airmail stamps for letters/ post cards to the USA.	Да́йте мне, пожа́луйста, де́сять ма́рок для а́виапи́сем/ а́виаоткры́ток в США.	DAYtyeh mnyeh pahZHALstah DYEHseet' MAH-rahk dlyah AHvee-ahPEEseem/ AHveeahahtKRIHT-ahk vsshah
I'd like to send this letter/post card by...	Я хоте́л(а) бы посла́ть э́то письмо́/ откры́тку...	yah khahtYEHL(ah) bih pahsLAHT' EHtah pees'MOH/ ahtKRIHTkoo
surface mail.	просто́й по́чтой.	prahsTOY POHCHtay
airmail.	авиапо́чтой.	ahveeahPOHCHtay
registered mail.	заказно́й по́чтой.	zahkahzNOY POHCHtay
special delivery.	сро́чной по́чтой.	SROHCHnay POHCHtay
Will this go out today?	Это уйдёт сего́дня?	EHtah ooyDYOHT seeVOHdnyah
I'd like to send this to...	Я хоте́л(а) бы посла́ть э́то в...	yah khahtYEHL(ah) bih pahsLAHT' EHtah f
America.	Аме́рику.	ahMYEHReekoo
Canada.	Кана́ду.	kahNAHdoo
England.	А́нглию.	AHNgleeyoo
Germany.	Герма́нию.	geerMAHneeyoo
France.	Фра́нцию.	FRAHNtseeyoo
I'd like to send this parcel.	Я хоте́л(а) бы посла́ть э́ту посы́лку.	yah khatYEHL(ah) bih pahsLAHT' EHtoo pahsIHLkoo

50

It contains books/ souvenirs/ fragile material.	Она́ соде́ржит кни́ги/ сувени́ры/ хру́пкий материа́л.	ahNAH sahdYEHR-zheet kneeGEE/ sooveeNEErih/ KHROOPkee mahteereeAHL
Wrap it up, please.	Заверни́те, пожа́луйста.	zahveerNEEtyeh pahZHAHLstah
Write the address here.	Напиши́те а́дрес вот здесь.	nahpeeSHEEtyeh AHdrees voht zdyehs'
Return address.	Обра́тный а́дрес.	ahbRAHTnihy AHdrees
Have I received any mail?	Есть ли для меня́ пи́сьма?	yehst' lee dlyah meenYAH PEEs'mah
My name is...	Моя́ фами́лия...	mahYAH fahMEEleeyah
Here's my passport.	Вот мой па́спорт.	vohtmoy PAHSpahrt

Telegrams

Most larger post offices have a telegraph department.

I'd like to send a telegram.	Я хочу́ посла́ть телегра́мму.	yah khahCHOO pahsLAHT' teeleeGRAHMmoo
Where can I send a telegram?	Отку́да мо́жно посла́ть телегра́мму?	ahtKOOdah MOHZH-nah pahsLAHT' teeleeGRAHMmoo
May I have an inter-national telegram form?	Да́йте мне, пожа́луйста, бланк междунаро́дной телегра́ммы.	DAYtyeh mnyeh pahZHAHLstah blahnk meezhdoo-nahROHDnay teeleeGRAHMmih
What is the rate per word?	Ско́лько сто́ит сло́во?	SKOHL'kah STOHeet SLOHvah
What will the total cost be?	Ско́лько бу́дет сто́ить телегра́мма?	SKOHL'kah BOOdeet STOHeet' teelee-GRAHMmah

How long will it take to reach the USA/ England?	Ско́лько вре́мени идёт телегра́мма в США / А́нглию?	SKOHL'kah VRYEH-meenee eedYOHT teeleeGRAHMmah vsshah/ VAHNglee-yoo

Telephones

Phone books are not very common in Russia. Local calls can be made at any time from any phone. International calls, however, can only be made by reservation at the telephone office of the main post office or through your hotel. They must be booked in advance. To make a local call from a phone booth you first drop in the necessary amount of change, pick up the phone, wait for a long, continuous buzz, then dial. Long signals mean the phone is ringing; shorter ones mean the line is busy.

Public phone.	Телефо́н-автома́т.	teeleeFOHN-ahftahMAHT
Where's the nearest telephone?	Где ближа́йший телефо́н?	gdyeh bleeZHAY-sheey teeleeFOHN
May I use your phone?	Мо́жно от вас позвони́ть?	MOHZHnah aht vahs pahzvahNEET'
Hello (on the phone).	Алло́./ Слу́шаю.	ahlLOH/ SLOOshahyoo
Who is this?	Кто говори́т?	ktoh gahvahREET
This is...	Это говори́т...	EHtah gahvahREET
My name is...	Меня́ зову́т...	meenYAH zahvOOT
I'd like to speak to...	Я хоте́л(а) бы поговори́ть с...	yah khahtYEHL(ah) bih pah-gahvahREET' s
He/She isn't in.	Его́/Её нет.	yeeVOH/yeeYOH nyeht
When will he/she return?	Когда́ он/она́ вернётся?	kahgDAH ohn/ahNAH veerNYOHtsah
Tell him/her that I called.	Переда́йте, что я звони́л(а).	peereeDAYtyeh shtoh yah zvahNEEL(ah)

Take a message, please.	Передáйте, пожáлуйста, что...	peereeDAYtyeh pahZHAHLstah shtoh
My number is...	Мой нóмер телефóна...	moy NOHmeer teeleeFOHNah
Ask him/her to call me back.	Попросúте егó/её позвонúть мне.	pahprahSEEtyeh yeeVOH/yeeYOH pahzvahNEET' mnyeh
I don't under-stand.	Я не понимáю.	yah nyeh pahneeMAHyoo
Do you speak English?	Вы говорúте по-англúйски?	vih gahvahREEtyeh pahahngLEEskee
I can't hear you.	Я вас не слы́шу.	yah vahs nee SLIHSHoo
Can you speak slowly/ louder?	Говорúте помéдленнее/ грóмче, пожáлуйста.	gahvahREEtyeh pahMYEHdleenneh -yeh/GROHMcheh pahZHAHLstah
With whom do you want to speak?	С кем вы хотúте говорúть?	skyehm vih khahTEEtyeh gahvahREET'
You've got the wrong number.	У вас непрáвильный нóмер.	oo vahs neePRAHveel'nihy NOHmeer
Dial again.	Наберúте ещё раз.	nahbeeREEtyeh yeeSHCHOH rahs
The number has been changed.	Нóмер телефóна поменя́лся.	NOHmeer teeleeFOHNah pahmeenYAHLsah
The phone is broken.	Телефóн не рабóтает.	teeleeFOHN nee rahBOHtaheet
Long-distance phone call.	Междугорóдный разговóр.	meezhdoogahROHD-nihy rahzgahv-OHR
International phone call.	Междунарóдный разговóр.	meezhdoonahROHD-nihy rahzgahv-OHR
Can I dial direct?	Могý ли я сам(á) набрáть?	mahGOO lee yah sahm(AH) nahbRAHT'

English	Russian	Pronunciation
Operator, please get me this number.	Телефони́стка, пожа́луйста, соедини́те меня́ с э́тим но́мером.	teeleefahnEESTkah pahZHAHLstah saheedeeNEEtyeh meenYAH SEHteem NOHmeerahm
I'd like to order a phone call to the USA.	Я хоте́л(а) бы заказа́ть разгово́р с США.	yah khahtYEHL(ah) bih zahkahzAHT' rahzgahvOHR ssshah
How much does a call to New York cost?	Ско́лько сто́ит телефо́нный разгово́р с Нью-Йо́рком?	SKOHL'kah STOHeet teeleeFOHNnihy rahzgahvOHR sn'yooYOHRkahm
I want to reverse the charges.	Я хочу́, что́бы разгово́р был за счёт вызыва́емого.	yah khaCHOO SHTOHbih rahzgahvOHR bihl zah shchoht vihzih- VAHeemahvah
What number are you calling?	Како́й но́мер?	kahKOY NOHmeer
Do I have to wait long?	Мне до́лго жда́ть?	mnyeh DOHLgah zhdaht'
How long do you want to speak?	Ско́лько мину́т вы хоти́те говори́ть?	SKOHL'kah meenOOT vih khahTEEtyeh gahvahrEET'
Wait a minute!	Подожди́те мину́точку!	pahdahzhDEEtyeh meeNOOtahchkoo
Your call is in booth #2.	Пройди́те в каби́ну но́мер два.	prahyDEEtyeh fkahBEEnoo NOHmeer dvah
Your time is up.	Вре́мя ко́нчилось.	VRYEHmyah KOHNcheelahs'
How much did the call cost?	Ско́лько сто́ил разгово́р?	SKOHL'kah STOHeel rahzgahvOHR
There's a call for you.	Вас вызыва́ют по телефо́ну.	vahs vihzihVAHyoot pah teeleeFOHNoo
Hold on, please.	Не веша́йте тру́бку.	nee veeSHAYtyeh TROOPkoo
It's busy.	Но́мер за́нят.	NOHmyehr ZAHNyaht

There's no answer.	Никто́ не отвеча́ет.	neeKTOH nee ahtveeCHAYyeht
I can't get through.	Я не могу́ дозвони́тся.	yah nee mahGOO dahzvahNEEtsah
We've been cut off.	Нас разъедини́ли.	nahs rahz"eedee-NEElee

Dry Cleaning and Laundry

Laundry and dry cleaning services are often available in the larger Intourist hotels. Ask your floor monitor (дежу́рная) for details and assistance.

Where can I get my laundry washed?	Куда́ отда́ть бельё в сти́рку?	kooDAH ahdDAHT' beel'YOH FSTEERkoo
Where is the nearest dry cleaner?	Где ближа́йшая химчи́стка?	gdyeh bleeZHAY-shahyah kheem-CHEESTkah
I need these things...	Эти ве́щи на́до...	EHtee VYEHshchee NAHdah
dry cleaned.	почи́стить.	pahCHEESTeet'
washed.	вы́стирать.	VIHsteeraht'
ironed.	погла́дить.	pahgLAHdeet'
No starch, please.	Не крахма́льте, пожа́луйста.	nee krahkhMAHL'tyeh pahZHAHLstah
Can you get this stain out?	Мо́жно вы́вести э́то пятно́?	MOHZHnah VIHveestee EHtah peetNOH
Can you mend/sew this?	Вы э́то мо́жете зашто́пать/ заши́ть?	vih EHtah MOHZH-ehtyeh zahSHTOH-paht'/zahSHEET'
Sew on this button, please.	Прише́йте, пожа́луйста, э́ту пу́говицу.	preeSHEYtyeh pah-ZHAHLstah EHtoo POOgahveetsoo
When will it be ready?	Когда́ э́то бу́дет гото́во?	kahgDAH EHtah BOOdeet gahTOHvah

Is my laundry ready?	Бельё готóво?	beel'YOH gahTOHvah
How much do I owe you? (f)	Скóлько я вам дóлжен (должнá)?	SKOHL'kah yah vahm DOHLzhehn (dahlzhNAH)
This isn't mine.	Это не моё.	EHtah nee mahYOH
I'm missing something.	Чегó-то не хватáет.	cheeVOHtah nee khvahTAHeet
This is torn.	Это пóрвано.	EHtah POHRvahnah
Can I borrow...	Мóжно попросúть на минýту...	MOHZHnah pahprahSEET' nah meeNOOtoo
a needle and thread?	игóлку и нúтку?	eegOHLkoo ee NEETkoo
scissors?	нóжницы?	NOHZHneetsih

Optician

Optician.	Оптика./Очкú.	OHPteekah/achKEE
Where can I find an optician?	Где мне найтú óптику?	gdyeh mnyeh nayTEE OHPteekoo
I have broken my glasses.	У меня разбúлись очкú.	oo meenYAH rahsBEElees' ahchKEE
The frame is broken.	Опрáва слóмана.	ahpRAHvah SLOHmahnah
The lenses are broken.	Стёкла разбúты.	STYOHKlah rahzBEEtih
Can you fix them?	Мóжно их починúть?	MOHZHnah eekh pahcheenEET'
How long will it take?	Когдá онú бýдут готóвы?	kahgDAH ahNEE BOOdoot gahTOHvih
Here's my prescription.	Вот мóй рецéпт.	vohtmoy reetsEHPT

I've lost/ damaged a contact lense.	Я потеря́л(а)/ испо́ртил(а) мою́ конта́ктную ли́нзу.	yah pahteerYAHL-(ah)/eesPOHRteel-(ah) mahYOO kahnTAHKTnooyoo LEENzoo
Can you replace it?	Есть ли у вас таки́е ли́нзы?	yehst' lee oo vahs tahKEEyeh LEENzih
I have hard/soft lenses.	У меня́ тве́рдые/ мя́гкие ли́нзы.	oo meenYAH TVYOHRdihyeh/ MYAHKHkeeyeh LEENzih
Do you sell contact lens fluid?	Есть ли у вас жи́дкость для конта́ктных линз?	yehst' lee oo vahs ZHEETkahst' dlyah kahnTAHKTnihkh leenz

Shoe Repair

Shoe repair.	Ремо́нт о́буви.	reemOHNT OHboovee
Shine my shoes, please.	Почи́сти́те ту́фли, пожа́луйста.	pahcheesTEEtyeh TOOflee pahZHAHLstah
Can these shoes be repaired?	Мо́жно почини́ть э́ти ту́фли?	MOHZHnah pahcheenEET' EHtee TOOflee
I need new soles/ heels.	Мне нужны́ но́вые подме́тки/ каблу́ки.	mnyeh noozhNIH NOHvihyeh pahd-MYOHTkee/ kahbLOOkee
The heel is broken.	Каблу́к сло́ман	kahbLOOK SLOHmahn
The strap is ripped.	Ремешо́к по́рван.	reemeeshOHK POHRvahn
Can this be sewn up?	Мо́жно э́то заши́ть?	MOHZHnah EHtah zahSHEET'
How much will it cost?	Ско́лько э́то бу́дет сто́ить?	SKOHL'kah EHtah BOOdeet STOHeet'
When will they be ready?	Когда́ они́ бу́дут гото́вы?	kahgDAH ahNEE BOOdoot gahTOHvih

Barber/Hairdresser

English	Russian	Pronunciation
Barber./Hair-dresser.	Парик-махерская.	pahreekMAHKHeer-skahyah
Where is the nearest barber?	Где ближайшая парик-махерская?	gdyeh bleeZHAY-shahyah pahreek-MAHKHeerskahyah
Is there a hair-dresser in the hotel?	В этой гостинице есть парик-махерская?	VEHtay gahsTEE-neetseh yehst' pahreek-MAHKHeerskahyah
Can I make an appoint-ment for Monday?	Можно записаться на понедельник?	MOHZHnah zahpee-SAHTsah nah pahneedYEHL'neek
Have a seat.	Садитесь.	sahDEEtees'
Hair cut.	Стрижка.	STREESHkah
Hair style.	Причёска.	preeCHOHSkah
Part (hair).	Пробор.	prahBOHR
Dye.	Покраска.	pahKRAHSkah
A hair cut, please.	Постригите меня, пожалуйста.	pahstreeGEEtyeh meenYAH pah-ZHAHLstah
Just a trim.	Меня только подстричь	meenYAH TOHL'kah pahtSTREECH
Take a little off the sides, please.	Подстригите немножко с боков, пожалуйста.	pahtstreeGEEtyeh neemNOHSHkah sbahkOHF pahZHAHLstah
Not too short.	Не слишком коротко.	nee SLEESHkahm KOHrahtkah
Just a little more, please.	Чуть побольше, пожалуйста.	choot' pahBOHL'-sheh pahZHAHL-stah
Shampoo and set, please.	Вымойте и уложите волосы, пожалуйста.	VIHmaytyeh ee oolahZHEEtyeh VOHlahsih pahZHAHLstah
Blow-dry my hair.	Уложите мне волосы феном.	oolahZHEEtyeh mnyeh VOHlahsih FYEHNahm

58

A shave, please.	Побре́йте меня́, пожа́луйста.	pahBREYtyeh meenYAH pahZHAHLstah
Trim my beard/ mustache/ sideburns.	Подстриги́те мою́ бо́роду/ мои́ усы́/ мои́ бакенба́рды.	pahtstreeGEEtyeh mahYOO BOHrah-doo/mahEE ooSIH/ mahEE bahkeen-BAHRdih
Dye my hair in this color.	Покра́сьте во́лосы в э́тот цвет.	pahKRAHS'tyeh VOHlahsih VEHtaht tsvyeht
I would like a facial/ manicure/ permanent.	Я хоте́ла бы произвести́ чи́стку и масса́ж лица́/ маникю́р/ пермане́нт.	yah khahtYEHlah bih praheezvyehsTEE CHEESTkoo ee mahsSAHSH leeTSAH/ mahneekYOOR/ peermahnYEHNT
Thank you.	Спаси́бо.	spahSEEbah
How much do I owe you? (f).	Ско́лько я вам до́лжен (должна́)?	SKOHL'kah yah vahm DOHLzhehn (dahlzhNAH)

Film Development

It is best to bring enough film and photography supplies from home. If you do purchase Russian film, be sure to have it developed at a "photo-laboratory" (фотолаборато́рия) before you leave, as their processing procedure differs from ours. Western film and batteries are now available for purchase in Russia, but they are very expensive. Remember that it is impolite to photograph people without their permission.

Photography.	Фотогра́фия.	fahtahGRAHfeeyah
Camera.	Фотоаппара́т.	fahtahahppahRAHT
Film.	Плёнка.	PLYOHNkah
Black and white film.	Чёрно-бе́лая плёнка.	CHOHRnah-BYEHlahyah PLYOHNkah
Color film.	Цветна́я плёнка.	tsveetNAHyah PLYOHNkah

59

Thirty-six exposure.	Три́дцать шесть ка́дров.	TREEtsaht' shehst' KAHDrahv
How much does processing cost?	Ско́лько сто́ит прояви́ть плёнку?	SKOHL'kah STOHeet praheeVEET' PLYOHNkoo
I'd like this enlarged.	Я хоте́л(а) бы увели́чить э́то.	yah khahtYEHL(ah) bih ooveelEECHeet' EHtah
I'd like another copy of this print.	Я хоте́л(а) бы ещё одну́ ко́пию.	yah khahtYEHL(ah) bih yeeSHCHOH ahdNOO KOHpee-yoo
When will they be ready?	Когда́ бу́дут гото́вы фотогра́фии?	kahgDAH BOOdoot gahTOHvih fahtah-GRAHfeeee

VIII. TRANSPORTATION

Public transportation in Russia is quite extensive and relatively efficient. Buses, street cars and trolleys all run from 6 am till 1 am. Tickets are usually purchased beforehand at subway stations, but it is not enough to simply have a ticket. The paper ticket must be punched once on board by puncher mechanisms located strategically throughout the bus or trolley. If the bus is crowded, it is common practice to merely pass your ticket towards the direction of the box and the punched ticket will be passed back to you. Spot checks are done occasionally and passengers without punched tickets are fined and sometimes expelled from the bus or trolley. Stops are marked with an 'A' for buses, 'T' for trolleys and a different capital 'T' for street cars. These signs also carry the name of the stop, the name of the terminal stop, and time table or interval between buses. The routes are denoted by numbers. If a passenger asks you if you are getting off and you are not, it is expected that you will move out of the way for him to get by.

Buses, Street Cars and Trolleys

Bus.	Автобус.	ahfTOHboos
Street car.	Трамвай.	trahmVAY
Trolley.	Троллейбус.	trahlLEYboos
Where is the bus/street car/trolley stop?	Где остановка автобуса/ трамвая/ троллейбуса?	gdyeh ahstahnOHF-kah ahfTOHboosah /trahmVAHyah /trahlLEYboosah
How often does the bus/ street car/ trolley run?	Как часто останавли- вается автобус/ трамвай/ троллейбус?	kahk CHAHstah ahstahNAHVlee-vaheetsah ahfTOHboos/ trahmVAY/ trahlLEYboos
When's the next bus?	Когда идёт следующий автобус?	kahgDAH eedYOHT SLYEHdooyooshch-eey ahfTOHboos

61

Where can I buy a ticket?	Где мне купить билет?	gdyeh mnyeh kooPEET' beeLYEHT
Bus driver.	Води́тель.	vahDEEteel'
Fare.	Пла́та за прое́зд.	PLAHtah zah prahYEHST
Monthly pass.	Ме́сячный билет.	MYEHseechnihy beelYEHT
Cash box.	Ка́сса.	KAHSsah
Pass me a ticket, please.	Переда́йте мне, пожа́луйста, билет.	peereeDAYtyeh mnyeh pahZHAHLstah beelYEHT
What bus do I take to get to Red Square?	Како́й абто́бус идёт до Кра́сной пло́щади?	kahKOY ahfTOHboos eedYOHT dah KRAHSnay PLOHshchahdee
Do I have to transfer?	Мне на́до пересе́сть?	mnyeh NAHdah peereeSYEHST'
Does this bus go past Moscow State University?	Пройдёт ли э́тот авто́бус ми́мо МГУ?	prahyDYOHT lee EHtaht ahfTOHboos MEEmah emgahoo
How many stops until we reach the center of town?	Ско́лько остано́вок до це́нтра го́рода?	SKOHL'kah ahstahNOHVahk dah TSEHNtrah GOHrahdah
You've gotten on the wrong bus.	Вы се́ли не на тот авто́бус.	vih SYEHlee nee nah toht ahfTOHboos
Can you tell me where to get off?	Вы не ска́жете, на како́й остано́вке мне на́до вы́йти?	vih nee SKAHzhehteh nah kahKOY ahstahNOHFkyeh mnyeh NAHdah VIHytee
You've missed your stop.	Вы прое́хали свою́ остано́вку.	vih prahYEHkhahlee svahYOO ahstahNOHFkoo
Are you getting off?	Вы сейча́с выхо́дите?	vih seeCHAHS vihKHOHdeetyeh

I want to get off here/at the next stop.	Я хочу́ сойти́ здесь/на сле́дующей остано́вке.	yah khahCHOO sahyTEE zdyehs/ nah SLYEHdooyoo- shchey ahstah- NOHFkyeh
Excuse me, can I get through?	Извини́те, мо́жно пройти́?	eezveeNEEtyeh MOHZHnah prahyTEE
Excuse me, I'm getting off at the next stop.	Извини́те, я вы́хожу на сле́дующей.	eezveeNEEtyeh yah VIHkhahzhoo nah SLYEHdooyoo- shchey
Just a minute!	Мину́точку!	meeNOOtahchkoo
I'm getting off now.	Я схожу́.	yah skhahZHOO

Subway

Russian subways are quick and efficient. The stations are marked by a large red 'M', which is illuminated at night. The Moscow system is a tourist attraction in itself, since each station is built from a different architectural design. In order to get to the trains, you must drop a subway token into a turnstile. These tokens, which are different in Moscow and St. Petersburg, must be purchased from cashiers in the vestibules of the subway stations. Trains run from 6 am till 1 am. Smoking is prohibited.

Subway.	Метро́.	meetROH
Entrance.	Вход.	fkhoht
Exit.	Вы́ход.	VIHkhaht
No entrance.	Нет вхо́да.	nyeht FKHOHdah
No exit.	Нет вы́хода.	nyeht VIHkhahdah
Way out.	Вы́ход в го́род.	VIHkaht VGOHraht
To the trains.	К поезда́м.	kpaheezDAHM
Transfer.	Перехо́д.	peereeKHOHT
Keep to the left/right.	Держи́тесь ле́вой/пра́вой сто́роны.	deerZHEEtyehs' LYEHvay/PRAHvay STOHrahnih

May I have change, please.	Разменяйте, пожалуйста.	rahzmeeNYAYtyeh pahZHAHLstah
Where's the nearest subway stop?	Где ближайшая станция метро?	gdyeh bleeZHAYshahyah STAHNtseeyah meetROH
Does this line go to...	Эта линия идёт до...	EHtah LEEneeyah eedYOHT dah
What line should I take to...	По какой линии мне доехать до...	pah kahKOY LEEneeee mnyeh dahYEHkhaht' dah
Do I have to transfer?	Надо пересесть?	NAHdah peereeSYEHST'
Can you tell me what the next station is?	Скажите, пожалуйста, какая следующая станция?	skahZHEEtyeh pahZHAHLstah kahKAHyah SLYEHdooyooshchahyah STAHNtseeyah
The next station is...	Следующая станция...	SLYEHdooyooshchahyah STAHNtseeyah
Can you tell me where to get off?	Вы мне скажете когда надо сходить?	vih mnyeh SKAHzhehtyeh kahgDAH NAHdah skhahDEET'
Careful, the doors are closing.	Осторожно, двери закрываются.	ahstahROHZHnah DVYEHree zahkrihVAHyootsah
The train goes as far as...	Поезд следует до станции...	POHeest SLYEHdooeet dah STAHNtseeee
This is the last stop.	Поезд дальше не пойдёт.	POHeest DAHL'sheh nee pahyDYOHT

Taxi

In addition to being ordered by phone, taxis can be found in front of major hotels and at taxi stands. A small, green light in the front window means that the cab is available. It is common to share a cab with strangers.

| Taxi. | Такси. | tahkSEE |

Taxi stand.	Стоянка такси.	stahYAHNkah tahkSEE
Where can I get a taxi?	Где мне поймать такси?	gdyeh mnyeh pahy-MAHT' tahkSEE
Where is the nearest taxi stand?	Где ближайшая стоянка такси?	gdyeh bleeZHAY-shahyah stah-YAHNkah tahkSEE
Please call me a taxi.	Пожалуйста, вызовите мне такси.	pahZHAHLstah VIHzahveetyeh mnyeh tahkSEE
Are you free?	Вы свободны?	vih svahBOHdnih
Where do you want to go?	Куда вам?	kooDAH vahm
Here's the address.	Вот адрес.	voht AHdrees
To the Bolshoi Theater, please.	Пожалуйста, к Большому театру.	pahZHAHLstah kbahl'SHOHmoo teeAHtroo
How much will the ride cost?	Сколько этот проезд будет стоить?	SKOHL'kah EHtaht prahYEHST BOOdeet STOHeet'
Can you get my bags, please.	Возьмите, пожалуйста, мои чемоданы.	vahz'MEEtyeh pah-ZHAHLstah mahEE chehmahDAHnih
I'm (not) in a hurry.	Я (не) спешу.	yah (nee) speeSHOO
Stop here.	Остановитесь здесь.	ahstahnahVEEtyehs' zdyehs'
Wait for me here.	Подождите меня.	pahdahzhDEEtyeh meenYAH
I'll be back in a couple of minutes.	Я вернусь через несколько минут.	yah veerNOOS' CHEHrees NYEHskahl'kah meeNOOT
Keep the change.	Возьмите себе сдачу.	vahz'MEEtyeh seeBYEH ZDAHchoo
Thankyou. Goodbye.	Спасибо. До свидания.	spahSEEbah dah sveeDAHneeyah

Boats

Boat.	Ло́дка.	LOHTkah
Motor boat.	Мото́рная ло́дка.	mahTOHRnahyah LOHTkah
Ship./ Steamship.	Кора́бль./ Парохо́д.	kahRAHBL'/ pahrahKHOHT
Hydrofoil.	Су́дно на подво́дных кры́льях.	SOODnah nah pahdVOHDnihkh KRIHL'eekh
Ferry.	Паро́м.	pahrOHM
Cruise.	Круи́з.	krooEEZ
Tour.	Экску́рсия.	ehksKOORseeyah
When does the next ship leave?	Когда́ отхо́дит сле́дующий парохо́д?	kahgDAH ahtKHOHdeet SLYEHdooyooshcheey pahrahKHOHT
Where do we get tickets?	Где мо́жно купи́ть биле́ты?	gdyeh MOHZHnah kooPEET' beelYEHTih
How much are the tickets?	Ско́лько сто́ят биле́ты?	SKOHL'kah STOHyeht beelYEHTih
Where is the pier?	Где при́стань?	gdyeh PREEstahn'
How long is the trip?	Ско́лько вре́мени дли́тся путеше́ствие?	SKOHL'kah VRYEHmeenee DLEETsah pooteeshEHSTveeyeh
Where do we stop?	В каки́е по́рты мы захо́дим?	fkahKEEyeh POHRtih mih zahKHOHdeem
Deck.	Па́луба.	PAHloobah
Cabin.	Каю́та.	kahYOOtah
Life jacket.	Спаса́тельный по́яс.	spahSAHteel'nihy POHyees
Lifeboat.	Спаса́тельная ло́дка.	spahSAHteel'nahyah LOHTkah
I feel seasick.	У меня́ морска́я боле́знь.	oo meenYAH mahrSKAHyah bahLYEHZN'

Trains

Like all long-distance travel in Russia, train trips must be reserved in advance. You can sometimes make reservations through your hotel.

Train.	По́езд.	POHeest
Train station.	Вокза́л.	vahkZAHL
Ticket office.	Биле́тная ка́сса.	beelYEHTnahyah KAHSsah
When does the ticket office open?	Когда́ откро́ется биле́тная ка́сса?	kahgDAH ahtKROHeetsah beelYEHTnahyah KAHSsah
Reservation office.	Предвари́тель- ная прода́жа биле́тов.	preedvahREEtyehl'- nahyah prahDAH- zhah beelYEHTahf
Information office.	Спра́вочное бюро́.	SPRAHvahchnahyeh byooROH
Express long- distance trains	Экспре́ссы по́езда да́льнего сле́дования.	ehksPRYEHSsih POHeesdah DAHL'- nehvah SLYEHD- ahvahneeyeh
Standard long- distance trains.	Ско́рый по́езд.	SKOHrihy POHeest
Local trains.	Электри́чки.	ehleekTREECHkee
Delux class.	Междунаро́дный ваго́н.	meezhdoonahROHD- nihy vahgOHN
First class.	Мя́гкий ваго́н.	MYAHKHkeey vahgOHN
Second class.	Купи́рованный ваго́н.	kooPEERahvahnnihy vahgOHN
Third class.	Плацка́ртный ваго́н.	plahtsKAHRTnihy vahgOHN
One-way ticket.	Биле́т в оди́н коне́ц.	beelYEHT vahdEEN kahnYEHTS
Round-trip ticket.	Биле́т туда́ и обра́тно.	beelYEHT tooDAH ee ahbRAHTnah
Time table.	Расписа́ние поездо́в	rahspeeSAHneeyeh paheezDOHF

67

English	Russian	Pronunciation
Departure time.	Время отправле́ния.	VRYEHmyah aht-prahvLYEHneeyah
Arrival time.	Время прибы́тия.	VRYEHmyah preeBIHTeeyah
When is the next train to Kiev?	Когда́ отхо́дит сле́дующий по́езд на Ки́ев?	kahgDAH ahtKHOHdeet SLYEHdoo-yooshcheey POHeest nah KEEeef
Is it a direct train?	Это прямо́й по́езд?	EHtah preeMOY POHeest
Do I have to change trains?	Мне на́до де́лать переса́дку?	mnyeh NAHdah DYEHlaht' peereeSAHTkoo
What's the fare to Tblisi?	Ско́лько сто́ит биле́т до Тбили́си?	SKOHL'kah STOHeet beelYEHT dah tbeeLEEsee
I'd like to reserve a seat.	Я хоте́л(а) бы заказа́ть платцка́рт.	yah khahtYEHL(ah) bih zahkahZAHT' plahtsKAHRT
I'd like to reserve a berth in the sleeping car.	Я хоте́л(а) бы купи́ть биле́т в спа́льный ваго́н.	yah khahtYEHL(ah) bih kooPEET' beelYEHT FSPAHL'nihy vahgOHN
From what platform does the train to St. Petersburg leave?	С како́й платфо́рмы отхо́дит по́езд на Са́нкт-Петербу́рг?	skahKOY plahtFOHRmih ahtKHOHdeet POHeest nah SAHNKT-peeteerBOORG
When does the train arrive in Erevan?	Когда́ по́езд прихо́дит в Ерева́н?	kahgDAH POHeest preeKHOHdeet veereeVAHN
Are we on time?	По́езд идёт по расписа́нию?	POHeest eedYOHT pah rahspeeSAHneeyoo
The train is twenty minutes late.	По́езд опа́здывает на два́дцать мину́т.	POHeest ahpAHZdihvaheet nah DVAHtsaht' meeNOOT
Where are we now?	Где мы сейча́с?	gdyeh mih seeCHAHS

68

How long do we stop here?	Ско́лько сто́ит здесь по́езд?	SKOHL'kah stahEET zdyehs' POHeest
Is there time to get off?	Я успе́ю сойти́?	yah oosPYEHyoo sahyTEE
Is this seat taken?	Это ме́сто за́нято?	EHtah MYEHstah ZAHneetah
This is my seat.	Это моё ме́сто.	EHtah mahYOH MYEHstah
Am I bothering you?	Я вам меша́ю?	yah vahm meeSHAHyoo
Can I open/ shut the window?	Мо́жно откры́ть/ закры́ть окно́?	MOHZHnah aht-KRIHT'/zahKRIHT' ahkNOH
Can I turn out/on the light?	Мо́жно вы́ключить/ включи́ть свет?	MOHZHnah VIHK-lyoocheet'/ vklyooCHEET' svyeht
I'd like the top/ bottom bunk.	Я хоте́л(а) бы ве́рхнюю/ ни́жнюю по́лку.	yah khahtYEHL(ah) bih VYEHRKH-nyooyoo/NEEZH-nyooyoo POHLkoo
We'd like some tea.	Принеси́те нам чай.	preeneeSEEtyeh nahm chay
Two glasses, please.	Два стака́на, пожа́луйста.	dvah stahKAHnah pahZHAHLstah
Where is the...	Где...	gdyeh
baggage check?	прие́м багажа́?	preeYOHM bahgahZHAH
lost and found?	бюро́ нахо́док?	byooROH nahKHOHDahk
baggage room?	ка́мера хране́ния?	KAHmeerah khrahNYEHneeyah
snack bar?	буфе́т?	boofYEHT
bathroom?	туале́т?	tooahlYEHT
conductor?	конду́ктор?	kahnDOOKtahr
ticket taker? (m/f)	проводни́к/ проводни́ца?	prahvahdNEEK/ prahvahdNEEtsah
ticket checker?	контролёр?	kahntrahlYOHR
porter?	носи́льщик?	nahSEEL'shcheek
platform?	платфо́рма?	plahtFOHRmah

gate?	вход?	fkhoht
waiting room?	зал ожида́ния?	zahl ahzheeDAH-neeyah
sleeping car?	спа́льный ваго́н?	SPAHL'nihy vahgOHN
dining car?	ваго́н-рестора́н?	vahgOHN-reestahRAHN
smoking car?	ваго́н для куря́щих?	vahgOHN dlyah kooRYAHshch-eekh
my sleeping compart-ment?	моё купе́?	mahYOH kooPYEH
Have a good trip!	Счастли́вого пути́!	shahstLEEvahvah pooTEE

Planes

Aeroflot, the Russian airline, now flies directly out of the United States, so be sure to ask your travel agent about them. You may find their rates to Russia are significantly less expensive than most other international carriers.

Plane.	Самолёт.	sahmahlYOHT
Airport.	Аэропо́рт.	ahehrahpOHRT
Arrival.	Прибы́тие.	preeBIHTeeyeh
Departure.	Вы́лет.	VIHlyeht
Boarding pass.	Поса́дочный тало́н.	pahSAHdahchnihy tahlOHN
I'd like to make a res-ervation.	Я хочу́ заказа́ть биле́т.	yah khahCHOO zahkahzAHT beelYEHT
I'd like a flight to Kiev.	Да́йте мне биле́т до Ки́ева.	DAYtyeh mnyeh beelYEHT dah KEEeevah
Is there a direct flight?	Есть ли прямо́й полёт?	yehst' lee preeMOY pahlYOHT
How long is the lay-over?	Как до́лго самолёт бу́дет стоя́ть?	kahk DOHLgah sahmahlYOHT BOOdeet stahYAHT'

70

English	Russian	Pronunciation
When is the next flight?	Когда́ вылета́ет сле́дующий самолёт?	kahgDAH vihleeTAHeet SLYEHdooyooshch- eey sahmahlYOHT
Is there a connection to Tblisi?	Есть ли переса́дка на Тбили́си?	yehst' lee peereeSAHTkah nah tbeeLEEsee
One-way ticket.	Биле́т в оди́н коне́ц.	beelYEHT vahdEEN kahnYEHTS
Round-trip ticket.	Биле́т туда́ и обра́тно.	beelYEHT tooDAH ee ahbRAHTnah
Is flight (#5) on time?	Ре́йс (но́мер пять) идёт по расписа́нию?	reys (NOHmeer pyaht') eedYOHT pah rahspee- SAHneeyoo
I'd like to change/ confirm my flight.	Я хоте́л(а) бы поменя́ть/ подтверди́ть ре́йс.	yah khatYEHL(ah) bih pahmeen- YAHT'/pahttveer- DEET' reys
I'd like to cancel my reserva- tion.	Я хоте́л(а) бы отказа́ться от биле́та.	yah khatYEHL(ah) bih ahtkahzAHT'- sah aht beelYEHTah
How much luggage am I allowed?	Како́й вес багажа́ разреша́ется провози́ть?	kahKOY vyehs bahgahZHAH rahzreeSHAHeet- sah prahvahzEET'
What's the flight number?	Како́й но́мер ре́йса?	kahKOY NOHmeer REYsah
What gate do we leave from?	Че́рез како́й вы́ход поса́дка на наш ре́йс?	CHEEryehz kahkOY VIHkhaht pahSAHTkah nah nahsh reys
Boarding gate.	Вы́ход на поса́дку.	VIHkhaht nah pahSAHTkoo
What time do we leave/ arrive?	Когда́ вы́лет/ прибы́тие?	kahgDAH VIHlyeht/ preeBIHTeeyeh
What time should I check in?	Во ско́лько на́до регистри́ровать багаж?	vah SKOHL'kah NAHdah reegeest- REERahvaht' bahgAHSH

71

Call the stewardess.	Вызовите стюардессу.	VIHzahveetyeh styooahrdYEHSsoo
Fasten your seat belts.	Пристегни́те ремни́.	preesteegNEEtyeh reemNEE
Will there be food served?	Бу́дут ли корми́ть в самолёте?	BOOdoot lee kahrMEET' fsahmahLYOHtyeh
Can I smoke on board?	Мо́жно кури́ть в полёте?	MOHZHnah koorEET' vpahLYOHtyeh
Is there a bus from the airport into the city?	Есть ли авто́бус от аэропо́рта до го́рода?	yehst' lee ahfTOHboos aht ahehrahPOHRtah dah GOHrahdah

IX. SIGHTSEEING AND RELAXING

Asking Directions

Generally speaking, Russians are tremendously helpful and will often do all they can to help you get where you are going; so do not be afraid to ask for information from people on the street.

I'm lost. (m/f)	Я заблуди́лся/ заблуди́лась.	yah zahblooDEELsah/zahblooDEELahs'
Excuse me.	Прости́те./ Извини́те.	prahsTEEtyeh/ eezveeNEEtyeh
Can you tell me how to get to...	Скажи́те пожа́луйста, как попа́сть...	skahZHEEtyeh pahZHAHLstah kahk pahpAHST'
Tverskaya Street?	на у́лицу Тверску́ю.	nah OOLeetsoo tveerSKOOyoo
the center of town?	в центр го́рода.	vtsehntr GOHrahdah
I'm looking for...	Я ищу́...	yah eeshchOO
Am I going in the right direction?	Я иду́ в пра́вильном направле́нии?	yah eedOO VPRAHVeel'nahm nahprahVLYEHneeee
Do you know where ... is?	Вы зна́ете где нахо́дится...?	vih ZNAHeetyeh gdyeh nahKHOHdeetsah
Is it far?	Это далеко́?	EHtah dahleeKOH
Is it close?	Это бли́зко?	EHtah BLEEskah
Can I walk there?	Мо́жно дойти туда́ пешко́м?	MOHZHnah dahytee tooDAH peeshKOHM
It would be best to take a bus or the metro.	Вам лу́чше дое́хать или на метро́ или на авто́бусе.	vahm LOOCHsheh dahYEHkhaht' eelee nah meetROH eelee nah ahfTOHboosyeh

73

English	Russian	Pronunciation
What bus can I take to get to...?	Каки́м автобусом мо́жно дое́хать до...?	kahKEEM ahfTOH-boosahm dah-YEHkhaht' dah
What street is this?	Кака́я э́то у́лица?	kahKAHyah EHtah OOLeetsah
Please show me on the map where I am.	Покажи́те мне, пожа́луйста, на ка́рте, где я нахожу́сь.	pahkahZHEEtyeh mnyeh pahZHAHL-stah nah KAHR-tyeh gdyeh yah nahkhahZHOOS'
Go straight ahead.	Иди́те пря́мо.	eeDEEtyeh PRYAHmah
Go in this/ that direc- tion.	Иди́те в э́ту/ту сто́рону.	eeDEEtyeh VEHtoo/ftoo STOHrahnoo
Turn left/ right...	Поверни́те нале́во/ напра́во...	pahveerNEEtyeh nahLYEHvah/ nahPRAHvah
at the next corner.	на сле́дующем углу́.	nah SLYEHD-ooyoushchem oogLOO
at the light.	у светофо́ра.	oo sveetahFOHrah
Take this road.	Поезжа́йте по э́той у́лице.	paheezhZHAYtyeh pah EHtay OOLeetseh
You have to go back.	Вам на́до верну́ться.	vahm NAHdah veerNOOT'syah
You're on the wrong bus.	Вы се́ли не на тот автобус.	vih SYEHlee nee nah toht ahfTOHboos
Do I have to transfer?	Мне на́до пересе́сть?	mnyeh NAHdah peereeSYEHST'
North./South.	Се́вер./Юг.	SYEHveer/yook
East./West.	Восто́к./За́пад.	vahsTOHK/zahPAHT
It's there...	Э́то там...	EHtah tahm
on the right/left.	напра́во/ нале́во.	nahPRAHvah/ nahLYEHvah
after/ behind...	по́сле/ позади́...	POHslee/ pahzahDEE
next to/ opposite...	ря́дом/ напро́тив...	RYAHdahm/ nahPROHteef
There it is. (m/f/n)	Вот он/она́/ оно́.	voht ohn/ahNAH/ ahNOH

This/That way.	Сюда́./Туда́.	syooDAH/tooDAH

Taking a Bus Trip

What sights should we see?	Каки́е достоприме ча́тельности сто́ит осмотре́ть?	kahKEEyeh dahstahpreemee-CHAHteel'nahstee STOHeet ahsmahTRYEHT'
Where can I sign up for an excursion?	Где мо́жно записа́ться на экску́рсию?	gdyeh MOHZHnah zahpeeSAHTsah nah ehksKOOR-seeyoo
What excursion do you suggest?	Каку́ю экску́рсию вы мне посове́туете?	kahKOOyoo ehks-KOORseeyoo vih mnyeh pahsahv-YEHtooeetyeh
I want to take a bus trip around the city.	Я хочу́ записа́ться на экску́рсию по го́роду.	yah khahCHOO zah-peeSAHTsah nah ehksKOORseeyoo pah GOHrahdoo
I'd like to sign up for this excursion.	Я хоте́л(а) бы записа́ться на эту экску́рсию.	yah khahtYEHL(ah) bih zapeeSAHT-sah nah EHtoo ehksKOORseeyoo
Do I have to sign up in advance?	Мне на́до зара́нее заказа́ть биле́ты?	mnyeh NAHdah zahRAHNeeyeh zahkahzAHT' beeLYEHtih
What does a ticket cost?	Ско́лько сто́ит биле́т?	SKOHL'kah STOHeet beelYEHT
When does the excursion leave?	На како́е вре́мя она́ назна́чена?	nah kahkOHyeh VRYEHMyah ahNAH nahzNACHehnah
How long does it last?	Как до́лго дли́тся экску́рсия?	kahk DOHLgah DLEEtsah ehksKOORseeyah
When do we get back?	Когда́ мы вернёмся?	kahgDAH mih veernYOHMsah

Will we stop somewhere for lunch?	Обе́д бу́дет где-нибу́дь?	ahBYEHT BOOdeet gdyeh-neeBOOT'
From where does the excursion leave?	Отку́да отхо́дит экску́рсия?	ahtKOOdah ahtKHOHdeet ehksKOORseeyah
Tour guide.	Экскурсово́д.	ehskoorsahvOHT
Is there an English-speaking guide?	Есть ли экскуросово́д, говоря́щий по-англи́йски?	yehst' lee ehskoorsahv-OHT gahvah-RYAHshcheey pahahngLEEYskee
Will we have free time there?	Бу́дет ли у нас там свобо́дное вре́мя?	BOOdeet lee oo nahs tahm svahBOHD-nahyeh VRYEHmyah
When should we be back on the bus?	Во ско́лько мы должны́ верну́ться к авто́бусу?	vahSKOHL'kah mih dahlzhNIH veerNYOOtsah kahfTOHboosoo

Taking a Walking Tour

Guided walking tours are available in most larger museums.

When does it open/close?	Когда́ открыва́ется/закрыва́ется?	kahgDAH ahtkrih-VAHeetsah/zah-krihVAHeetsah
I want to sign up for a tour.	Я хочу́ записа́ться на экску́рсию.	yah khahCHOO zah-peeSAHTsah nah ehksKOORseeyoo
When does it start/end?	Когда́ она́ начина́ется/конча́ется?	kahgDAH ahNAH nahchehNAHeetsah /kahnCHAHeetsah
What is the cost?	Ско́лько сто́ит биле́т?	SKOHL'kah STOHeet beelYEHT
Free admission.	Вход беспла́тный.	fkhoht beesPLAHTnihy

Do you sell guidebooks in English?	У вас есть путеводитель на английском языке?	oo vahs yehst' pooteevahDEEteel' nah ahngLEEYskahm yeezIHKyeh
Is there a map?	Есть у вас карта?	yehst' oo vahs KAHRtah
In front of...	Впереди...	vpeereeDEE
To the rear of...	Позади...	pahzahDEE
In the middle of...	Посередине...	pahseereeDEEnyeh
On the left of...	Слева...	SLYEHvah
On the right of...	Справа...	SPRAHvah
Where can I buy post cards?	Где можно купить открытки?	gdyeh MOHZHnah kooPEET' ahtKRIHTkee
May I see what post cards you have for sale?	Можно посмотреть, какие у вас открытки?	MOHZHnah pahsmahtRYEHT' kahKEEyeh oo vahs ahtKRIHTkee
I'd like to buy this set.	Я куплю этот комплект.	yah koopLYOO EHtaht kahmpLYEHKT
How much is it?	Сколько это стоит?	SKOHL'kah EHtah STOHeet
Can I take pictures?	Можно здесь фотографировать?	MOHZHnah zdyehs fahtahgrahFEERahvaht'
No cameras allowed.	Фотографировать воспрещается.	fahtahgrahFEERahvaht' vahspreeSHCHAHeetsah

Taking in the Sights

| I want to see the sights. | Я хочу осмотреть достопримечательности. | yah khahCHOO ahsmahtRYEHT' dahstahpreemeeCHAHteel'nahstee |
| Let's go for a walk. | Давайте погуляем. | dahVAYtyeh pahgooLYAHeem |

English	Russian	Pronunciation
What kind of ... is that?	Что э́то за...?	shtoh EHtah zah
animal/bird/ fish/ flower/ tree.	живо́тное/ пти́ца/ ры́ба/ цвето́к/ де́рево.	zheeVOHTnahyeh/ PTEEtsah/ RIHBah/ tsveeTOHK/ deeRYEHvah
We don't have those at home.	У нас таки́х нет.	oo nahs tahkEEKH nyeht
What a beautiful view!	Како́й прекра́сный вид!	kahKOY preeKRAHSnihy veet
What's that building?	Что э́то за зда́ние?	shtoh EHtah zah ZDAHneeyeh
When was it built?	Когда́ оно́ бы́ло постро́ено?	kahgDAH ahNOH BIHlah pahst-ROHeenah
Who built it?	Кто его́ постро́ил?	ktoh yeeVOH pahstROHeel
Who was the architect/ artist?	Кто был архите́ктором/ худо́жником?	ktoh bihl ahrkheeTYEHK-tahrahm/khood-OHZHneekahm
When did he/she live?	Когда́ он/она́ жил(а́)?	kahgDAH ohn/ahNAH zheel(AH)
Where's the house where ... lived?	Где дом, в кото́ром жил(а́)...?	gdyeh dohm fkah-TOHrahm zheel(AH)
Can we go in?	Мо́жно войти́?	MOHZHnah vahyTEE
Very inter-esting.	О́чень интере́сно.	OHcheen' eenteerYEHSnah
It's...	Э́то...	EHtah
beautiful.	краси́во.	krahSEEvah
ugly.	безобра́зно.	beezahbRAHZnah
wonderful.	прекра́сно.	preeKRAHSnah
horrible.	ужа́сно.	ooZHAHSnah
great.	великоле́пно.	veeleekahLYEHPnah
terrible.	стра́шно.	STRAHSHnah
amazing.	удиви́тельно.	oodeeVEEtyehl'nah
strange.	стра́нно.	STRAHNnah

cute.	ми́ло.	MEElah
sinister.	жу́тко.	ZHOOTkah
Let's rest.	Дава́йте отдохнём.	dahVAYtyeh ahtdahkhNYOHM
I'm tired.	Я уста́л(а).	yah oostAHL(ah)
I'm bored.	Мне ску́чно./ надое́ло.	mnyeh SKOOCHnah/ nahdahYEHLah

Worship Services

Most places of worship do not mind visitors, as long as you observe their customs and do not disturb their services. Orthodox churches demand that women wear skirts and cover their heads with a kerchief or hat. Taking pictures inside churches is usually not permitted.

Worship services.	Богослуже́ния.	bahgahsloozh-EHNeeyah
Monastary.	Ла́вра.	LAHVrah
Cathedral.	Собо́р.	sahbOHR
Church.	Це́рковь.	TSEHRkahf'
Synagogue.	Синаго́га.	seenahGOHgah
Temple.	Храм.	khrahm
Mosque.	Мече́ть.	meechEHT'
Orthodox.	Правосла́вный.	prahvahSLAHVnihy
Old-Believers.	Старо-обря́дцы.	stahrah-ahbRYAHTtsih
Saint.	Свято́й.	sveeTOY
Altar.	Алта́рь.	ahlTAHR'
Iconostasis.	Иконоста́с.	eekahnahSTAHS
Icons.	Ико́ны.	eeKOHnih
Incense.	Ла́дан.	LAHdahn
Candle.	Свеча́.	sveeCHAH
Contribution.	Поже́ртвование.	pahzhEHRTvahvah-neeyeh
Prayers.	Моли́твы.	mahLEETvih
Prayer book.	Моли́твенник.	mahLEETveenneek
Rabbi.	Равви́н.	rahvVEEN
Priest.	Свяще́нник.	sveeshchEHNneek
When's the service?	Когда́ слу́жба?	kahgDAH SLOOSHbah

I want to look around the church.	Я хочу́ осмотре́ть це́рковь.	yah khahCHOO ahsmahtRYEHT' TSEHRkahf'
You must cover your head.	Вам на́до покры́ть го́лову.	vahm NAHdah pahKRIHT' GOHlahvoo
Are women allowed?	Же́нщины допуска́ются?	ZHEHNshcheenih dahpoosKAHyoot-sah
May I take a picture?	Мо́жно здесь фото-графи́ровать?	MOHZHnah zdyehs fahtahgrahFEER-ahvaht'
No cameras allowed.	Фото-графи́ровать воспреща́ется.	fahtahgrahFEER-ahvaht' vahspree-SHCHAHeetsah
Cemetary.	Кла́дбище.	KLAHTbeeshcheh
Grave.	Моги́ла.	mahGEElah
Tombstone.	Надгро́бный ка́мень.	nahdGROHBnihy KAHmeen'

Outdoor Recreation

I enjoy...	Мне нра́вится...	mnyeh NRAHveetsah
running.	бе́гать.	BYEHgaht'
cycling.	велоспо́рт.	veelahSPOHRT
tennis.	те́ннис.	TYEHNnees
horseback riding.	ката́ться верхо́м.	kahTAHTsah veerkhAHM
swimming.	пла́вание.	PLAHvahneeyeh
sailing.	ката́ние на пару́сной ло́дке.	kahTAHneeyeh nah PAHroosnay LOHTkyeh
mountain climbing.	альпини́зм.	ahl'peeNEEZM
skiing.	ката́ться на лы́жах.	kahTAHTsah nah LIHZHahkh
skating.	ката́ться на конька́х.	kahTAHTsah nah kahn'KAHKH
I want to play tennis.	Я хочу́ игра́ть в те́ннис.	yah khahCHOO eegRAHT' FTYEHNnees

English	Russian	Pronunciation
Can we rent rackets?	Мо́жно взять напрока́т раке́тки?	MOHZHnah vzyaht' nahprahKAHT rahKYEHtkee
Are there courts here?	Есть ли здесь ко́рты?	yehst' lee zdyehs KOHRtih
Is there a swimming pool here?	Есть ли здесь бассе́йн?	yehst' lee zdyehs bahsSEYN
Can one go swimming here?	Мо́жно здесь купа́ться?	MOHZHnah zdyehs kooPAHTsah
Is it safe to swim here?	Здесь не опа́сно купа́ться?	zdyehs nee ahpAHSnah kooPAHTsah
Is the water here deep?	Здесь глубоко́?	zdyehs gloobahKoH
Is the water cold?	Вода́ холо́дная?	vahDAH khahLOHDnahyah
No Swimming.	Купа́ться воспреща́ется.	kooPAHTsah vahspreeSHCHAHeetsah
I want to lie on the beach.	Я хочу́ полежа́ть на пля́же.	yah khahCHOO pahleezhAHT' nah PLYAHzheh
I want to sunbathe.	Я хочу́ загора́ть.	yah khahCHOO zahgahrYAHT'
Can I rent...	Мо́жно взять напрока́т...	MOHZHnah vzyaht' nahprahKAHT
a beach chair?	шезло́нг?	shehzLOHNG
a sun umbrella?	зо́нтик?	ZOHNteek
a row boat?	ло́дку?	LOHTkoo
water skis?	во́дные лы́жи?	VOHDnihyeh LIHZHee
skiing equipment?	лы́жное снаряже́ние?	LIHZHnahyeh snahreeZHEHneeyeh
skates?	ко́ньки?	KOHN'kee
What's the charge per hour/per day?	Ско́лько сто́ит на час/день?	SKOHL'kah STOHeet nah chahs/dyehn'

81

| Is there a skating rink here? | Есть ли здесь като́к? | yehst' lee zdyehs kahTOHK |
| Where can I go skiing? | Где мо́жно ката́ться на лы́жах? | gdyeh MOHZHnah kahTAHTsah nah LIHZHahkh |

Camping

Camping.	Ке́мпинг.	KYEHMpeeng
Camping equipment.	Обору́дование для ке́мпинга.	ahbahROOdahvah-neeyeh dlyah KYEHMpeengah
Camping permit.	Разреше́ние на ке́мпинг.	rahzreeSHEHneeyeh nah KYEHMpeeng
Can we camp here?	Мо́жно здесь устро́ить стоя́нку?	MOHZHnah zdyehs' oosTROHeet' stahYAHNkoo
What's the charge per day?/per person?	Ско́лько сто́ит на день?/на челове́ка?	SKOHL'kah STOHeet nah dyehn'/nah chehlahVYEHKah
Are there showers/toilets?	Есть душ/убо́рная?	yehst' doosh/oobOHRnahyah
Where are the toilets?	Где убо́рная?	gdyeh ooBOHRnahyah
Can we light a fire here?	Мо́жно здесь разже́чь костёр?	MOHZHnah zdyehs' rahzZHEHCH kahstYOHR
Is there electricity?	Есть электри́чество?	yehst' ehleekTREE-chehstvah
Is swimming allowed?	Здесь мо́жно купа́ться?	zdyehs' MOHZHnah kooPAHTsah
Can we fish here?	Здесь мо́жно лови́ть ры́бу?	zdyehs' MOHZHnah lahvEET' RIHBoo
Do we need a license to fish?	На́до ли име́ть разреше́ние на ры́бную ло́влю?	NAHdah lee eemYEHT' rahzreeSHEHnee-yeh nah RIHBnoo-yoo LOHVlyoo

Can we rent equipment?	Мо́жно ли взять напрока́т обору́дование для ке́мпинга?	MOHZHnah lee vzyaht' nahprahKAHT ahbahROOdahvahneeyeh dlyah KYEHMpeengah
Where can we get (a) ...	Где мо́жно доста́ть...	gdyeh MOHZHnah dahsTAHT'
corkscrew?	што́пор?	SHTOHpahr
candles?	све́чки?	SVYEHCHkee
can opener?	консе́рвный нож?	kahnSYEHRVnihy nohsh
charcoal?	древе́сный у́голь?	dreeVYEHSnihy OOGahl'
compass?	ко́мпас?	KOHMpahs
cooking utensils?	ку́хонные принад- ле́жности?	KOOkhahnnihyeh preenahd- LYEHZHnahstee
cooler?	су́мку- те́рмос?	SOOMkoo- TYEHRmahs
fire wood?	дрова́?	drahVAH
first-aid kit?	апте́чку?	ahpTYEHCHkoo
flashlight?	карма́нный фона́рь?	kahrMAHNnihy fahnAHR'
groundsheet?	подсти́лку под пала́тку?	pahdsTEELkoo paht pahLAHTkoo
kerosene?	кероси́н?	keerahSEEN
lantern?	фона́рь?	fahnAHR'
mattress?	матра́с?	mahtRAHS
sleeping bag?	спа́льный мешо́к?	SPAHL'nihy meeshOHK
tent?	пала́тку?	pahLAHTkoo
thermos?	те́рмос?	TYEHRmahs

Public Baths

The larger Russian public baths often have saunas and pools where you can relax Russian-style. After sitting for awhile in the sauna, it is a Russian custom to beat oneself lightly with dried birch switches.

| Public bath. | Ба́ня. | BAHNyah |

Men.	Мужчи́ны.	mooshCHEEnih
Women.	Же́нщины.	ZHEHNshcheenih
What does admission cost?	Ско́лько сто́ит входно́й биле́т?	SKOHL'kah STOHeet fkhahdNOY beeLYEHT
I'd like to rent...	Я хоте́л(а) бы взять...	yah khahtYEHL(ah) bih vzyaht'
a towel.	полете́нце.	pahleeTYEHNtseh
a sheet.	простыню́.	prahstihnYOO
It's too hot/cold here.	Здесь сли́шком жа́рко/ хо́лодно.	zdyehs SLEESHkahm ZHAHRkah/ KHOHlahdnah
Shower.	Душ.	doosh
Pool.	Бассе́йн.	bahsSEYN
Bathing cap.	Купа́льная ша́почка.	kooPAHL'nahyah SHAHPahchkah
Bathing suit.	Купа́льный костю́м.	kooPAHL'nihy kahstYOOM
Soap.	Мы́ло.	MIHlah
Bucket.	Ведро́.	veedROH
Steam room.	Пари́лка	pahrEELkah
Birch switches.	Берёзовый ве́ник.	beerYOHZahvihy VYEHneek
Massage.	Масса́ж.	mahsSAHSH

84

X. ENTERTAINMENT

Tickets

Tickets can be purchased most easily from Intourist for dollars. You can also try your luck at buying tickets from kiosks on the street, but do not expect to get your first choice. Russians are avid theater-goers and most performances sell out quickly. If you really want to see a particular performance, you can go down to the theater a little early and try to buy spare tickets (лишние билеты) from people outside the theater. This is not only accepted behavior, it is actually quite common.

Tickets.	Билеты.	beelYEHTih
(Theater) box office.	(Театральная) касса.	(teeahTRAHL'nah-yah) KAHSsah
Ticket window.	Билетная касса.	beelYEHTnahyah KAHSsah
Can you recommend a(n) opera/ concert/ play?	Можете ли вы посоветовать мне оперу/ концерт/ пьесу?	MOHZHehtyeh lee vih pahsahVYEHT-ahvaht' mnyeh OHPeeroo/kahnts-EHRT/P'YEHsoo
Have you any tickets for tonight's performance?	У вас есть билеты на сегодняшний спектакль?	oo vahs yehst' beelYEHTih nah seeVOHDneesh-neey speekTAHKL'
How much are they?	Сколько они стоят?	SKOHL'kah ahNEE STOHyaht
I'd like two for...	Я хотел(а) бы два на...	yah khahtYEHL(ah) bih dvah nah
We're sold out.	Все билеты проданы.	vsyeh beelYEHTih PROHdahnih
What time does it begin?	Во сколько начинается спектакль?	vah SKOHL'kah nahcheeNAHeetsah speekTAHKL'

85

How do I get to this theater?	Как мне добра́ться до э́того теа́тра?	kahk mnyeh dahBRAHT'sah dah EHtahvah teeAHtrah
The Bolshoi Theater.	Большо́й Теа́тр.	bahl'SHOY teeAHTR
The Kremlin Palace of Congresses.	Кремлёвский Дворе́ц съе́здов.	kreemLYOHFskeey dvahrYEHTS S"YEHSdahf
Chaikovsky Conservatory.	Конце́ртный зал и́мени Чайко́вского.	kahntsEHRTnihy zahl EEMeenee chayKOHFskahvah
No admittance after the third bell.	Вход в зри́тельный зал по́сле тре́тьего звонка́ воспрещён.	fxoht VZREEteel'-nihy zahl POHslee TRYEHt'ehvah zvahnKAH vahs-preeshchOHN
Orchestra stalls.	Парте́р.	pahrtYEHR
Amphitheater.	Амфитеа́тр.	ahmfeeteeAHTR
Balcony.	Балко́н.	bahlKOHN
Box.	Ло́жа.	LOHzhah
Left side.	Ле́вая сторона́.	LYEHvahyah stahrahNAH
Right side.	Пра́вая сторона́.	PRAHvahyah stahrahNAH
Middle.	Середи́на.	seereeDEEnah
Lobby.	Фойе́.	foyYEH
Snack bar.	Буфе́т.	boofYEHT
Smoking room.	Кури́тельная ко́мната.	kooREEteel'nahyah KOHMnahtah
Cloakroom.	Гардеро́б.	gahrdeerOHP
Cloakroom attendant. (f)	Гардеро́бщик/ Гардеро́бщица.	gahrdeerOHP-shcheek/gahrdeer-OHPshcheetsah
Entrance to auditorium.	Вход в зри́тельный зал.	fxoht VZREEteel'-nihy zahl
Exit.	Вы́ход.	VIHkhat

Theater and Movies

Russian theater is often first-rate and tickets are relatively inexpensive compared to western standards. Movies are shown all day long at most movie theaters. No one is admitted after the lights are turned off and Russians typically keep their coats on in movie theaters, but leave them in coat rooms while at plays or concerts.

Play.	Пьéса.	P'YEHsah
Performance.	Спектáкль.	speekTAHKL'
Movie.	Кинó.	keeNOH
Theater.	Теáтр.	teeAHTR
What's at the... ?	Что идёт в... ?	shtoh eedYOHT f
What kind of play/movie is it?	Что э́то за пьéса/ фильм?	shtoh EHtah zah P'YEHsah/ feel'm
It's a...	Это...	EHtah
cartoon.	мультфи́льм.	mool'tFEEL'M
comedy.	комéдия.	kahMYEHdeeyah
documentary.	документáльный фильм.	dahkoomeentAHL'- nihy feel'm
drama.	фильм-дрáма.	feel'm-DRAHmah
Who's the director?	Кто режиссёр?	ktoh reezheesSYOHR
Who's playing the lead?	Кто игрáет глáвную роль?	ktoh eegRAHeet GLAHVnooyoo rohl'
Are there any tickets left?	Остáлись ли ли́шние билéты?	ahSTAHlees' lee LEESHneeyeh beelYEHTih
Is there a matinee?	Есть ли дневнóй спектáкль?	yehst' lee dneevNOY speekTAHKL'
When does the show begin?	Когдá начинáется спектáкль?	kahgDAH nahcheeNAHeet- sah speekTAHKL'
Do you have any extra tickets?	У вас éсть ли́шние билéты?	oo vahs yehst' LEESHneeyeh beelYEHTih

Opera, Concerts and Ballet

Tickets to the Bolshoi Theater are practically impossible to get unless you buy them for dollars at the box office or from the theater agent in an international hotel.

Opera.	О́пера.	OHPeerah
Concert.	Конце́рт.	kahntsEHRT
Ballet.	Бале́т.	bahlYEHT
Orchestra.	Орке́стр.	ahrkYEHSTR
Folk songs/ dances.	Наро́дные пе́сни/ та́нцы.	nahROHDnihyeh PYEHSnee/ TAHNtsih
Here is my ticket.	Вот мой биле́т.	voht moy beelYEHT
Where is my seat?	Где моё ме́сто?	gdyeh mahYOH MYEHstah
Follow me.	Сле́дуйте за мно́й.	SLYEHdooytyeh zah mnoy
How much for a program?	Ско́лько сто́ит програ́мма?	SKHOL'kah STOHeet prahgRAHMmah
May I have a program, please?	Да́йте, пожа́луйста, програ́мму.	DAYtyeh pahZHAHLstah prahgRAHMmoo
Want to rent opera glasses?	Бино́кль вам ну́жен?	beeNOHKL' vahm NOOZHehn
No, thank you. I don't need them.	Нет, спаси́бо. Он мне не ну́жен.	nyeht spahSEEbah ohn mnyeh nee NOOzhehn
Who is the conductor?	Кто дирижёр?	ktoh deereezhOHR
Who is dancing the lead?	Кто танцу́ет гла́вную па́ртию?	ktoh tahnTSOOeht GLAHVnooyoo PAHRteeyoo
Who is the soloist?(f)	Кто соли́ст(ка)?	ktoh sahlEEST(kah)
When is the inter- mission?	Когда́ антра́кт?	kahgDAH ahnTRAHKT

How long is the inter- mission?	Ско́лько дли́тся антра́кт?	SKOHL'kah DLEETsah ahnTRAHKT
Pardon me, can I get by?	Прости́те, мо́жно пройти́?	prahsTEEtyeh MOHZHnah prahyTEE
That's my seat.	Это мое́ ме́сто.	EHtah mahYOH MYEHstah

Circus and Puppet Show

Circus.	Цирк.	tseerk
Puppet theater.	Ку́кольный теа́тр.	KOOkahl'nihy teeAHTR
Do you have tickets for the circus/ puppet theater?	У вас есть биле́ты в цирк/ ку́кольный теа́тр?	oo vahs yehst' beelYEHTih vtseerk/ VKOOkahl'nihy teeAHTR
How do I get to the circus?	Как мне добра́ться до ци́рка?	kahk mnyeh dahBRAHT'sah dah TSEERkah
Is there a matinee today?	Есть ли сего́дня дневно́й спекта́кль?	yehst' lee seeVOHdnyah dneevNOY speekTAHKL'
Do you have a spare ticket?	У вас есть ли́шний биле́т?	oo vahs yehst' LEESHneey beelYEHT
Give me a program, please.	Да́йте мне, програ́мму, пожа́луйста..	DAYtyeh mnyeh prahgRAHMmoo pahZHAHLstah

Sporting Events

Sporting events.	Спорти́вные соревнова́ния.	spahrTEEVnihyeh sahreevnahVAH- neeyah
Sports fan.	Боле́льщик.	bahlYEHL'shcheek
I want to see a hockey/ soccer game.	Я хочу́ посмотре́ть хокке́йный/ футбо́льный матч.	yah khahCHOO pahsmahTRYEHT' khahkKEYnihy/ footBOHL'nihy mahtch

How much are the tickets?	Ско́лько сто́ят биле́ты?	SKOHL'kah STOHyaht beelYEHTih
Are there any tickets for today's game?	Есть ли биле́ты на сего́дняшний матч?	yehst' lee beelYEHTih nah seeVOHdnyee-shneey mahtch
How do I get to Lenin Stadium?	Как мне дое́хать до Ле́ни́нского стадио́на?	kahk mnyeh dahYEHkhat' dah leenEENskahvah stahdeeOHNah
Who is playing?	Каки́е кома́нды игра́ют?	kahKEEyeh kahMAHNdih eegRAHyoot
Scoreboard.	Табло́.	tahbLOH
Who is winning?	Кто выи́грывает?	ktoh vihEEGrih-vaheet
What's the score?	Како́й счёт?	kahKOY shchoht
Dynamo are ahead 3-1.	Три оди́н в по́льзу Дина́мо.	tree ahdEEN FPOHL'zoo deeNAHmoh
It's score-less.	Счёт нулево́й/ По нуля́м.	EHtah nooleeVOY/ pah noolYAHM
Score a point.	Вы́играть очко́.	VIHeegraht' ahchKOH
Score a goal.	Забить гол.	zahBEET' gohl
Who won?	Кто вы́играл?	ktoh VIHeegrahl
Scoreless tie.	Нулева́я ничья́.	nooleeVAHyah neechYAH
Do you want to play chess?	Вы хоти́те игра́ть в ша́хматы?	vih khahTEEtyeh eegRAHT' FSHAHKHmahtih
Check mate.	Мат.	maht

XI. STORES

Moscow has two large department stores, known as GUM (State Department Store) and TSUM (Central Department Store), which are open from 8 am to 9:30 pm. Food stores typically open at 9 am and close at 8 pm. Other shops, like bookstores and souvenir shops, are open from around 10 or 11 am to 8 pm. Most stores, except those selling food, are closed on Sundays.

Finding the Right Store

The easiest and most convenient, although also the most expensive, stores for foreigners are the hard-currency stores or Beryozkas. These stores used to only accept foreign currency and credit cards, but some are beginning to take rubles as well. The staff usually speaks some English and the stock usually includes some items not found in Russian stores.

Where can I buy...?	Где можно купить...?	gdyeh MOHZHnah kooPEET'
Where can I find a...?	Где мне найти...?	gdyeh mnyeh nahyTEE
Is there a ... near here?	Есть ли поблизости...	yehst' lee pahbLEEzahstee
bakery.	булочная.	BOOlahchnahyah
bookstore.	книжный магазин.	KNEEZHnihy mahgahZEEN
candy shop.	кондитерская.	kahnDEEteer-skahyah
clothes store.	одежда.	ahdYEHZHdah
dairy.	молочная.	mahLOHCHnahyah
department store.	универмаг.	ooneeveerMAHK
drug store.	аптека.	ahpTYEHkah
farmers' market.	рынок.	RIHnahk
fish market.	рыбный магазин.	RIHBnihy mahgahZEEN

91

fruit and vegetable store.	фру́кты и о́вощи.	FROOKtih ee OHVahchshee
furrier.	меха́.	meeKHAH
gift shop.	пода́рки.	pahdAHRkee
greengrocer.	зеленщи́к.	zeeleenSHCHEEK
grocery.	проду́кты.	prahDOOKtih
Beryozka.	Берёзка.	beerYOHSkah
hat shop.	магази́н головны́х убо́ров.	mahgahZEEN gahlahvNIHKH ooBOHrahf
jeweler.	ювели́рный магази́н.	yooveelEERnihy mahgahZEEN
liquor store.	вино́.	veeNAH
newsstand.	газе́тный кио́ск.	gahzYEHTnihy keeOHSK
record store.	грампласти́нки.	grahmplahstEENkee
secondhand bookstore.	букинисти́ческий магази́н.	bookeeneestEECHeh-skeey mahgahZEEN
secondhand store.	комисси́онный магази́н.	kahmeesseeOHNnihy mahgahZEEN
shoe store.	О́бувь.	OHBoof'
souvenirs.	сувени́ры.	sooveeNEErih
stationary.	канцтова́ры.	kahntstahVAHrih
tobacconist.	таба́к.	tahBAHK
toy store.	магази́н игру́шек.	mahgahZEEN eegROOSHehk

Looking Around

Service.	Обслужива́ние.	ahpsloozheeVAH-neeyeh
Can you help me...	Бу́дьте добры́...	BOOt'tyeh dahbRIH
Where's the ... department?	Где нахо́дится отде́л...	gdyeh nahKHOHdee-tsah ahtTYEHL
Can I help you?	Слу́шаю вас.	slooSHAHyoo vahs
Do you have...	Есть ли у вас...	yehst' lee oo vahs

What kind of ... would you like?	Какой ... вы хотите?	kahKOY ... vih khahTEEtyeh
I'd like...	Я хотел(а) бы...	yah khahtYEHL(ah) bih
I'm sorry, we don't have any.	Простите, этого у нас нет.	prahsTEEtyeh EHtahvah oo nahs nyeht
We're sold out.	Всё распродано.	vsyoh rahsPROH-dahnah
Anything else?	Ещё что-нибудь?	yeeSHCHOH SHTOH-neeboot'
Show me (this/that), please.	Покажите мне (это/то), пожалуйста.	pahkahZHEEtyeh mneyh (EHtah/toh) pahZHAHLstah
No, not that, but that there...next to it.	Нет, не это, а вот это...рядом.	nyeht nee EHtah ah voht EHtah... RYAHdahm
It's not what I want.	Это не то, что я хочу.	EHtah nee toh shtoh yah khahCHOO
I don't like it.	Это мне не нравится.	mnyeh EHtah nee NRAHveetsah
I'm just looking.	Я только смотрю.	yah TOHL'kah smahtRYOO
I prefer...	Я предпочитаю...	yah preetpahchee-TAHyoo
Something not too expensive.	Что-нибудь не очень дорогое.	shtahneeBOOT' nee OHcheen' dahrahGOHyeh
How much is it?	Сколько это стоит?	SKHOL'kah EHtah STOHeet
Repeat that, please.	Повторите, пожалуйста.	pahftahREEtyeh pahZHAHLstah
Please write it down.	Пожалуйста, напишите.	pahZHAHLstah nahpeeSHEEtyeh

Making a Purchase

Shopping in Russia is an adventure. There are usually several steps involved in making a purchase. First, you choose your merchandise and take note of the price. Next, you go to the register

93

and pay for it, receiving a чек (receipt) in return. Finally, you take this receipt to another counter where you receive your purchase.

Have you decided?	Вы решили?	vih reeSHEElee
Yes, I want this.	Да, я хочу э́то.	dah yah khahCHOO EHtah
I'll take it.	Я возьму́ э́то.	yah vahz'MOO EHtah
Will I have problems with customs?	Бу́дут ли у меня́ тру́дности на тамо́жне?	BOOdoot lee oo meenYAH TROO-dnahstee nah tahMOHZHnyeh
Pay at the cashier.	Плати́те в ка́ссу.	plahTEEtyeh FKAHSsoo
Do you accept traveler's checks/ credit cards/ dollars?	Вы принима́ете доро́жные че́ки/ креди́тные ка́рточки/ до́ллары?	vih preenee-MAHyehtyeh dahROHZHnihyeh SHEHkee/ kreeDEETnihyeh KAHRtahchkee/ DOHLlahrih
Can I have a receipt, please.	Да́йте, пожа́луйста, квита́нцию.	DAYtyeh pahZHAHL-stah kveeTAHN-tseeyoo
Wrap it up for me, please.	Заверни́те, пожа́луйста.	zahveerNEEtyeh pahZHAHLstah
Please give me a bag.	Да́йте мне су́мку, пожа́луйста.	DAYtyeh mnyeh SOOMkoo pah-ZHAHLstah

XII. SHOPPING

Gifts and Souvenirs

Before buying gifts for hard currency at the Beryozkas, you might try shopping in a Подарки or Сувениры store, where you can often find the same merchandise for cheaper prices in rubles.

Amber.	Янта́рь.	yeenTAHR'
Balalaika.	Балала́йка.	bahlahLAYkah
Books.	Кни́ги.	KNEEgee
Box of candy.	Коро́бка конфе́т.	kahROHPkah kahnFYEHT
Caviar.	Икра́.	eekRAH
Ceramics.	Кера́мика.	keeRAHmeekah
Chess set.	Ша́хматы.	SHAHKHmahtih
Chocolate.	Шокола́д.	shahkahLAHT
Cigarettes.	Сигаре́ты.	seegahRYEHtih
Cigarette case.	Папиро́сница.	pahpeeROHSneetsah
Cigarette lighter.	Зажига́лка.	zahzheeGAHLkah
Coins.	Моне́ты.	mahNYEHtih
Fur hat.	Мехова́я ша́пка.	meekhahVAHyah SHAHPkah
Icon.	Ико́на.	eeKOHnah
Jewelry.	Драгоце́нности.	drahgahTSEHNahstee
Lace.	Кружева́.	kroozhehVAH
Nested wooden doll.	Матрёшка.	mahtRYOHSHkah
Palekh boxes.	Па́лехские шкату́лки.	PAHleekhskeeyeh shkahTOOlkee
Perfume.	Духи́.	dooKHEE
Postcards.	Откры́тки.	ahtKRIHTkee
Posters.	Плака́ты.	plahKAHtih
Records.	Пласти́нки.	plahstEENkee
Samovar.	Самова́р.	sahmahVAHR
Scarf.	Шарф.	shahrf
Shawl.	Плато́к.	plahTOHK
Stamps.	Ма́рки.	MAHRkee

Tapes.	Кассе́ты.	kahsSYEHtih
Tea caddy.	Ча́йница.	CHAYneetsah
Toys.	Игру́шки.	eegROOSHkee
Vodka.	Во́дка.	VOHTkah
Wine.	Вино́.	veeNOH
Wood carvings.	Резьба́ по де́реву.	rees'BAH pah DYEHreevoo
Wooden spoons and bowls.	Деревя́нные ло́жки и ми́ски.	deereevYAHNnihyeh LOSHkee ee MEESkee

Jewelry

Jewelry department.	Ювели́рные изде́лия.	yooveelEERnihyeh eezDYEHleeyah
Jewelry.	Драгоце́нности.	drahgahTSEHN-nahstee
Bracelet.	Брасле́т.	brahsLYEHT
Brooch.	Брошь.	brohsh
Chain.	Цепо́чка.	tseePOHCHkah
Charm.	Брело́к.	breeLOHK
Clips.	Кли́псы.	KLEEPsih
Cufflinks.	За́понки.	ZAHpahnkee
Earrings.	Се́рьги.	SYEHR'gee
Money clip.	Де́нежная скре́пка.	DYEHneezhnahyah SKRYEHPkah
Necklace.	Ожере́лье.	ahzheeRYEHL'yeh
Pendant.	Куло́н.	kooLOHN
Ring.	Кольцо́.	kahl'TSOH
Tie pin.	Була́вка для га́лстука.	booLAHFkah dlyah GAHLstookah
Watch.	Часы́.	cheeSIH

Stones and Metals

What's it made of?	Из чего́ э́то сде́лано?	ees cheeVOH EHtah ZDYEHlahnah
Is it real silver/ gold?	Э́то настоя́щее серебро́/ зо́лото?	EHtah nahstahYAH-shchehyeh seereebROH/ ZOHlahtah

How many carats is this?	Ско́лько здесь кара́т?	SKOHL'kah zdyehs' kahRAHT
What kind of metal/ stone is it?	Что э́то за мета́лл/ ка́мень?	shtoh EHtah zah meetAHL/ KAHmeen'
Amber.	Янта́рь.	yeenTAHR'
Amethyst.	Амети́ст.	ahmeetEEST
Copper.	Ме́дь.	myeht'
Coral.	Кора́лл.	kahrAHL
Crystal.	Хруста́ль.	khroosTAHL'
Diamond.	Бриллиа́нт.	breelleeAHNT
Ebony.	Чёрное де́рево.	CHOHRnahyeh DYEHreevah
Emerald.	Изумру́д.	eezoomROOT
Garnet.	Грана́т.	grahNAHT
Gilded.	Позоло́ченный.	pahzahLOHCH- ehnnihy
Glass.	Стекло́.	steekLOH
Gold.	Зо́лото.	ZOHlahtah
Ivory.	Слоно́вая кость.	slahNOHvahyah kohst'
Jade.	Нефри́т.	neefREET
Onyx.	О́никс.	OHNeeks
Pearl.	Же́мчуг.	ZHEHMchook
Pewter.	О́лово.	OHlahvah
Platinum.	Пла́тина.	PLAHteenah
Ruby.	Руби́н.	rooBEEN
Sapphire.	Сапфи́р.	sahpFEER
Silver.	Серебро́.	seereeBROH
Silver plated.	Сере́бряный.	seeREEbreenihy
Topaz.	Топа́з.	tahPAHS
Turquoise.	Бирюза́.	beeryooZAH

Books and Stationary Supplies

Bookstore.	Кни́жный магази́н.	KNEEZHnihy mahgahZEEN
Newsstand.	Газе́тный кио́ск.	gahzYEHTnihy keeOHSK
Secondhand bookstore.	Букинисти́ч- еский магази́н.	bookeeneestEECHeh- skeey mahgahZEEN

Stationary store.	Канцтова́ры.	kahntstahVAHrih
Do you have any books in English?	Есть ли у вас книги на англи́йском языке́?	yehst' lee oo vahs KNEEgee nah ahngLEEYskahm yeeZIHkyeh
Do you have any children's books /art books?	Есть ли у вас де́тские книги/ книги по иску́сству?	yehst' lee oo vahs DYEHTskeeyeh KNEEgee/KNEEgee pah eesKOOSTvoo
Where are the guide-books/dic-tionaries?	Где нахо́дятся путеводи́тели/ словари́?	gdyeh nahKHOH-deetsah pootee-vahDEEteelee/ slahvahREE
How much is this book?	Ско́лько сто́ит э́та кни́га?	SKOHL'kah STOHeet EHtah KNEEgah
Where do I pay?	Где мне плати́ть?	gdyeh mnyeh plahTEET'
Have you got...	Есть ли у вас...	yehst' lee oo vahs
calendars?	календа́ри?	kahleenDAHree
envelopes?	конве́рты?	kahnVYEHRtih
magazines in English?	журна́лы на англи́йском языке́?	zhoorNAHlih nah ahngLEEYskahm yeeZIHkyeh
maps?	пла́ны/ка́рты?	PLAHnih/KAHRtih
notebooks?	блокно́ты?	blahkNOHtih
paper?	бума́га?	booMAHgah
pens?	ру́чки?	ROOCHkee
pencils?	карандаши́?	kahrahndahSHEE
post cards?	откры́тки?	ahtKRIHTkee
stationary?	почто́вая бума́га?	pachTOHvahyah booMAHgah

Records

Records.	Пласти́нки.	plahstEENkee
Cassettes.	Kacсе́ты.	kahsSYEHtih
Have you got any rec-ords by...	Есть ли у вас пласти́нки...	yehst' lee oo vahs plahstEENkee
Do you have any...	Есть ли у вас...	yehst' lee oo vahs

98

English	Russian	Pronunciation
Russian folk songs?	ру́сские наро́дные пе́сни?	ROOskeeyeh nah-ROHDnihyeh PYEHsnee
poets reading their work?	поэ́ты, чита́ющие свои́ стихи́?	pahEHtih cheeTAH-yooshcheeyeh svahEE steeKHEE
classical music?	класси́ческая му́зыка?	klahsSEEchehskah-yah MOOzihkah
popular music?	эстра́дная му́зыка?	ehstRAHDnahyah MOOzihkah
recordings of operas and plays?	за́писи о́пер и спекта́клей?	ZAHpeesee OHpeer ee speekTAHkley
rock?	рок-н-ролл?	rohk-n-rohl
Can I listen to this record?	Мо́жно прослу́шать э́ту пласти́нку?	MOHZHnah prahs-LOOshaht' EHtoo plahstEENkoo

Toys

Toys./Games.	Игру́шки./Игры.	eegROOshkee/EEGrih
For a boy.	Для ма́льчика.	dlyah MAHL'cheekah
For a girl.	Для де́вочки.	dlyah DYEHvahchkee
Ball.	Мяч.	myahch
Blocks.	Ку́бики.	KOObeekee
Cards.	Игра́льные ка́рты.	eegRAHL'nihyeh KAHRtih
Checkers.	Ша́шки.	SHAHSHkee
Chess.	Ша́хматы.	SHAHKHmahtih
Doll.	Ку́кла.	KOOklah
Electronic game.	Электро́нная игра́.	ehleekTROHNnahyah eegRAH
Stuffed animal.	Чу́чело.	CHOOchehlah
Teddy bear.	Ми́шка.	MEESHkah
Wooden toys.	Деревя́нные игру́шки.	deereeVYAHNnihyeh eegROOSHkee

Clothes

English	Russian	Pronunciation
Clothes.	Оде́жда.	ahDYEHZHdah
Where can I find a...	Где мне найти́...	gdyeh mnyeh nahyTEE

99

bathing cap?	купа́льную шапочку?	koopAHL'nooyoo SHAHPahchkoo
bathing suit?	купа́льник?	koopAHL'neek
bathrobe?	хала́т?	khahlAHT
belt?	по́яс?	POHyees
blouse?	блу́зку?	BLOOSkoo
bra?	бюстга́льтер?	byoozKHAHL'teer
children's clothes?	де́тскую оде́жду?	DYEHTskooyoo ahDYEHZHdoo
coat?	пальто́?	pahl'TOH
dress?	пла́тье?	PLAHt'yeh
fur coat?	шу́бу?	SHOOboo
fur hat?	мехову́ю ша́пку?	meekhahVOOyoo SHAHPkoo
gloves?	перча́тки?	peerCHAHTkee
handker- chief?	носово́й плато́к?	nahsahVOY plahTOHK
hat?	шля́пу?	SHLYAHpoo
jacket?	ку́ртку?	KOORTkoo
panties?	тру́сики?	TROOSeekee
pants?	брю́ки?	BRYOOkee
pygamas?	пижа́му?	peeZHAHmoo
raincoat?	плащ?	plahshch
scarf?	шарф?	shahrf
shirt?	руба́шку?	rooBAHSHkoo
shorts?	шо́рты?	SHOHRtih
skirt?	ю́бку?	YOOPkoo
slip?	комбина́цию?	kahmbeeNAH- tseeyoo
socks?	носки́?	nahsKEE
stockings?	чулки́?	choolKEE
suit?	костю́м?	kahstYOOM
sweater?	сви́тер?	SVEEteer
sweatsuit?	трениро́вочный костю́м?	treeneeROHVahch- nihy kahstYOOM
swimming trunks?	пла́вки?	PLAHFkee
tie?	га́лстук?	GAHLstook
t-shirt?	ма́йку?	MAYkoo
underwear?	ни́жнее бельё?	NEEZHnehyeh beel'YOH

100

Fit

I don't know my size.	Я не зна́ю мой разме́р.	yah nee ZNAHyoo moy rahzMYEHR
I take a size...	Мой разме́р...	moy rahzMYEHR
Is there a mirror?	Есть ли у вас зе́ркало?	yehst' lee oo vahs ZYEHRkahlah
Can I try it on?	Мо́жно поме́рить?	MOHZHnah pahMYEHreet'
Where is the fitting-room?	Где приме́рочная?	gdyeh preemYEHR-ahchnahyah
Does it fit?	Вам годи́тся?/ Хорошо́ сиди́т?	vahm gahDEEtsah/ khahrahSHOH seeDEET
It fits well.	О́чень хорошо́ сиди́т.	OHcheen' khahrah-SHOH seeDEET
It doesn't suit me.	Не годи́тся.	nee gahDEEtsah
It's too...	Сли́шком...	SLEESHkahm
big/small.	велико́/мало́.	veeleeKOH/mahLOH
long/short.	длинно́/коротко́.	dleeNOH/kahrahtKOH
loose/tight.	широко́/узко́.	sheerahKOH/oosKOH

Colors

Color.	Цвет.	tsvyeht
What color is it?	Како́го э́то цве́та?	kahKOHvah EHtah TSVYEHtah
I don't like the color.	Мне не нра́вится э́тот цвет.	mnyeh nee NRAH-veetsah EHtaht tsvyeht
Do you have other colors?	Есть ли у вас други́е цвета́?	yehst' lee oo vahs drooGEEyeh tsvyehTAH
I'd like something bright.	Я хоте́л(а) бы что́-нибудь я́ркое.	yah khahtYEHL(ah) bih SHTOHneeboot' YAHRkahyeh
Do you have anything in red?	У вас есть что́-нибудь кра́сного цве́та?	oo vahs yehst' SHTOH-neeboot' KRAHS-nahvah TSVYEHtah

Red.	Кра́сный.	KRAHSnihy
Pink.	Ро́зовый.	ROHzahvihy
Violet.	Фиоле́товый.	feeahLYEHtahvihy
Purple.	Пурпу́рный.	poorPOORnihy
Blue.	Си́ний.	SEEneey
Light blue.	Голубо́й.	gahlooBOY
Green.	Зелёный.	zeeLYOHnihy
Orange.	Ора́нжевый.	ahrAHNzhehvihy
Yellow.	Жёлтый.	ZHOHLtihy
Brown.	Кори́чневый.	kahrEECHneevihy
Beige.	Бе́жевый.	BYEHzhehvihy
Grey.	Се́рый.	SYEHrihy
Black.	Чёрный.	CHOHRnihy
White.	Бе́лый.	BYEHlihy
Light- (+color).	Све́тло-...	SVYEHTlah-
Dark- (+color).	Тёмно-...	TYOHMnah-

Materials and Fabrics

Aluminum.	Алюми́ний.	ahlyooMEEneey
Brass.	Лату́нь.	lahtOON'
Ceramics.	Кера́мика.	keeRAHmeekah
Chiffon.	Шифо́н.	sheeFOHN
China.	Фарфо́р.	fahrFOHR
Copper.	Медь.	myeht'
Corduroy.	Вельве́т.	veel'VYEHT
Cotton.	Хлопчато бума́жный.	khlahpchahtah-booMAHZHnihy
Crepe.	Креп.	kryehp
Crystal.	Хруста́ль	khroosTAHL'
Fabric.	Ткань.	tkahn'
Felt.	Фетр.	fyehtr
Flannel.	Ба́йка.	BAYkah
Fur.	Мех.	myehkh
Glass.	Стекло́.	steekLOH
Gold.	Зо́лото.	ZOHlahtah
Iron.	Желе́зо.	zheeLYEHzah
Lace.	Кружева́.	kroozhehVAH
Leather.	Ко́жа.	KOHzhah
Linen.	Полотно́.	pahlahtNOH
Metal.	Мета́лл.	meetAHL

Nylon.	Нейлон.	neyLOHN
Plastic.	Платмасса.	plahtMAHSsah
Satin.	Атлас.	ahtLAHS
Silk.	Шёлк.	shohlk
Silver.	Серебро.	seereeBROH
Steel.	Сталь.	stahl'
Stone.	Камень.	KAHmeen'
Suede.	Замша.	ZAHMshah
Synthetic.	Синтетика.	seenTYEHteekah
Terrycloth.	Махровая ткань.	mahkhROHvahyah tkahn'
Velvet.	Бархат.	BAHRkhaht
Wood.	Дерево.	DYEHreevah
Wool.	Шерсть.	shehrst'

Shoes

Shoes.	Обувь.	OHboovee
Boots.	Сапоги.	sahpahGEE
Felt boots.	Валенки.	VAHleenkee
Sandals.	Сандалии.	sahnDAHleeee
Slippers.	Тапочки.	TAHpahchkee
Children's shoes.	Детская обувь.	DYEHTskeeyeh OHboovee
Shoelaces.	Шнурки.	SHNOORkee
Are these made of cloth/ suede/ leather/ rubber?	Они сделанны из ткани/ замши/ кожи/ резины?	ahNEE ZDYEHlahnnih ees TKAHNee/ ZAHMshee/ KOHzhee/ reeZEEnih
I take a size...	У меня номер...	oo meenYAH NOHmeer
I don't know my size.	Я не знаю мой номер.	yah nee ZNAHyoo moy NOHmeer
Can I try these on in a size...	Я хочу примерить эти, номер...	yah khahCHOO preeMEEReet' EHtee, NOHmeer
These are too big/ small/ narrow/ wide.	Они слишком большие/ маленькие/ узкие/ широкие.	ahNEE SLEESHkahm bahl'SHEEyeh/ mahlYEHN'keeyeh/ OOSkeeyeh / sheeROHkeeyeh

103

Groceries

Groceries.	Продукты.	prahDOOKtih
I'd like...	Я хотéл(а) бы...	yah khahtYEHL(ah) bih
a piece of that.	кусóк этого.	koosOHK EHtahvah
a half kilo...	полкилó...	pohlkeeLOH
a kilo...	килогрáмм...	keelahgRAHMM
one-and-a-half kilos...	полторá килó...	pohltahRAH keeLOH
50 grams...	пятьдесят грамм...	peet'deesYAHT grahm
100 grams...	сто грамм...	stoh grahm
a liter of...	литр...	leetr
a bottle of...	бутылку...	bootlHLkoo
ten eggs.	десяток яиц.	deeSYAHtahk yaheets
a packet of cookies/ tea.	пáчку печéнья/ чáя.	PAHCHkoo peechEHN'yah/ CHAHyah
a can of pears.	бáнку консервирóванных груш.	BAHNkoo kahnseerveerOHVahnnihk groosh
a jar of sour cream.	бáнку сметáны.	BAHNkoo smeeTAHnih
a loaf of bread.	бухáнку хлéба.	bookhAHNkoo KHLYEHbah
a box of candy.	корóбку конфéт.	kahROHPkoo kahnFYEHT
a bar of chocolate.	плитку шоколáда.	PLEETkoo shahkahLAHdah

Health and Beauty Aides

Absorbent cotten.	Вáта.	VAHtah
Antiseptic.	Антисептическая мазь.	ahnteeseepTEECHeeskahyah mahs'
Aspirin.	Аспирин.	ahspeerEEN
Ace-bandage.	Эластичный бинт.	ehlahsTEECHnihy beent
Band-Aides.	Плáстырь.	PLAHStihr'
Bobby-pins.	Закóлки.	zahKOHLkee

Comb.	Расчёска.	rahsCHOHSkah
Condoms.	Презервативы.	preezeervahTEEvih
Contra-ceptives.	Противоза-чаточные средства.	prahteevahzah-CHAHtahchnihyeh SRYEHTstvah
Cough drops.	Таблетки от кашля.	tahbLYEHTkee aht KAHSHlyah
Curlers.	Бигуди.	beegooDEE
Deodorant.	Дезодорант.	deezahdahRAHT
Diapers.	Пелёнки.	peelYOHNkee
Disinfectant.	Дизинфицир-ующее средство.	deezeenfeeTSEER-ooyooshchehyeh SRYEHTstvah
Ear drops.	Ушные капли.	ooshNIHyeh KAHPlee
Eye drops.	Глазные капли.	glahzNIHyeh KAHPlee
Eye liner.	Тушь для век.	toosh dlyah vyehk
Eye shadow.	Тени для век.	TYEHnee dlyah vyehk
Hair brush.	Щётка для волос.	SHCHOHTkah dlyah VOHlahs
Hair dye.	Краска.	KRAHSkah
Hair spray.	Лак.	lahk
Hand cream.	Крем для рук.	kryehm dlyah rook
Insect repelent.	Средство от насекомых.	SRYEHTstvah aht nahseeKOHmihkh
Iodine.	Йод.	yoht
Laxative.	Слабительное.	slahBEEteel'nahyeh
Lipstick	Губная помада.	goobNAHyah pahMAHdah
Make-up.	Косметика.	kahsMYEHteekah
Mascara.	Тушь для ресниц.	toosh dlyah reesNEETS
Nail clipper.	Ножницы для ногтей.	NOHZHneetsih dlyah nahkTEY
Nail file.	Пилочка.	PEElahchkah
Nail polish.	Лак для ногтей.	lahk dlyah nahkTEY
Nail polish remover.	Ацетон.	ahtseeTOHN
Pacifier.	Соска.	SOHSkah
Perfume.	Духи.	dooKHEE
Razor.	Бритва.	BREETvah

English	Russian	Pronunciation
Razor blades.	Лезвия.	LYEHZveeyah
Rouge.	Румяна.	roomYAHnah
Safety pins.	английские булавки.	ahngLEEYskeeyeh boolAHFkee
Sanitary napkins.	Гигиенические салфетки.	geegeeeehnEECH-eeskeeyeh sahlFYEHTkee
Shampoo.	Шампунь.	shahmpOON'
Shaving cream.	Крем для бритья.	kryehm dlyah breet'YAH
Sleeping pills.	Снотворное.	snahTVOHnahyeh
Soap.	Мыло.	MIHlah
Sponge.	Губка.	GOOPkah
Sun-tan lotion.	Крем для загара.	kryehm dlyah zahGAHrah
Thermo-meter.	Градусник.	GRAHdoosneek
Throat lozengers.	Таблетки для горла.	tahbLYEHTkee dlyah GOHRlah
Toilet paper.	Туалетная бумага.	tooahlYEHTnahyah booMAHgah
Tooth brush.	Зубная щётка.	zoobNAHyah SHCHOHTkah
Tooth paste.	Зубная паста.	zoobNAHyah PAHStah
Tranquil-lizer.	Успокоительное.	oospahkahEET-eel'nahyeh
Tweezers.	Пинцет.	peentsEHT
Vitamins.	Витамины.	veetahMEEnih

106

XIII. ACCIDENTS AND EMERGENCIES

Help

I need help.	Мне нужна́ по́мощь.	mnyeh noozhNAH POHmahshch
There's been an accident.	Произошёл несча́стный слу́чай.	praheezahSHOHL neeSHAHSTnih SLOOchay
Please call the...	Вы́зовите, пожа́луйста...	VIHzahveetyeh pahZHAHLstah
American/ British/ Canadian embassy.	америка́нское/ англи́йское/ кана́дское посо́льство.	ahmeereeKAHN-skahyeh/ahngLEEY -skahyeh/kah-NAHTskahyeh pahSOHL'stvah
consulate.	ко́нсульство.	KOHNsool'stvah
ambulance.	ско́рую по́мощь.	SKOHrooyoo POHmahshch
Please get...	Пожалуйста, вы́зовите...	pahZHAHLstah VIHzahveetyeh
a doctor.	врача́.	vrahCHAH
the police.	мили́цию.	meeLEEtseeyoo
Please notify...	Пожа́луйста, сообщи́те...	pahZHAHLstah sahahpSHCHEEtyeh
my husband.	моему́ му́жу.	maheeMOO MOOzhoo
my wife.	мое́й жене́.	maheey zhehNYEH
my family.	мое́й семье́.	maheey seem'YEH
my hotel.	в мою гости́ницу.	vmahyoo gahSTEEneetsoo
I've had my ... stolen.	У меня́ укра́ли...	oo meenYAH ookRAHlee
I've lost my...	Я потеря́л(а)...	yah pahteer-YAHL(ah)
passport.	па́спорт.	PAHSpahrt
wallet.	бума́жник.	booMAHZHneek
purse.	су́мку.	SOOMkoo
keys.	ключи́.	klyooCHEE
money.	де́ньги.	DYEHN'gee

Illness and Injury

He/She is hurt.	Он бо́лен./Она́ больна́.	ohn BOHleen/ ahNAH bahl'NAH
He/She is bleeding badly.	У него́/неё си́льное кровотече́ние.	oo neeVOH/neeYOH SEEL'nahyeh krahvahtee- CHEHneeyeh
He/She is unconscious.	Он/Она́ потеря́л(а) созна́ние.	ohn/ahNAH pahteer- YAHL(ah) sahz- NAHneeyeh
He/She is seriously injured.	У него́/неё серьёзное поврежде́ние.	oo neeVOH/neeYOH seer'YOHZnahyeh pahvreezhDYEH- neeyeh
I'm in pain.	Мне бо́льно.	mnyeh BOHL'nah
My ... hurts.	У меня́ боли́т...	oo meenYAH bahlEET
I can't move my...	Я не могу́ дви́нуть...	yah nee mahGOO DVEEnoot'
I'm ill. (f)	Я бо́лен/ больна́.	yah BOHleen/ (bahl'NAH)
I'm dizzy.	У меня́ кру́жится голова́.	oo meenYAH KROOZHeetsah gahlahVAH
I'm nauseous.	Меня́ тошни́т.	meenYAH tahshNEET
I feel feverish.	Меня́ лихора́дит.	meenYAH leekhah- RAHdeet
I've vomited.	Меня́ вы́рвало.	meenYAH VIHRvahlah
I've got food poisoning.	У меня́ пищево́е отравле́ние.	oo meenYAH peeshchehVOHyeh ahtrahvLYEH- neeyeh
I've got diarrhea.	У меня́ поно́с.	oo meenYAH pahNOHS
I'm constipated.	У меня́ запо́р.	oo meenYAH zahpOHR
It hurts to swallow.	Мне бо́льно глота́ть.	mnyeh BOHL'nah glahtAHT'
I'm having trouble breathing.	Мне тру́дно дыша́ть.	mnyeh TROOdnah dihshAHT'

108

English	Russian	Pronunciation
I have chest pain.	У меня боль в груди.	oo meenYAH bohl' fgrooDEE
I've got indigestion.	У меня несварение желудка.	oo meenYAH nee-svahRYEHneeyeh zheelOOTkah
I've got a bloody nose.	У меня кровотечение из носа.	oo meenYAH krahvahteeCHEH-neeyeh ees NOHsah
I've got sun stroke.	У меня солнечный удар.	oo meenYAH SOHLneechnihy ooDAHR
I'm sunburned.	я загорал(а).	yah zahgahrAHL(ah)
I've got a cramp/ cramps.	У меня судороги/ схватки.	oo meenYAH SOOdahrahgee/ SKHVAHTkee
I've got a bladder/ vaginal infection.	У меня воспаление пузыря / влагалища.	oo meenYAH vahspahlYEHNee-yeh poozihRYAH/ vlahGAHleeshchah
I've broken my arm.	Я сломал(а) руку.	yah slahMAHL(ah) ROOkoo
I've sprained my ankle.	Я подвернул(а) ногу.	yah pahdveerNOOL-(ah) NOHgoo
I've dislocated my shoulder.	Я вывихнул(а) лопатку.	yah VIHveekhnool-(ah) lahPAHTkoo
I've been stung by a wasp/bee.	Меня укусила оса/пчела.	meenYAH ookoo-SEElah ahSAH/ pchehLAH
I've got...	У меня...	oo meenYAH
arthritis.	артрит.	ahrtREET
asthma.	астма.	AHSTmah
diabetis.	диабет.	deeahbYEHT
high blood pressure.	высокое давление.	VIHsahkahyeh dahvLYEHneeyeh
an ulcer.	язва.	YAHZvah

Parts of the Body

English	Russian	Pronunciation
Ankle.	Лодыжка.	lahDIHSHkah
Appendix.	Аппендикс.	ahPYEHNdeeks
Arm.	Рука.	rooKAH

English	Russian	Pronunciation
Back.	Спина́.	speeNAH
Bladder.	Мочево́й пузы́рь.	mahchehVOY poozIHR'
Blood.	Кровь.	krohf'
Body.	Те́ло.	TYEHlah
Bone.	Кость.	kohst'
Breasts.	Грудь.	groot'
Calves.	И́кры	EEKrah
Cheek.	Щека́.	shchehKAH
Chest cavity.	Грудна́я по́лость.	groodNAHyah POHlahst'
Ear/Ears.	Ухо/Уши.	OOkah/OOshee
Elbow.	Ло́коть.	LOHkaht'
Eye.	Глаз.	glahs
Face.	Лицо́.	leeTSOH
Finger.	Па́лец.	PAHleets
Foot.	Нога́.	nahGAH
Gall bladder.	Жёлчный пузы́рь.	ZHOHLCHnihy poozIHR'
Genitals.	Половы́е о́рганы.	pahlahVIHyeh OHRgahnih
Glands.	Же́лезы.	ZHEHlehzih
Hand.	Рука́.	rooKAH
Heart.	Се́рдце.	SYEHRTtseh
Heel.	Пя́тка.	PYAHTkah
Hip.	Бедро́.	beedROH
Intestines.	Кишки́.	keeshKEE
Jaw.	Че́люсть.	CHEHlyoost'
Joint.	Суста́в.	soosTAHF
Kidney.	По́чка.	POHCHkah
Knee.	Коле́но.	kahLYEHnah
Leg.	Нога́.	nahGAH
Lip.	Губа́.	gooBAH
Liver.	Пе́чень.	PYEHchehn'
Lungs.	Лёгкие.	LYOHKHkeeyeh
Mouth.	Рот.	roht
Muscle.	Мы́шца.	MIHSHtsah
Neck.	Ше́я.	SHEHyah
Nerve.	Нерв.	nyehrf
Nose.	Нос.	nohs
Rib.	Ребро́.	reebROH
Shoulder.	Плечо́.	pleeCHOH
Skin.	Ко́жа.	KOHzhah

Spine.	Позвоно́чник.	pahzvahNOHCHneek
Stomach.	Живо́т.	zheeVOHT
Teeth.	Зу́бы.	ZOObih
Tendon.	Сухожи́лие.	sookhahZHEEleeyeh
Throat.	Го́рло.	GOHRlah
Thumb.	Большо́й па́лец.	bahl'SHOY PAHleets
Toe.	Па́лец ноги́.	PAHleets nahGEE
Tongue.	Язы́к.	yeezIHK
Tonsils.	Минда́лины.	meenDAHleenih
Vein.	Ве́на.	VYEHnah
Wrist.	Запя́стье.	zahPYAHST'yeh

Seeing a Doctor

I'd like an appointment... for tomorrow.	Я хочу́ записа́ться на приём... на за́втра.	yah khahCHOO zapeeSAHTsah nah preeYOHM nah ZAHFtrah
as soon as possible.	как мо́жно скоре́е.	kahk MOHZHnah skahRYEHyee
Where does it hurt?	Что у вас боли́т?	shtoh oo vahs bahLEET
Is the pain sharp/dull /constant?	Боль о́страя/ тупа́я/ постоя́нная?	bohl' OHStrahyah/ tooPAHyah/pahstahYAHnahyah
How long have you felt this way?	Вы давно́ так себя́ чу́вствуете?	vih dahvNOH tahk seeBYAH CHOOSTvooyehtyeh
I'll take your temperature.	Я изме́рю вашу температу́ру.	yah eezMYEHryoo vashoo teempeerahTOOroo
I'll measure your blood pressure.	Я изме́рю ваше давле́ние.	yah eezMYEHryoo vahsheh dahvLYEHneeyeh
I'll take your pulse.	Я пошу́паю ваш пульс.	yah pahSHOOpahyoo vahsh pool's
Roll up your sleeve.	Засучи́те рука́в.	zahsooCHEEtyeh rookAHF
Undress to the waist.	Разде́ньтесь до по́яса.	rahzDYEHN'tees' dah POHyeesah

111

Breathe deeply.	Сде́лайте глубо́кий вдох.	ZDYEHlaytyeh glooBOHkeey vdohkh
Open your mouth.	Откро́йте рот.	ahtKROYtyeh roht
Cough.	Пока́шляйте.	pahKAHSHlyahtyeh
I'll need an X-ray.	На́до сде́лать рентге́н.	NAHdah ZDYEHlaht' reentGYEHN
Is it serious?	Это серьёзно?	EHtah seer'YOHZnah
Do I need surgery?	Мне нужна́ опера́ция?	mnyeh noozhNAH ahpeeRAHTSeeyah
It's broken/ sprained.	Это слома́но/ подверну́то.	EHtah slahMAHnah/ pahdveerNOOtah
You need a cast.	Вам ну́жен гипс.	vahm NOOzhen geeps
You've pulled a muscle.	Вы растяну́ли мы́шцу.	vih rahstyahNOOlee MIHSHtsoo
It's infected.	У вас зараже́ние.	oo vahs zahrah-ZHEHneeyeh
It's not contagious.	Это не зара́зно.	EHtah nee zahRAHZnah
Get well!	Поправля́йтесь!	pahprahvLYAYtees'

Seeing a Dentist

Dentist.	Зубно́й врач.	zoobNOY vrahch
I need a dentist.	Мне ну́жен зубно́й врач.	mnyeh NOOzhen zoobNOY vrahch
What are the clinic's hours?	Когда́ приёмные часы́ в поликли́нике?	kahgDAH preeYOHMnihyeh cheeSIH vpahlee-KLEEneekeh
I want to make an appoint-ment.	Я хочу́ записа́ться на приём.	yah khahCHOO zahpeeSAHTsah nah preeYOHM
Will I have to wait long?	Мне придётся до́лго ждать?	mnyeh preedYOHT-sah DOHLgah zhdaht'
I have...	У меня́...	oo meenYAH
an abscess.	нары́в.	nahrIHF

112

English	Russian	Pronunciation
a broken tooth.	сломáлся зуб.	slahMAHLsah zoop
a broken denture.	сломáлся протéз.	slahMAHLsah prahTYEHS
lost a filling.	вы́пала плóмба.	VIHpahlah PLOHMbah
a toothache.	болѝт зуб.	bahLEET zoop
a cavity.	дуплó.	doopLOH
sore and bleeding gums.	дёсны óчень воспалены́ и кровоточáт.	DYOHSnih OHcheen' vahspahlyohNIH ee krahvahtahchAHT
Don't pull it out.	Не вырывáйте егó.	nee vihrihVAYtyeh yeeVOH
Can you fix it temporarily?	Мóжно ли егó врéменно залечѝть?	MOHZHnah lee yeeVOH VRYEHMeenhah zahlee-CHEET'
When will my denture be ready?	Когдá бýдет готóв протéз?	kahgDAH BOOdeet gahTOHF prahtYEHZ
May I have an anesthetic?	Мóжно сдéлать обезбóливание?	MOHZHnah ZDYEHlaht' ahbeesBOHleevahneeyeh

Treatment

English	Russian	Pronunciation
I'm taking medication.	Я принимáю лекáрство.	yah preeneeMAHyoo leekAHRSTvah
What medicine are you taking?	Какóе лекáрство вы принимáете?	kahKOHyeh leekAHRstvah vih preeneeMAHeetyeh
I'm taking antibiotics.	Я принимáю антибиóтики.	yah preeneeMAHyoo ahnteebeeOHteekee
I'm on the Pill.	Я принимáю противозачáточные пилю́ли.	yah preeneeMAHyoo prahteevahzahchAHTahchnihyeh peelYOOlee
I'm allergic to penicillin.	У меня́ аллергѝя на пеницилли́н.	oo meenYAH ahlleerGEEyah nah peeneetseelLEEN

113

English	Russian	Pronunciation
I'll prescribe an antibiotic/a painkiller.	Я пропишу́ вам антибио́тик/ болеутоля́ющее сре́дство.	yah prahpeeSHOO vahm ahnteebeeOHteek/bahleeootahLYAHyooshchehyeh SRYEHTstvah
Where can I have this prescription filled?	Где мо́жно доста́ть пека́рство по э́тому реце́пту?	gdyeh MOHZHnah dahsTAHT' leekAHRSTvah pah EHtahmoo reetsEHPtoo
When should I take the medicine?	Когда́ мне принима́ть э́то лека́рство?	kahgDAH mnyeh preeneemAHT' EHtah leekAHRSTvah
Take...	Принима́йте...	preeneeMAYtyeh
2 pills.	по две табле́тки.	pah dvyeh tahbLYEHTkee
3 teaspoons.	по три ча́йных ло́жки.	pah tree CHAYnihkh LOHSHkee
every 2/6 hours.	ка́ждые два часа́/шесть часо́в.	KAHZHdihyeh dvah cheeSAH/shehst' cheesOHF
twice a day.	два ра́за в день.	dvah RAHzah vdyehn'
before meals.	пе́ред едо́й.	PYEHreet yeeDOY
after meals.	по́сле еды́.	POHSlee yeeDIH
as needed.	когда́ вам на́до.	kahgDAH vahm NAHdah
for 5/10 days	пять/де́сять дне́й	pyaht'/DYEHsaht' dnyay
I feel better/ worse/ the same.	Я чу́вствую себя́ лу́чше/ ху́же/ так же.	yah CHOOSTvooyoo seeBYAH LOOCHsheh/KHOOzheh/ tahk zheh
Can I travel on Friday?	Могу́ ли я отпра́виться в путь в пя́тницу?	mahGOO lee yah ahtPRAHVeet'sah fpoot' FPYAHTneetsoo

At the Hospital

Hospital.	Больни́ца.	bahl'NEEtsah
Clinic.	Поликли́ника.	pahleeKLEEneekah
Doctor.	Врач.	vrahch
Surgeon.	Хиру́рг.	kheerOORK
Gynecologist.	Гинеко́лог.	geeneeKOHlahk
Ophtha-mologist.	Офтальмо́лог.	ahftahl'MOHlahk
Pediatrician.	Педиа́тр.	peedeeAHTR
Nurse.	Медсестра́.	meedseesTRAH
Patient. (f)	Пацие́нт(ка).	pahtseeEHNT(kah)
Anesthesia.	Анестези́я.	ahneesteeZEEyah
Bedpan.	Подкладно́е су́дно.	pahtklahdNOHyeh SOODnah
Injection.	Уко́л.	ookOHL
Operation.	Опера́ция.	ahpeerAHTSeeyah
Transfusion.	Перелива́ние кро́ви.	peereeleeVAH-neeyeh KROHvee
Thermo-meter.	Гра́дусник.	GRAHdoosneek
I can't sleep/eat.	Я не могу́ спать/есть.	yah nee mahGOO spaht'/yehst'
When will the doctor come?	Когда́ придёт врач?	kahgDAH preedYOHT vrahch
When can I get out of bed?	Когда́ я смогу́ встава́ть?	kahgDAH yah smahGOO fstahVAHT'
When are visiting hours?	Мо́жно навести́ть больно́го?	MOHZHnah nahvehsTEET' bahl'NOHvah

115

XIV. NUMBERS AND TIME EXPRESSIONS

Cardinal Numbers

Russian numbers are highly irregular. The number "one" agrees in gender with the noun it modifies, so that it can be either masculine, feminine or neuter. The number "two" has two forms: one serves as both masculine and neuter, while the other form is reserved for feminine subjects. All the remaining numbers have only one form.

0	Ноль/Нуль.	nohl'/nool'
1(m/f/n)	Один/Одна́/Одно́.	ahdEEN/ahdNAH/ahdNOH
2 (m/n, f)	Два/Две.	dvah/dvyeh
3	Три.	tree
4	Четы́ре.	chehTIHree
5	Пять.	pyaht'
6	Шесть.	shehst'
7	Семь.	syehm'
8	Во́семь.	VOHseem'
9	Де́вять.	DYEHveet'
10	Де́сять.	DYEHseet'
11	Оди́ннадцать.	ahDEENnahtsaht'
12	Двена́дцать.	dveeNAHtsaht'
13	Трина́дцать.	treeNAHtsaht'
14	Четы́рнадцать.	chehTIHRnahtsaht'
15	Пятна́дцать.	peetNAHtsaht
16	Шестна́дцать.	sheesNAHtsaht'
17	Семна́дцать.	seemNAHtsaht'
18	Восемна́дцать.	vahseemNAHtsaht'
19	Девятна́дцать.	deeveetNAHtsaht'
20	Два́дцать.	DVAHtsaht'
21	Два́дцать оди́н.	DVAHtsaht' ahdEEN
22	Два́дцать два.	DVAHtsaht' dvah
23	Два́дцать три.	DVAHtsaht' tree
24	Два́дцать четы́ре.	DVAHtsaht' chehTIHree
25	Два́дцать пять.	DVAHtsaht' pyaht'
26	Два́дцать шесть.	DVAHtsaht' shehst'

27	Двадцать семь.	DVAHtsaht' syehm'
28	Двадцать восемь.	DVAHtsaht' VOHseem'
29	Двадцать девять.	DVAHtsaht' DYEHveet'
30	Тридцать.	TREEtsaht'
31	Тридцать один.	TREEtsaht' ahdEEN
40	Сорок.	SOHrahk
41	Сорок один.	SOHrahk ahdEEN
50	Пятьдесят.	peet'deesYAHT'
60	Шестьдесят.	sheezdeesYAHT'
70	Семьдесят.	SYEHM'deeseet
80	Восемьдесят.	VOHseem'deeseet
90	Девяносто.	deeveeNOHstah
100	Сто.	stoh
200	Двести.	DVYEHstee
300	Триста.	TREEstah
400	Четыреста	chehTIHreestah
500	Пятьсот.	peet'SOHT
600	Шестьсот.	sheesSOHT
700	Семьсот.	seem'SOHT
800	Восемьсот.	vahseem'SOHT
900	Девятьсот.	deeveet'SOHT
1,000	Тысяча.	TIHseechah
2,000	Две тысячи.	dvyeh TIHseechee
5,000	Пять тысяч.	pyaht' TIHseech
100,000	Сто тысяч.	stoh TIHseech
1,000,000	Миллион.	meelleeOHN

Ordinal Numbers

Since they act as adjectives grammatically, all ordinal numbers have masculine (-ый, -ой), feminine (-ая) and neuter forms (-ое), which can be identified by their endings. The number "three" has irregular ("soft") endings.

First.	Первый. (-ая, -ое)	PYEHRvihy (-ahyah, -ahyeh)
Second.	Второй. (-ая, -ое)	vtahROY (-ahyah, -ahyeh)
Third.	Третий. (-ья, -ье)	TRYEHteey (-'yah, -'yeh)

117

English	Russian	Pronunciation
Fourth.	Четвёртый.	chehtVYOHRtihy
Fifth.	Пятый.	PYAHtihy
Sixth.	Шестой.	sheesTOY
Seventh.	Седьмой.	seed'MOY
Eighth.	Восьмой.	vahs'MOY
Ninth.	Девятый.	deevYAHtihy
Tenth.	Десятый.	deesYAHtihy
Eleventh.	Одиннадцатый.	ahDEEnahtsahtihy
Twelfth.	Двенадцатый.	dveeNAHtsahtihy
Thirteenth.	Тринадцатый.	treeNAHtsahtihy
Fourteenth.	Четырнадцатый.	chehTIHRnaht-sahtihy
Fifteenth.	Пятнадцатый.	peetNAHtsahtihy
Sixteenth.	Шестнадцатый.	sheesNAHtsahtihy
Seventeenth.	Семнадцатый.	seemNAHtsahtihy
Eighteenth.	Восемнадцатый.	vahseemNAH-tsahtihy
Nineteenth.	Девятнадцатый.	deeveetNAHtsahtihy
Twentieth.	Двадцатый.	dvahTSAHtihy
Thirtieth.	Тридцатый.	treeSAHtihy
Fortieth.	Сороковой.	sahrahkahVOY
Hundredth.	Сотый.	SOHtih
Thousandth	Тысячный.	TIHseechnihy

Quantities and Measurements

Quantity.	Количество.	kahLEEchehstvah
A lot./Much.	Много.	MNOHgah
A little./	Мало./	MAHlah/
Few.	Несколько.	NYEHskahl'kah
More./	Больше./	BOHL'sheh/
Less.	Меньше.	MYEHN'sheh
Most/	Больше/	BOHL'sheh/
least/	меньше/	MYEHN'sheh/
best/	лучше/	LOOCHsheh/
worst	хуже	KHOOzheh
of all.	всего.	vseeVOH
Majority./	Большинство./	bahl'sheenstVOH/
Minority.	Меньшинство.	meen'sheenstVOH
Enough./	Достаточно./	dahsTAHtahchnah/
Too much.	Слишком много.	SLEESHkahm MNOHgah
A third.	Треть.	tryeht'

English	Russian	Pronunciation
A quarter.	Че́тверть.	CHEHTveert'
A half.	Полови́на.	pahlahVEEnah
Three-quarters.	Три че́тверти.	tree CHEHTveertee
The whole.	Це́лое.	TSEHlahyeh
Once.	Раз.	rahs
Twice.	Два ра́за.	dvah RAHzah
Three times.	Три ра́за.	tree RAHzah
Five times.	Пять ра́з.	pyaht' rahs
Early./Late.	Ра́но./По́здно.	RAHnah/POHZnah
Now.	Сейча́с.	seeCHAHS
Still.	Ещё.	yeeSHCHOH
Never.	Никогда́.	neekahgDAH
Seldom.	Ре́дко.	RYEHTkah
Sometimes.	Иногда́.	eenahgDAH
Usually.	Обы́чно.	ahblHCHnah
Often.	Ча́сто.	CHAHStah
Always.	Всегда́.	FSYEHGdah
In the past.	В про́шлом.	FPROHSHlahm
In the future.	В бу́дущем.	FBOOdooshchehm
A long time ago.	Да́вным давно́.	DAHVnihm dahvNOH
A short while ago.	Не так давно́.	nee tahk dahvNOH

Days and Weeks

English	Russian	Pronunciation
Sunday.	Воскресе́нье.	vahskreeSYEHN'yeh
Monday.	Понеде́льник.	pahneedYEHL'neek
Tuesday.	Вто́рник.	FTOHRneek
Wednesday.	Среда́.	sreeDAH
Thursday.	Четве́рг.	chehtVYEHRK
Friday.	Пя́тница.	PYAHTneetsah
Saturday.	Суббо́та.	soobBOHtah
On Wednesday.	В сре́ду.	FSRYEHdoo
On Monday.	В понеде́льник.	fpahneedYEHL'neek
Last Saturday.	В про́шлую суббо́ту.	FPROHSHlooyoo soobBOHtoo
Next Thursday.	В бу́дущий четве́рг.	FBOOdooshcheey chehtVYEHRK

119

English	Russian	Pronunciation
From Monday to Friday.	С понедельника до пятницы.	spahneedYEHL'nee-kah dah PYAHT-neetsih
What day is it today?	Какой сегодня день недели?	kahKOY seeVOH-dnyah dyehn' neeDYEHlee
It's Tuesday.	Сегодня вторник.	seeVOHdnyah FTOHRneek
Week.	Неделя.	neeDYEHlyah
Last week.	На прошлой неделе.	nah PROHSHlay neeDYEHlyeh
This week.	На этой неделе.	nah EHtay nee-DYEHlyeh
Next week.	На будущей неделе.	nah BOOdooshchey neeDYEHLyeh
In two weeks.	Через две недели.	CHEHrees dvyeh neeDYEHlee
In five weeks.	Через пять недель.	CHEHrees pyaht' neeDYEHL'
Every week.	Каждую неделю.	KAHZHdooyoo neeDYEHlyoo
For 3 weeks.	На три недели.	nah tree neeDYEHlee
Two weeks ago.	Две недели назад.	dvyeh neeDYEHlee nahzAHT

Months

English	Russian	Pronunciation
Month.	Месяц.	MYEHseets
This month.	В этом месяце.	VEHtahm MYEHseetseh
Last month.	В прошлом месяце.	FPROHSHlahm MYEHseetseh
Next month.	В будущем месяце.	FBOOdooshchehm MYEHseetseh
Every month.	Каждый месяц.	KAHZHdihy MYEHseets
In a month.	Через месяц.	CHEHrees MYEHseets
January.	Январь.	yeenVAHR'
February.	Февраль.	feevRAHL'
March.	Март.	mahrt
April.	Апрель.	ahpRYEHL'
May.	Май.	mahy
June.	Июнь.	eeYOON'

120

English	Russian	Pronunciation
July.	Июль.	eeYOHL'
August.	Август.	AHVgoost
September.	Сентябрь.	seenTYAHBR'
October.	Октябрь.	ahkTYAHBR'
November.	Ноябрь.	nahYAHBR'.
December.	Декабрь.	deeKAHBR'
In July...	В июне...	veeYOONyeh
Since January...	С января...	syeenvahrYAH
In the beginning of October...	В начале октября...	vnahCHAHlyeh ahkteebRYAH
In the middle of December...	В середине декабря...	fseereeDEEnyeh deekahbRYAH
In the end of April...	В конце апреля...	fkahnTSEH ahpRYEHlyah
We'll be here from June to August.	Мы здесь будем с июня до августа.	mih zdyehs' BOOdeem seeYOONyah dah AHVgoostah
We'll be here from the 3rd of May through the 19th of July.	Мы здесь будем с третьего мая по девятнадцатое июля.	mih zdyehs' BOOdeem STRYEHt'eevah MAHyah pah deeveetNAHtsahtahyeh eeYOOL'yah
I've been here since October 14th.	Я здесь с четырнадцатого октября.	yah zdyehs' schehtIHRnahtsahtahvah ahkteebRYAH
What's the date?	Какое сегодня число?	kahKOHyeh seeVOHdnyah cheesLOH
It's January 22nd.	Сегодня двадцать второе января.	seeVOHdnyah DVAHtsaht' vtahROHyeh yeenvahrYAH
When did he come?	Когда он приехал?	kahgDAH ohn preeYEHkhahl
He arrived on May 20th.	Он приехал двадцатого мая.	ohn preeYEHkhahl dvahTSAHtahvah MAHyah

121

Years

Year.	Год.	goht
Decade.	Десятилéтие.	deeseeteeLYEHteeyeh
Century.	Век.	vyehk
This year.	В э́том году́.	VEHtahm gahDOO
Next year.	В бу́дущем году́.	FBOOdooshchehm gahDOO
Last year.	В про́шлом году́.	FPROHSHlahm gahDOO
In a year.	Че́рез год.	CHEHrees goht
For a year.	На год.	NAH goht
Three years ago.	Три го́да наза́д.	tree GOHdah nahzAHT
Year round.	Кру́глый год.	KROOGlihy goht
In the 19th century.	В девятна́дцатом ве́ке.	vdeeveetNAHtsahtahm VYEHkyeh
In the 20th century.	В двадца́том ве́ке.	vdvahTSAHtahm VYEHkyeh
In the 21st century.	В два́дцать пе́рвом ве́ке.	VDVAHtsaht' PYEHRvahm VYEHkyeh
In 2010.	В две ты́сячи деся́том году́.	vdvyeh TIHseechee deeSYAHtahm gahDOO
In 1991.	В ты́сяча девятьсо́т девяно́сто пе́рвом году́.	FTIHseechah deeveetSOHT deeveeNOHstah PYEHRvahm gahDOO
In 1985.	В ты́сяча девятьсо́т во́семьдесят пя́том году́.	FTIHseechah deeveetSOHT VOHseem'deeseet PYAHTahm gahDOO
How old are you?	Ско́лько вам лет?	SKOHL'kah vahm lyeht

122

I'm 28/51 years old.	Мне двáдцать вóсемь лет /пятьдеся́т оди́н год.*	mnyeh DVAHtsaht' VOHseem' lyeht/ peet'deeSYAHT ahDEEN goht
When was he/she born?	Когдá он роди́лся?/ Когдá онá родилáсь?	kahgDAH ohn rahDEELsah/ kahgDAH ahNAH rahdeeLAHS'
He was born in...1936/ 1960.	Он роди́лся в... ты́сяча девятьсо́т три́дцать шесто́м году́/ ты́сча девятьсо́т шестидеся́том году́.	ohn rahDEELsah VTIHseechah deeveet'SOHT TREEtsaht' shehs-TOHM gahDOO/ TIHseechah deev-eetSOHT sheezdee-deeSYAHtahm gahDOO

Other Time Expressions

Today.	Сего́дня.	seeVOHdnyah
Tomorrow.	За́втра.	ZAHFtrah
Yesterday.	Вчера́.	vchehRAH
Day after tomorrow.	Послеза́втра.	pahsleeZAHFtrah
Day before yesterday.	Позавчера́.	pahzahvchehRAH
The next day.	На друго́й день.	nah drooGOY dyehn'
Three/Five days ago.	Три дня/Пять дне́й наза́д.	tree dnyah/pyaht' dnyey nahzAHT
Morning.	У́тро.	OOtrah
In the morning.	У́тром.	OOtrahm
This morning.	Сего́дня у́тром.	seeVOHdnyah OOtrahm

---

* The word for year changes depending on the number that precedes it. For one year or numbers that end in a one (41, 621 etc) the word for year is год (goht). For two, three, four and numbers that end in any of those numbers, the word is го́да and for five and above, as well as numbers that end in five or higher, the word for year is лет (lyeht).

123

Yesterday morning.	Вчера́ у́тром.	vchehRAH OOtrahm
Tomorrow morning.	За́втра у́тром.	ZAHFtrah OOtrahm
All morning.	Всё у́тро.	fsyoh OOtrah
Every morning.	Ка́ждое у́тро.	KAHZHdahyeh OOtrah
Day.	День.	dyehn'
In the afternoon.	Днём./ По́сле обе́да.	dnyohm/POHSlee ahBYEHdah
This afternoon.	Сего́дня по́сле обе́да.	seeVOHdnyah POHSlee ahBYEHdah
Yesterday afternoon.	Вчера́ по́сле обе́да.	vchehRAH POHSlee ahBYEHdah
Tomorrow afternoon.	За́втра по́сле обе́да.	ZAHFtrah POHSlee ahBYEHdah
All day.	Весь день.	vyehs' dyehn'
Every day.	Ка́ждый день.	KAHZHdihy dyehn'
Evening.	Ве́чер.	VYEHchehr
In the evening.	Ве́чером.	VYEHchehrahm
This evening.	Сего́дня ве́чером.	seeVOHdnyah VYEHchehrahm
Yesterday evening.	Вчера́ ве́чером.	vchehRAH VYEHchehrahm
Tomorrow evening.	За́втра ве́чером.	ZAHFtrah VYEHchehrahm
All evening.	Весь ве́чер.	vyehs' VYEHchehr
Every evening.	Ка́ждый ве́чер.	KAHZHdihy VYEHchehr
Night.	Ночь.	nohch
At night.	Но́чью.	NOHCHyoo
Tonight.	Сего́дня но́чью.	seeVOHdnyah NOHCHyoo
All night.	Всю ночь.	fsyoo nohch
Every night.	Ка́ждую ночь.	KAHZHdooyoo nohch
Weekend.	Уик-е́нд.	ooeek-EHNT
Holiday.	Пра́здник.	PRAHZneek
Vacation.	О́тпуск.	OHTpoosk
School holiday.	Кани́кулы.	kahNEEkoolih
Birthday.	День рожде́ния.	dyehn' rahzhDYEHneeyah

124

Telling Time

Moscow and St. Petersburg are eight hours ahead of Eastern Standard Time.

Time.	Время.	VRYEHmyah
Half hour.	Полчаса́.	pahlcheeSAH
Hour.	Час.	chahs
Minute.	Мину́та.	meeNOOtah
Second.	Секу́нда.	seekOONdah
Early./Late.	Ра́но./По́здно.	RAHnah/POHZnah
I'm sorry, I'm late.	Прости́те за опозда́ние.	prahsTEEtyeh zah ahpahzDAHneeyeh
On time.	Во́время.	VOHvreemyah
What time is it?	Ско́лько вре́мени?	SKOHL'kah VRYEHmeenee
It's...	Сейча́с...	seeCHAHS
one o'clock.	час.	chahs
five past three.	пять мину́т четвёртого.	pyaht' meeNOOT chehtVOHRtahvah
ten past six.	де́сять мину́т седьмо́го.	DYEHseet' meeNOOT seedMOHvah
quarter after four.	пятна́дцать мину́т пя́того.	peetNAHtsaht' meeNOOT PYAHTahvah
twenty past twelve.	два́дцать мину́т пе́рвого.	DVAHtsaht' meeNOOT PYEHRvahvah
twenty-five after two.	два́дцать пять мину́т тре́тьего.	DVAHtsaht' pyaht' meeNOOT TRYEHt'ehvah
seven thirty.	полови́на восьмо́го.	pahlahVEEnah vahs'MOHvah
twenty-five to nine.	без двадцати́ пяти́ де́вять.	byehs dvahtsahTEE peeTEE DYEHveet'
twenty to eleven.	без двадцати́ оди́ннадцать.	byehs dvahtsahTEE ahDEENnahtsaht'
quarter to one.	без че́тверти час.	byehs chehtveerTEE chahs
ten of eight.	без десяти́ во́семь.	byehs deeseeTEE VOHseem'
five of two.	без пяти́ два.	byehs peeTEE dvah

125

twelve o'clock.	двена́дцать часо́в.	dveeNAHtsaht' cheeSOHF
midnight.	по́лночь.	POHLnahch
noon.	по́лдень.	POHLdeen'
A.M.	Утра́.	ootRAH
P.M.	Ве́чера.	VYEHchehrah
At what time?	В кото́ром часу́?	fkahTOHrahm cheeSOO
At one.	В час.	fchahs
At 3:05.	В пять мину́т четвёртого.	fpyaht' meeNOOT chehtVOHRtahvah
At 2:10.	В де́сять мину́т тре́тьего.	VDYEHsaht' meeNOOT TRYEHt'ehvah
At 5:30.	В полови́не шесто́го.	vpahlahVEENyeh sheesTOHvah
At 7:40.	Без двадцати́ во́семь.	byehs dvahstahTEE VOHseem'
At 12:50	Без десяти́ час.	byehs deeseeTEE chahs

Seasons

Seasons.	Времена́ го́да.	vreemeeNAH GOHdah
Spring./In the spring.	Весна́./Весно́й.	veesNAH/veesNOY
Summer./In the summer.	Ле́то./Ле́том.	LYEHtah/LYEHtahm
Fall./In the fall.	О́сень./О́сенью.	OHseen'/OHseen'yoo
Winter./In the winter.	Зима́./Зимо́й.	zeeMAH/zeeMOY

126

XV. REFERENCE

Some Russian National Holidays

Jan. 1-2	New Years Day.	Но́вый год.
Jan. 7	Christmas.	Рождество́.
Mar. 8	International Women's Day.	Междунаро́дный день же́нщин.
May 1-2	May Day.	Пра́здник весны́ и труда́.
May 9	V-E Day.	Де́нь Побе́ды.

Weather

The weather.	Пого́да.	pahGOHdah
What is it like outside?	Кака́я сего́дня пого́да?	kahKAHyah seeVOHdnyah pahGOHdah
What's the forecast (for tomorrow)?	Како́й прогно́з пого́ды (на за́втра?)	kahKOY prahgNOHS pahGOHdih (nah ZAHFtrah)
Tomorrow it will rain.	За́втра бу́дет дождь.	ZAHFtrah BOOdeet dohsht'
Today it's...	Сего́дня...	seeVOHdnyah
sunny.	све́тит со́лнце.	SVYEHteet SOHNtseh
overcast.	па́смурно.	PAHsmoornah
cool.	прохла́дно.	prahkhLAHdnah
warm.	тепло́.	teepLOH
hot.	жа́рко.	ZHAHRkah
cold.	хо́лодно.	KHOHlahdnah
humid.	вла́жно.	VLAHZHnah
foggy.	тума́н.	tooMAHN
windy.	ве́тер.	VYEHteer
What's it usually like here?	Кака́я здесь быва́ет пого́да ?	kahKAHyah zdyehs' bihVAHeet pahGOHdah
It's raining/ snowing.	Идёт дождь/ снег.	eedYOHT dohsht'/ snyehk
What a beautiful day!	Како́й прекра́сный день!	kahKOY preeKRAHSnihy dyehn'

127

What awful weather!	Кака́я ужа́сная пого́да!	kahKAHyah oozhAHSnahyah pahGOHdah

Directions

North.	Се́вер.	SYEHveer
In the north.	На се́вере.	nah SYEHveeryeh
To the north.	На се́вер.	nah SYEHveer
Northward.	К се́веру.	KSYEHveeroo
South.	Юг.	yook
In the south.	На ю́ге.	nah YOOgyeh
To the south.	На юг.	nah yook
Southward.	К ю́гу.	KYOOgoo
East.	Восто́к.	vahsTOHK
In the east.	На восто́ке.	nah vahsTOHKyeh
To the east.	На восто́к.	nah vahsTOHK
Eastward.	К восто́ку.	kvahsTOHKoo
West.	За́пад.	ZAHpaht
In the west.	На за́паде.	nah ZAHpahdyeh
To the west.	На за́пад.	nah ZAHpaht
Westward.	К за́паду.	KZAHpahdoo

Family

Family.	Семья́.	seem'YAH
Relatives.	Ро́дственники.	ROHTSTveeneekee
Children.	Де́ти.	DYEHtee
Adults.	Взро́слые.	VZROHSlihyeh
Wife./ Spouse. (f)	Жена́./ Супру́га.	zhehNAH/ soopROOgah
Husband./ Spouse. (m)	Муж./ Супру́г.	moosh/ soopROOK
Mother.	Мать.	maht'
Father.	Оте́ц.	ahtYEHTS
Baby.	Ребёнок.	reebYOHnahk
Daughter.	Дочь.	dohch
Son.	Сын.	sihn
Sister.	Сестра́.	seesTRAH
Brother.	Брат.	braht
Grandmother.	Ба́бушка.	BAHbooshkah
Grandfather.	Де́душка.	DYEHdooshkah
Granddaughter.	Вну́чка.	VNOOCHkah

128

Grandson.	Внук.	vnook
Aunt.	Тётя.	TYOHtyah
Uncle.	Дядя.	DYAHdyah
Niece.	Племянница.	pleemYAHNneetsah
Nephew.	Племянник.	pleemYAHNneek
Cousin. (m/f)	Двоюродный брат/ Двоюродная сестра.	dvahYOOrahdnihy braht/dvahYOO-rahdnahyah seesTRAH
Husband's mother.	Свекровь.	sveekROHF'
Husband's father.	Свёкор.	SVYOHKahr
Wife's mother.	Тёща.	TYOHshchah
Wife's father.	Тесть.	tyehst'

Signs

Information.	Справки./ Справочное бюро.	SPRAHFkee/SPRAH-vahchnahyeh byooROH
Bathroom (M/W).	Туалет (М/Ж).	tooahlYEHT
Don't touch.	Не прикасаться.	nee preekahsAHT'syah
Push./ Pull.	От себя./ К себе.	ahtseeBYAH/ kseeBYEH
No admittance.	Не входить.	neefkhahDEET'
Entrance.	Вход.	fkhoht
Exit.	Выход.	VIHkhaht
No entry.	Нет входа.	nyeht FKHOHdah
No exit.	Нет выхода.	nyeht VIHkhahdah
Emergency exit.	Запасный выход.	zahpahsNIHY VIHkhaht
Employees' entrance.	Служебный вход.	sloozhEHBnihy fkhoht
Elevator.	Лифт.	leeft
Stairs.	Лестница.	LYEHSTneetsah
Up./Down.	Вверх./Вниз.	vyehrkh/vnees

Keep to the left/right.	Держи́тесь ле́вой/пра́вой стороны́.	deerZHEEtyehs LYEHvay/PRAHvay stahrahNIH
Don't lean against.	Не прислоня́ться	nee preeslahn-YAHTsah
Stop.	Стоп.	stohp
Wait.	Сто́йте.	STOYtyeh
Go.	Иди́те.	eeDEEtyeh
Careful!	Осторо́жно!	ahstahROHZHnah
Attention!	Внима́ние!	vneeMAHneeyeh
Prohibited.	Воспреща́ется.	vahspreeSHCHAH-eetsah
Danger!	Опа́сно!	ahPAHSnah
Police.	Мили́ция.	meeLEEtseeyah
Quiet!	Не шуме́ть.	nee shoomYEHT'
Self-serve.	Самообслу́жи-вание.	sahmahahpSLOO-zheevahneeyeh
Occupied.	За́нято.	ZAHneetah
No smoking.	Не кури́ть.	nee kooREET'
Closed for lunch/ repairs/ cleaning.	Закры́то на обе́д/ремо́нт/ санита́рный день.	zahKRIHtah nah ahbYEHT/reem-OHNT/sahnee-TAHRnihy dyehn'
Closed for a break from 1 to 2.	Переры́в с 1 до 2.	peereeRIHF SCHAH-soo dahdVOOKH
Office hours.	Приёмные часы́.	preeYOHMnihyeh cheeSIH
Men working.	Ремо́нтные рабо́ты.	reeMOHNTnihyeh rahBOHTih
Watch out for cars.	Береги́сь автомоби́ля.	beereeGEES' ahftahmahBEElyah

Abbreviations and Acronyms

АЗС	автозапра́вочная ста́нция.	gas station.
бульв.	бульва́р.	boulevard.
в.	век.	century.
г.	год./го́род./ грамм./ гора́./ господи́н.	year./city./ gram./mountain. /Mr.
г-жа.	госпожа́.	Mrs.

гр.	граждани́н.	citizen.
Г У М	Госуда́рст-венный универса́льный магагзи́н.	State Department Store (in Moscow).
д.	дом.	house.
до н.э.	до на́шей э́ры.	B.C.
ж.	же́нский	women.
и т. д.	и так да́лее.	etc.
им.	и́мени.	named after...
к., коп.	копе́йка.	kopeck.
к., корп.	ко́рпус.	corpus.
кв.	кварти́ра.	apartment.
м.	метр./мужско́й.	meter./men.
М Г У	Моско́вский госуда́рствен-ный университе́т.	Moscow State University.
наб.	на́бережная.	embankment.
напр.	наприме́р.	for example.
н.э.	на́шей э́ры.	A.D.
обл.	о́бласть	oblast.
оз.	о́зеро.	lake.
пл.	пло́щадь.	square.
пр., просп.	проспе́кт.	prospect.
р.	рубль.	rouble.
Р Ф	Росси́йская Федера́ция	The Russian Federation
с., стр.	страни́ца.	page.
С Ш А	Соединённые Шта́ты Аме́рики.	USA - United States of America.
И Т А Р-Т А С С	Телегра́фное аге́нство России.	Telegraph Agency of Russia.
т.е.	то есть.	that is, ie.
ул.	улица.	street.
Ц У М	Центра́льный универса́льный магази́н.	Central Department Store (in Moscow).
ч.	час.	hour.

Metric Conversions

Temperature:
To convert Celsius into Fahrenheit, multiply degree Celsius by 1.8 and add 32. To convert Fahrenheit into Celsius, subtract 32 from degree Fahrenheit and divide by 1.8.

Distance:
To convert miles into kilometers, divide miles by 5 and multiply by 8. To convert kilometers into miles, divide kilometers by 8 and multiply by 5.

1 km = 5/8 mile
1 centimeter = 0.39 inches
1 meter = 3.28 feet
1 kilometer = .675 mile
1 inch = 2.54 centimeters
1 foot = 30.5 centimeters
1 mile = 1609 meters

Weight:
1 kilogram = 2.2 pounds
1 gram = 0.0352 ounces
1 ounce = 28.35 grams
1 pound = 453.60 grams

Volume:
1 liter = 0.264 gallons
1 liter = 1.06 quarts
1 quart = .95 liter
1 gallon = 3.8 liters

As in all standard dictionaries, verbs are listed in the infinitive form. Adjectives are given in the masculine form and are marked by the abbreviation (adj). Nouns are given without articles. When both masculine and feminine forms exist, the masculine form is given first, followed by the feminine (f) version.

Russian-English Dictionary

А

авария ahVAHreeyah - breakdown; accident.

авеню ahveenYOO - avenue.

авиапочта ahveeah-POHCHtah - airmail.

автобус ahfTOHboos - bus.

автозаправочная станция ahftahzahPRAHvahchnahyah STAHNtseeyah - service station.

автомат ahftahMAHT - vending machine.

автомобилист ahftahmahbeeLEEST - motorist.

автомобиль ahftahmah-BEEL' - car.

автор AHFtahr - author.

адвокат ahdvahKAHT - lawyer.

администратор ahdmeeneesTRAHtahr - manager.

адрес AHdrees - address.

азбука AHSbookah - alphabet.

аккуратный ahkooRAHTnihy - neat, tidy, punctual (adj).

акт ahkt - act.

актёр ahkTYOHR - actor.

актриса ahkTREEsah - actress.

актуальный ahktooAHL'nihy - current (adj).

акушёр ahkooSHOHR - obstetrician.

акцент ahkTSEHNT - accent.

алкоголь ahlkahGOHL' - alcohol.

аллергия ahlleerGEEyah - allergy.

алло ahlLOH - hello (on the telephone).

амбулатория ahmboolah-TOHreeyah - outpatient clinic.

американец/(-канка) ahmeereeKAHneets/ (-KAHNkah) - American/ (f).

американский ahmeeree-KAHNskeey - American (adj).

ананас ahnahNAHS - pineapple.

английская булавка ahng-LEEskahyah booLAHFkah - safety pin.

английский ahngLEEYskeey - English, British (adj).

англичанин/(-чанка) ahngleeCHAHneen (-CHAHNkah) Englishman/(f).

анкета ahnKYEHtah - form, blank, survey.

антибиотик ahnteebeeOHteek - antibiotic.

133

антра́кт ahnTRAHKT -
intermission.
апельси́н ahpeel'SEEN -
orange.
аппе́ндикс ahpYEHNdeeks -
appendix.
аппендици́т ahppeendee-
TSEET - appendicitis.
аппети́т (прия́тного
аппети́та!) ahpeeTEET
(preeYAHTnahvah ahpee-
TEEtah!) appetite (Hearty
appetite!)
апте́ка ahpTYEHkah -
drugstore.
апте́чка ahpTYEHCHkah -
first-aid kit.
арбу́з ahrBOOZ - water-
melon.
арома́тный ahrahMAHT-
nihy - fragrant (adj).
арте́ль ahrTYEHL' -
workers' cooperative.
арте́рия ahrTYEHreeyah -
artery.
арти́ст ahrTEEST -
performer.
артри́т ahrtREET -
arthritis.
архите́ктор
ahrkheeTYEHKtahr -
architecht.
архитекту́ра ahrkheeteek-
TOOrah - architechture.
аспира́нт/(-ка) ahspee-
RAHNT/(-kah) - graduate
student/(f).
аспири́н ahspeeREEN -
aspirin.
а́стма AHSTmah - asthma.
атеи́зм ahteeEEZM -
atheism.
атле́тика ahtLYEHTeekah -

athletics.
атлети́чский ahtleeTEE-
chskeey - athletic (adj).
афи́ша ahFEEshah - poster;
play bill.
аэропо́рт ahehrahPOHRT -
airport.

Б

ба́бушка BAHbooshkah -
grandmother.
бага́ж bahgAHSH - baggage.
база́р bahZAHR - market;
bazaar.
баклажа́н bahklahzhAHN -
eggplant.
балала́йка bahlahLAYkah -
balalaika.
бале́т bahLYEHT - ballet.
балко́н bahlKOHN -
balcony.
бана́н bahNAHN - banana.
бандеро́ль bahndeeROHL' -
wrapping for mailing
printed matter.
банк bahnk - bank.
ба́нка BAHNkah - jar; can.
банке́т bahnKYEHT -
banquet.
ба́ня BAHNyah - public
bath.
бара́нина bahRAHneenah -
mutton; lamb.
бассе́йн bahsSEYN - pool.
батаре́я bahtahREEyah -
battery.
ба́шня BAHSHnyah - tower.
бег byehk - run; race.
бе́гать BYEHgaht' - to run.
беда́ beeDAH - misfortune.
бе́дный BYEHDnihy - poor
(adj).
бедро́ beedROH - hip; thigh.

134

без byehs - without

безалкого́льный beezahl-kahGOHL'nihy - nonalcoholic (adj).

безбо́жие beesBOHzheeyeh - atheism.

безбо́жник beesBOHZHneek - atheist.

безви́нный beezVEENnihy - innocent (adj).

безвку́сный beezVKOOSnihy - tasteless (adj).

безопа́сно beezahPAHSnah - safely.

безусло́вно beezoosLOHVnah - certainly; absolutely.

беко́н beeKOHN - bacon.

бе́лый BYEHlihy - white (adj).

бельё beel'YOH - laundry; linen.

бензи́н beenZEEN - gas.

бензоба́к beenzahBAHK - gas tank.

бензозапра́вочная ста́нция beenzahzahPRAHvahchnahyah STAHNtseeyah - gas station.

бе́рег BYEHreek - coast; bank; shore.

береги́сь beereeGEES' - caution.

берёза beerYOHzah - birch.

Берёзка beerYOHSkah - hard-currency store.

бере́менная beeRYEHmeennahyah - pregnant (adj).

бере́чь beeRYEHCH - to save, keep; to guard.

бес byehs - demon.

бесе́да beeSYEHdah - conversation.

бесе́довать beeSYEHdahvaht' - to talk, chat.

беспереса́дочный beespeereeSAHdahchnihy - without transfer (adj).

беспла́тный beesPLAHTnihy - free of charge (adj).

беспоко́ить beespahKOHeet' - to worry, trouble, bother, disturb.

беспоко́йный beespahKOYnihy - worried; troubled (adj).

беспол́езный beespahlYEHZnihy - useless (adj).

беспоса́дочный beespahSAHdahchnihy - nonstop (of a flight) (adj).

беспо́шлинный beesPOHSHleennihy - dutyfree (adj).

бессозна́тельный beessahzNAHteel'nihy - unconscious (adj).

бессо́ница beesSOHNeetsah - insomnia.

бесцве́тный beesTSVYEHTnihy - colorless; dull (adj).

библиоте́ка beebleeah-TYEHkah - library.

Би́блия BEEbleeyah - Bible.

бизнесме́н beezneesMYEHN - businessman.

биле́т beeLYEHT - ticket.

биле́тная ка́сса beeLYEHTnahyah KAHSsah - ticket office.

бино́кль beeNOHKL' - binoculars; opera glasses.

бинт beent - bandage.

бить beet' - to beat, strike.

би́ться BEETsah - to fight.

бифштéкс beefSHTYEHKS - steak.

благодарúть blahgahdah-REET' - to thank.

благодáрный blahgah-DAHRnihy - thankful; grateful (adj).

благополýчно blahgah-pahLOOCHnah - safely; without mishap.

благословéние blahgah-slahVYEHneeyeh - blessing.

бланк blahnk - form; blank.

блéдный BLYEHDnihy - pale (adj).

ближáйший bleeZHAY-sheey - nearest; next (adj).

блúзко BLEESkah - near; close; nearby.

блин bleen - pancake.

блондúн/(-ка) blahnDEEN/(-kah) - blonde/(f).

блýзка BLOOSkah - blouse.

блюдо BLYOOdah - dish; food; course.

Бóг bohkh- God.

богáтый bahGAHtihy - rich (adj).

богослужéние bahgahsloo-ZHEHneeyeh - worship service.

бóдрый BOHdrihy - cheerful (adj).

бок bohk - side.

бóком BOHKahm - sideways.

бóлее BOHleeyeh - more.

болéзнь bahLYEHZN' - illness; disease.

болéльщик bahlYEHL'-shcheek - sports fan.

болéть bahlYEHT' - to be ill.

болеутоляющее срéдство bahleeoootahlYAHyooshch-ehyeh SRYEHTstvah - painkiller.

болтлúвый bahltLEEvihy - talkative (adj).

боль bohl' - pain.

больнúца bahl'NEEtsah - hospital.

больнóй bahl'NOY - sick (adj).

бóльше BOHL'sheh - larger; bigger; greater.

большинствó bahl'sheenst-VOH - majority.

большóй bahl'SHOY - big; large; great (adj).

большóй пáлец bahl'SHOY PAHleets - thumb.

большóе спасúбо bahl'-SHOHyeh spahSEEbah - thanks a lot!

бородá bahrahDAH - beard.

борщ bohrshch - borsch; beet soup.

борьбá bahr'BAH - fight, struggle.

ботанúческий сад bahtah-NEEchehskeey saht - botanical garden.

боя́ться bahYAHTsah - to fear, be afraid.

брак brahk - marriage.

брат braht - brother

брать braht' - to take, seize.

бриллиáнт breeleeAHNT - diamond.

брúтва BREETvah - razor.

брúться BREETsah - to shave; get a shave.

136

бровь brohf' - eyebrow.
брошь brohsh - brooch.
брюки BRYOOkee - pants.
брюнет/(-ка) bryooNYEHT/
(-kah) - brunette/(f).
будильник booDEEL'neek -
alarm clock.
будний день BOODneey
dyehn' - weekday.
будущий BOOdooshcheey -
the future.
буква BOOKvah - letter of
the alphabet.
букинист bookeenEEST -
secondhand book dealer.
булавка booLAHFkah - pin.
булка BOOLkah - roll; bun.
булочная BOOlahchnahyah
- bakery.
бульвар bool'VAHR -
boulevard.
бульон bool'OHN -
bouillon.
бумага booMAHgah - paper.
бумажник booMAHZHneek -
wallet; billfold.
бурный BOORnihy -
stormy; violent (adj).
буря BOORyah - storm.
бусы BOOsih - beads.
бутерброд booteerBROHT -
sandwich.
бутылка booTIHLkah -
bottle.
буфет boofYEHT - snack
bar.
буханка bookhAHNkah -
loaf of bread.
бывший BIHFsheey -
former (adj).
быстро BIHStrah - fast;
quickly; rapidly.
бюро byooROH - office;
bureau.
бюро Интуриста byooROH
eentooREESTah - Intourist
office.
бюстгальтер
byoozKHAHL'teer - bra.

B
в v - in, at, for, to.
в один конец vahDEEN
kahNYEHTS - one-way
(ticket).
вагон vahGOHN - railroad
car.
важность VAHZHnahst' -
importance.
важный VAHZHnihy -
important (adj).
вазелин vahzeeLEEN -
vaseline.
вальдшнеп VAHL'Tshneep -
woodcock.
валюта vahLYOOtah - hard-
currency.
валютный курс vahLYOO-
tnihy koors - rate of
exchange.
ваниль vahNEEL' - vanilla.
ванна VAHNnah - bathtub.
ванная VAHNnahyah -
bathroom.
вареник vahRYEHneek -
filled dumpling.
варёный vahRYOHnihy -
boiled (adj).
варенье vahRYEHN'yeh -
jam.
варить vahrEET' - to cook,
boil.
вата VAHtah - absorbent
cotton.
введение vveeDYEHneeyeh -
introduction.

137

вверх vvyehrkh - up, upwards (destination).
вверху́ vveerKHOO - above; overhead (location).
вдали́ vdahLEE - in the distance.
вдова́ vdahVAH - widow.
вдове́ц vdahvYEHTS - widower.
вдруг vdrook - suddenly.
вегетариа́нец veegeetahreeAHNeets - vegetarian.
ведро́ veedROH - bucket.
ве́ер VYEHeer - fan.
ве́жливый VYEHZHleevihy - polite; courteous (adj).
везде́ veezDYEH - everywhere.
век vyehk - century; age.
вели́кий veeLEEkeey - great (adj).
велосипе́д veelahseePYEHT - bicycle.
ве́на VYEHnah - vein.
ве́ра VYEHrah - belief; faith.
верблю́д veerBLYOOT - camel.
верёвка veeRYOHFkah - rope; string; cord.
ве́рить VYEHreet' - to believe, have faith.
ве́рный VYEHRnihy - true; faithful (adj).
вероя́тно veerahYAHTnah - probably.
верх vyehrkh - top
ве́рхний VYEHRkhneey - upper; top (adj).
вес vyehs - weight.
весели́ться veeseeLEEtsah - to enjoy oneself; have fun.
весе́нний veesYEHNneey - spring (adj).
весна́ veesNAH - spring.
весь vyehs' - all; the whole.
ве́тер VYEHteer - wind.
ве́треный VYEHTreenihy - windy (adj).
ветрово́е стекло́ veetrahvOHyeh steekLOH - windshield.
ветчина́ veetcheeNAH - ham.
ве́чер VYEHcheer - evening.
вече́рний veeCHEHRneey - evening (adj.).
ве́чно VYEHCHnah - eternally.
ве́шалка VYEHshahlkah - hanger.
взаимопонима́ние vzaheemahpahneeMAHneeyeh - mutual understanding.
взгляд vzglyaht - look; glance.
вздор vzdohr - nonsense.
взлёт vzlyoht - takeoff (in a plane).
взро́слый VZROHSlihy - adult.
взя́тка VZYAHTkah - bribe.
взять напрока́т vzyaht' nahprahKAHT - to rent.
вид veet - appearance.
ви́дение VEEdeeneeyeh - sight; vision.
ви́деть VEEdeet' - to see.
ви́димо VEEdeemah - apparently; evidently.
ви́дно VEEDnah - visible; clear; obvious.
ви́за VEEzah - visa.
ви́лка VEELkah - fork.
вина́ veeNAH - guilt.
винегре́т veeneegRYEHT -

vegetable salad.
вино́ veeNOH - wine.
винова́тый veenahVAHtihy
- guilty (adj).
виногра́д veenahGRAHT -
grapes.
ви́рус VEEroos - virus.
витами́н veetahMEEnih -
vitamin.
ви́шня VEESHnyah - sour
cherries.
включа́ть vklyooCHAHT' -
to turn, switch on.
вку́сный VKOOSnihy -
tasty (adj).
влага́лище vlahGAH-
leeshcheh - vagina.
вла́жность VLAHZHnahst' -
humidity.
вла́жный VLAHZHnihy -
humid (adj).
влия́ние vleeYAHneeyeh -
influence.
влия́тельный
vleeYAHTeel'nihy -
influential (adj).
вме́сте VMYEHStyeh -
together.
вме́сто VMYEHStah -
instead of.
вне vnyeh - outside; out of.
вне́шний VNYEHSHneey -
outward; external (adj).
вниз vnees - down;
downward (destination).
внизу́ vneeZOO - down
below (location).
внима́ние vneeMAHneeyeh
- attention.
внук vnook - grandson.
вну́тренний VNOOtreen-
neey - internal (adj).
внутри́ vnooTREE - inside.

вну́чка VNOOCHkah -
granddaughter.
во́время VOHvreemyah - on
time.
вода́ vahDAH - water.
води́тель vahDEEteel' -
driver.
во́дка VOHTkah - vodka.
водопа́д vahdahPAHT -
waterfall.
водопрово́дчик vahdah-
prahVOHTcheek -
plumber.
вое́нный vahYEHNnihy -
military (adj).
возбуждённый vahzboozh-
DYOHNnihy - excited.
возвраща́ть vahzvrah-
SHCHAHT' - to return.
во́здух VOHZdookh - air.
возмо́жность vahzMOHZH-
nahst' - opportunity.
возмущённый vahzmoo-
shchOHNnihy - out-raged
(adj).
возраже́ние vahzrahZHEH-
neeyeh - objection.
во́зраст VOHZrahst - age.
война́ voyNAH - war.
вокза́л vahkZAHL - station.
вокру́г vahkROOK - around
(location).
волна́ vahlNAH - wave.
волнова́ться vahlnahVAH-
tsah - to be worried,
agitated.
во́лосы VOHlahsih - hair.
во́льно VOHL'nah - freely;
voluntarily.
вольта́ж vahl'TAHSH -
voltage.
во́ля VOHLyah - freedom.
воображе́ние vahahbrah-

ZHEHneeyeh - imagination.

вообще vahahpSHCHEH - in general.

вопрос vahpROHS - question.

вор vohr - thief.

ворота vahROHtah - gate.

воспаление vahspahLYEHneeyeh - inflamation.

воспаление влагалища vahspahLYEHneeyeh vlahGAHleeshchah - vaginal infection.

воспаление лёгких vahspahLYEHneeyeh LYOHKHkeekh - pneumonia.

воспоминание vahspahmeeNAHneeyeh - memory; recollection.

воспрещаться vahspreeSHCHAHtsah - to be forbidden.

восстание vahsSTAHneeyeh - uprising; revolt.

восток vahsTOHK - east.

восточный vahsTOHCHnihy - eastern (adj).

восход vahsKHOHT - sunrise.

вот voht - here (is).

впервые fpeerVIHyeh - for the first time; first.

вперёд fpeeRYOHT - forward; ahead.

впереди fpeereeDEE - in front; ahead.

впечатление fpeechahtLYEHneeyeh - impression.

вполне fpahlNYEH - fully; completely; quite.

впуск fpoosk - admission; admittance.

впускать fpoosKAHT' - to admit, let in.

враг vrahk - enemy.

врать vraht' - to lie, tell lies.

врач vrahch - doctor.

вредный VRYEHDnihy - harmful (adj).

временно VRYEHmeennah - temporarily.

время VRYEHmyah - time.

всегда fseegDAH - always.

всеобщий fseeOHPshcheey - universal; general (adj).

всё-таки VSYOHtahkee - still; all the same.

вслух fslookh - aloud.

вставать fstahVAHT' - to get, stand up.

встреча FSTRYEHchah - meeting; encounter.

встречать fstreechAHT' - to meet.

вход fkhoht - entrance.

входить fkhahDEET' - to enter.

вчера fcheeRAH - yesterday.

вчерашний fcheeRAHSHneey - yesterday's (adj).

выбор VIHbahr - choice; assortment; selection.

выборы VIHbahrih - elections.

выгодный VIHgahdnihy - profitable; favorable (adj).

вызолоченный VIHzahlahchehnnihy - gilded (adj).

выключать vihklyooCHAHT' - to turn out, switch off.

выпуск VIHpoosk - issue; edition; output.

высокий vihSOHkeey - high; tall; lofty (adj).

высота vihsahTAH - height; altitude.

выставка VIHstahfkah - exhibition; display.

выход VIHkhaht - exit.

выходить vihkhahDEET' - to leave, go out, exit.

выходной день vihkhahd-NOY dyehn' - day off.

вышитый VIHsheetihy - embroidered (adj).

Г

гадкий GAHTkeey - nasty; foul; vile (adj).

газета gahZYEHtah - newspaper.

газомер gahzahMYEHR - gas meter.

галоши gahLOHshee - rubbers; galoshes.

галстук GAHLstook - tie.

гараж gahRAHSH - garage.

гардероб gahrdeeROHP - cloakroom.

гардеробщик gahrdee-ROHPsheek - cloakroom attendant.

гастрит gahstREET - gastritis.

гастроном gahstrahNOHM - grocery store.

гвоздика gvahzDEEkah - carnation.

гвоздь gvohst' - nail, tack.

где gdyeh - where.

где-нибудь GDYEHneeboot' - somewhere.

геморрой geemahrROY - hemorrhoids.

гемофилия geemahFEElee-yah - hemophilia.

гепатит geepahTEET - hepatitis.

гериатрический geeree-ahtREEcheeskeey - geriatric (adj).

германец geerMAHneets - German.

германский geerMAHN-skeey - German (adj).

герой geeROY - hero.

гибкий GEEPkeey - flexible (adj).

гид geet - guide.

гинеколог geeneeKOHlahk - gynecologist.

гипертония geepeertah-NEEyah - high blood pressure.

гипс geeps - cast.

гитара geeTAHrah - guitar.

главный GLAHVnihy - main; principle (adj).

глагол glahGOHL - verb.

гладить GLAHdeet' - to iron.

гладкий GLAHTkeey - smooth (adj).

глаз glahs - eye.

гланды GLAHNdih - tonsils.

глина GLEEnah - clay.

глотать glahTAHT' - to swallow.

глубокий glooBOHkeey - deep; in depth (adj).

глупый GLOOpihy - stupid; silly (adj).

глухой glooKHOY - deaf (adj).

гнев gnyehf - anger.

говори́ть gahvahrEET' - to speak, talk (about).

говя́дина gahvYAHDeenah - beef.

год goht - year.

голова́ gahlahVAH - head.

головна́я боль gahlahv-NAHyah bohl' - headache.

го́лод GOHlaht - hunger.

голо́дный gahLOHDnihy - hungry (adj).

го́лос GOHlahs - voice.

голосова́ть gahlahsahVAHT' - to vote.

голубо́й gahlooBOY - light blue (adj).

голубцы́ gahloopTSIH - stuffed cabbage.

го́лубь GOHloop' - pigeon; dove.

го́лый GOHlihy - naked (adj).

гомосексуали́зм gahmah-seeksooahlEEZM - homo-sexuality.

гора́ gahRAH - mountain.

гора́здо gahRAHZdah - much, far.

го́рдый GOHRdihy - proud (adj).

го́ре GOHRyeh - grief.

го́рло GOHRlah - throat.

го́рничная GOHRneech-nahyah - maid.

го́род GOHraht - city.

горо́х gahROHKH - peas.

горчи́ца gahrCHEEtsah - mustard.

го́рький GOHR'keey - bitter (adj).

горя́чий gahrYAHcheey - hot (of food and drink) (adj).

господи́н gahspahDEEN - Mr. (pre-revolutionary).

госпожа́ gahspahZHAH - Mrs. (pre-revolutionary).

гости́ница gahsTEEneetsah - hotel.

гость gohst' - guest.

госуда́рственный gahsoo-DAHRstveennihy - state; government (adj).

госуда́рство gahsooDAHR-stvah - the State.

гото́вить gahTOHveet' - to prepare.

гото́вый gahTOHvihy - ready (adj).

гра́дус GRAHdoos - temp-erature.

гра́дусник GRAHdoosneek - thermometer.

граждани́н grahzhdahNEEN - citizen.

гражда́нка grahzhDAHNkah - citizeness.

гражда́нский grahzhDAHN-skeey - civil; civilian (adj).

гражда́нство grahzhDAHN-stvah - citizenship.

грамм grahm - gram.

грамма́тика grahmMAHtee-kah - grammar.

грампласти́нка grahmplahs-TEENkah - record.

грана́т grahNAHT - garnet.

грани́ца grahNEEtsah - border.

гребёнка greebYOHNkah - comb.

гре́йпфрут GREYPfroot - grapefruit.

грех gryehkh - sin.

грибы́ greeBIH - mush-

142

rooms.

грипп greep - flu.

гроза grahZAH - thunder-
storm.

грозный GROHZnihy -
threatening (adj).

гром grohm - thunder.

громкий GROHMkeey - loud
(adj).

грубый GROObihy - rude;
course (adj).

грудь groot' - chest; breast.

грузовик groozahVEEK -
truck.

группа GROOPpah - group.

группа крови GROOPpah
KROHvee - blood type.

грустный GROOSTnihy -
sad; melancholy (adj).

груша GROOshah - pear.

грыжа GRIHzhah - hernia.

грязный GRYAHZnihy -
dirty; filthy (adj).

грязь gryahs' - dirt; filth.

губа gooBAH - lip.

гудок gooDOHK - horn;
whistle.

гулять goolYAHT' - to
stroll, walk.

гуляш goolYAHSH -
goulash.

густой goosTOY - thick,
dense (adj).

гусь goos' - goose.

Д

да dah - yes.

давай dahVAY - let's; go
ahead!

давать dahVAHT' - to give.

давление dahvLYEHneeyeh
- (blood) pressure.

давно dahvNOH - long ago.

далее DAHleeyeh - further;
farther.

далеко dahleeKOH - far
away.

дальше DAHL'sheh -
farther; continue.

дамский DAHMskeey -
ladies (adj).

дарить dahrEET' - to give
(as a gift).

дары моря DAHrih
MOHryah - sea food.

дача DAHchah - cottage.

дверь dvyehr' - door.

движение dveeZHEHnee-
yeh - movement; traffic.

дворец dvahrYEHTS -
palace.

двоюродный брат dvah-
YOOrahdnihy braht -
cousin (m).

двоюродная сестра dvah-
YOOrahdnahyah sees-
TRAH - cousin (f).

двуспальный dvoo-
SPAHL'nihy - double
occupency (adj).

девочка DYEHvahchkah -
little girl.

девушка DYEHvooshkah -
young lady; waitress.

дедушка DYEHdooshkah -
grandfather.

дежурная deezhOORnahyah
- hall monitor.

дезинфицировать deezeen-
feetsEERahvaht' - to
disinfect.

дезодорант deezahdah-
RAHNT - deoderant.

действие DEYSTveeyeh -
action.

действительно deystVEE-

143

teel'nah - really; truly.
действительный
deystVEE-teel'nihy - real;
actual; effective (adj).
действовать DEYSTvahvaht'
- to act, take action.
делать DYEHlaht' - to do.
делить deelEET' - to share,
divide.
дело DYEHlah - matter;
affair; business.
деловой deelahVOY -
business (adj).
денежный перевод DYEH-
neezhnihy peereeVOHT -
money order.
день dyehn' - day.
день рождения dyehn'
rahzhDYEHneeyah -
birthday.
деньги DYEHN'gee - money.
деревня deeRYEHVnyah -
countryside.
дерево DYEHreevah - tree.
деревянный deereevYAHN-
nihy - wooden (adj).
держать deerZHAHT' - to
hold, keep, support.
десерт deeSYEHRT -
dessert.
детектив deeteekTEEF -
mystery (story/movie).
дети DYEHtee - children.
детский DYEHTskeey -
children's (adj).
дефицит deefeeTSEET -
deficit.
дешёвый deeSHOHvihy -
inexpensive; cheap (adj).
джинсы DZHEENsih - jeans.
диабет deeahBYEHT -
diabetes.
диагноз deeAHGnahs -

diagnosis.
диван deeVAHN - sofa.
диета deeYEHtah - diet.
дикий DEEkeey - wild
(adj).
директор deeRYEHKtahr -
director; manager.
дирижёр deereezhOHR -
conductor (music).
дичь deech' - wild game.
длина dleeNAH - length.
длинный DLEENnihy - long
(physically) (adj).
длиться DLEEtsah - to last.
для dlyah - for.
дневной dneevNOY -
daytime (adj).
до dah - to; before; until.
до свидания dahsveeDAH-
neeyah - goodbye.
доброта dahbrahTAH -
kindness.
добрый DOHbrihy - good;
kind (adj).
довольно dahVOHL'nah -
rather; fairly.
договор dahgahVOHR -
contract; agreement.
дождь dohsht' - rain.
дозировка dahzeeROHFkah
- dosage.
долгий DOHLgeey - long (in
time) (adj).
долго DOHLgah - for a long
time.
должен DOHLzhehn -
should; must; ought to.
долина dahLEEnah - valley.
доллар DOHLlahr - dollar.
доля DOHLyah - share; lot.
дом dohm - house; home.
дорога dahROHgah - road.
дорогой dahrahGOY - dear;

expensive; valuable (adj).
достáточно dahsTAHtahch-
nah - enough.
достóинство dahsTOHeen-
stvah - value; worth.
дóступ DOHstoop - access.
дохóд dahKHOHT - income.
дочь dohch - daughter.
драгоцéнность drahgah-
TSEHNnahst' - jewel.
драматýрг drahmahTOORK
- playwright.
дрвéвний DRYEHVneey -
ancient (adj).
дрýг drook - friend.
другóй drooGOY - other;
another; the other.
дрýжба DROOZHbah -
friendship.
дрýжный DROOZHnihy -
friendly; amicable (adj).
дуплó doopLOH - cavity.
дýра DOOrah - fool (f).
дурáк dooRAHK - fool (m).
духи́ dooKHEE - perfume.
душ doosh - shower.
душá dooSHAH - soul.
душéвный dooshEHVnihy -
mental; emotional (adj).
дýшно DOOSHnah - stuffy.
дым dihm - smoke.
ды́мный DIHMnihy -
smokey (adj).
ды́ня DIHNyah - melon.
дырá dihRAH - hole.
дыхáние dihKHAHneeyeh -
breathing; respiration.
дышáть dihshAHT' - to
breath.
дю́жина DYOOzheenah -
dozen.
дю́йм dyooym - inch.
дя́дя DYAHdyah - uncle.

E
еврéй/(-ка) yeevREY/
(-kah) - Jew/(f).
еврéйский yeevREYskeey -
Jewish; Hebrew (adj).
европéец yeevrahPYEHeets
- European (f).
европéйский yeevrah-
PEYskeey - European
(adj).
егó yeeVOH - his; its.
едá yeeDAH - food.
едвá yeedVAH - hardly;
scarsely; barely.
её yeeYOH - her; its.
ёж yohsh - hedgehog.
ежеви́ка yeezhehVEEkah -
blackberries.
ежегóдный yeezhehGOHD-
nihy - yearly; annual
(adj).
ежеднéвный yeezhehd-
NYEHVnihy - daily (adj).
ежемéсячный yeezheh-
MYEHseechnihy - monthly
(adj).
ездá yeezDAH - ride; drive.
éздить YEHZdeet' - to
drive.
ёлка YOHLkah - spruce;
Christmas tree.
ермóлка yeerMOHLkah -
skullcap.
éсли YEHSlee - if; when;
whereas.
естéственно yeestYEHST-
veennah - naturally.
есть yehst' - to eat.
éхать YEHkhaht' - to drive.
ещё yeeSHCHOH - still; yet;
else; more; another.
ещё раз yeeSHCHOH rahs -

once again.

Ж

жа́дный ZHAHDnihy - greedy (adj).

жа́жда ZHAHZHdah - thirst.

жале́ть zhahLYEHT' - to feel sorry for; pity.

жа́лоба ZHAHlahbah - complaint.

жаль zhahl' - pity.

жар zhahr - fever.

жа́рить ZHAHReet' - to fry, roast, broil.

жа́ркий ZHAHRkeey - hot (of the weather) (adj).

ждать zhdaht' - to wait.

железа́ zhehleeZAH - gland.

жёлтый ZHOHLtihy - yellow (adj).

жёмчуг ZHEHMchook - pearl.

жена́ zhehNAH - wife.

жена́т zhehNAHT - married (men) (adj.)

же́нский ZHEHNskeey - feminine; woman's (f.)

же́нщина ZHEHNshcheenah - woman.

жесто́кий zhehsTOHkeey - cruel; brutal (adj).

жечь zhehch - to burn.

жи́вопись ZHEEvahpees' - painting.

живо́т zheeVOHT - stomach.

живо́тное zheeVOHTnah-yeh - animal.

жизнь zheezn' - life.

жи́ла ZHEElah - vein.

жиле́т zheeLYEHT - vest.

жир zheer - fat; grease.

жи́рный ZHEERnihy - fatty; greasy; oily (adj).

жи́тель ZHEEteel' - resident.

жить zheet' - to live.

журна́л zhoorNAHL - magazine.

журнали́ст zhoornahLEEST - journalist.

З

за zah - behind; beyond; past; for; in; after.

заболе́ть zahbahLYEHT' - to fall ill.

забо́та zahBOHtah - care; concern.

забыва́ть zahbihVAHT' - to forget.

забы́тый zahBIHTihy - forgotten (adj).

заведе́ние zahveeDYEHneeyeh - institution.

заве́дующий zahVYEHdoo-yooshcheey - manager.

заво́д zahVOHT - factory.

за́втра ZAHFtrah - tomorrow.

за́втрак ZAHFtrahk - breakfast.

за́втракать ZAHFtrahkaht' - to eat breakfast.

за́втрашний ZAHFtrahsh-neey - tomorrow's (adj).

зага́р zahGAHR - sunburn; sun tan.

за́дний ZAHDneey - rear; back; hind (adj).

зажига́лка zahzhee-GAHLkah - cigarette lighter.

заказа́ть zahkahzAHT' - to order.

заключе́ние zahklyooCHEH-neeyeh - conclusion.

закон zahKOHN - law.
законный zahKOHNnihy - legal; legitimate (adj).
законченный zahKOHNchehnnihy - finished; completed (adj).
закрытый zahKRIHtihy - closed (adj).
закуска zahKOOSkah - appetizer; snack.
закусочная zahKOOSahchnahyah - snackbar.
зал zahl - hall.
залив zahLEEF - bay; gulf.
замена zahMYEHnah - substitution.
заметка zahMYEHTkah - note; mark; notice.
замок zahMOHK - lock.
замужем ZAHmoozhehm - married (women).
занавес ZAHnahvees - curtain.
занятие zahnYAHteeyeh - occupation; work; studies.
занятый ZAHNyahtihy - busy; occupied (adj).
запад ZAHpaht - west.
западный ZAHpahdnihy - western (adj).
запах ZAHpahkh - smell.
записаться zahpeeSAHTsah - to sign up (for).
запись ZAHpees' - recording (record/tape).
запор zahPOHR - constipation.
запрещать zahpreeshch-AHT' - to forbid.
заражение zahrahZHEHneeyeh - infection.
заранее zahRAHnehyeh - in advance.

заяц ZAHeets - hare.
звезда zvyehzDAH - star.
звук zvook - sound; noise.
здание ZDAHneeyeh - building.
здесь zdyehs' - here.
здоровый zdahROHvihy - healthy (adj).
здоровье zdahROHv'yeh - health.
зеленщик zeeleenSHCHEEK - greengrocer.
зелёный zeeLYOHnihy - green (adj).
земля zeemLYAH - ground; dirt; earth.
земляника zeemleeNEEkah - strawberries.
зеркало ZYEHRkahlah - mirror.
зерно zeerNOH - grain.
зима zeeMAH - winter.
зимний ZEEMneey - winter (adj).
злобный ZLOHBnihy - malicious; spiteful (adj).
злой zloy - evil; wicked; mean; malicious (adj).
знак znahk - sign; signal.
знакомство znahKOHMstvah - acquaintance.
знакомый znahKOHmihy - acquainted; familiar (adj).
знаменитый znahmeeNEEtihy - famous (adj).
знание ZNAHneeyeh - knowledge.
знать znaht' - to know.
значение znahCHEHneeyeh - meaning; sense.
значительный znahCHEEteel'nihy - considerable; significant (adj).

значить ZNAHcheet' - to
mean.
значо́к znahCHOHK - badge.
зо́лото ZOHlahtah - gold.
золото́й zahlahTOY - gold
(adj).
зо́нтик ZOHNteek -
umbrella.
зоопа́рк zahahPAHRK - zoo.
зре́лый ZRYEHlihy - ripe;
mature (adj).
зре́ние ZRYEHneeyeh -
eyesight.
зри́тель ZREEteel' -
spectator.
зуб zoop - tooth.
зубна́я боль zoobNAHyah
bohl' - toothache.
зубна́я па́ста zoobNAHyah
PAHStah - toothpaste.
зубна́я щётка zoobNAHyah
SHCHOHTkah - tooth-
brush.
зубно́й врач zoobNOY
vrahch - dentist.
зять zyaht' - son-in-law;
brother-in-law.

И

и ee - and; also.
иго́лка eeGOHLkah -
needle.
игра́ eegRAH - game.
игра́ть eegRAHT' - to play.
игру́шка eegROOSHkah -
toy.
иде́я eedYEHyah - idea.
идти́ eetTEE - to go, walk.
изба́ eesBAH - peasant's
hut; cabin.
изве́стие eezVYEHSteeyeh -
news.
извини́те eezveeNEEtyeh -

sorry; excuse me.
извиня́ть eezveenYAHT' -
to excuse, pardon.
из-за eezzah - because of.
изли́шний eezLEESHneey -
excessive; superfluous
(adj).
изумру́д eezoomROOT -
emerald.
изю́м eezYOOM - raison.
ико́на eekOHnah - icon.
иконоста́с eekahnahSTAHS
- iconostasis.
икра́ eekRAH - caviar.
и́ли EElee - or.
и́менно EEMeennah -
exactly; precisely.
иму́щество eemOOSHCH-
ehstvah - property.
и́мя EEMyah - first name.
ина́че eeNAHcheh -
differtly; otherwise.
инвали́д eenvahLEET -
disabled person.
инвали́дность eenvah-
LEEDnahct' - disability.
инде́йка eenDEYkah -
turkey.
инжене́р eenzheeNYEHR -
engineer.
иногда́ eenahgDAH -
sometimes.
иностра́нец eenahsTRAH-
neets - foreigner.
иностра́нный eenahs-
TRAHNnihy - foreign
(adj).
инстру́кция eenSTROOK-
tseeyah - instructions.
инсу́льт eenSOOL'T -
stroke.
интере́сный eenteeRYEHS-
nihy - interesting (adj).

148

искренний EESkreenneey - sincere (adj).
искусственный eesKOOSTveennihy - artificial (adj).
искусство eesKOOSTvah - art; skill.
испорченный eesPOHRchehnnihy - spoiled; rotten; tainted (adj).
исследование eesSLYEHdahvahneeyeh - research.
история eesTOHreeyah - history; story.

Й

йод yoht - iodine.

К

к k - to; toward.
кабина kahBEEnah - booth; cubicle.
каблук kahbLOOK - heel.
каждый KAHZHdihy - every (adj).
как kahk - how.
как далеко kahk dahleeKOH - how far.
как долго kahk DOHLgah - how long.
какао kahKAHoh - cocoa.
какой kahKOY - which.
как-то KAHKtah - somehow.
календарь kahleenDAHR' - calendar.
калория kahLOHreeyah - calorie.
кальсоны kahl'SOHnih - long underwear.
камбала KAHMbahlah - flounder; sole.
камень KAHmeen' - rock.
камера хранения KAHmeerah khrahNYEHneeyah - baggage room.
канадец/(-надка) kahNAHdeets/(-NAHTkah) Canadian/(f).
канадский kahNAHTskeey - Canadian (adj).
канал kahNAHL - canal.
каникулы kahNEEkoolih - school vacation.
капля KAHPlyah - drop.
капуста kahPOOStah - cabbage.
карандаш kahrahnDAHSH - pencil.
карат kahRAHT - carat.
караул kahrahOOL - guard; sentry.
карман kahrMAHN - pocket.
карманный фонарь kahrMAHNnihy fahNAHR' - flash light.
карнавал kahrnahVAHL - carnival.
карта KAHRtah - map.
картина kahrTEEnah - picture; drawing.
картофель kahrTOHfeel' - potato.
касса KAHSsah - ticket office; cashier's booth.
кассета kahsSYEHtah - cassette.
кассир kahsSEER - cashier.
кастрюля kahstRYOOLyah - pot; sausepan.
каток kahTOHK - skating rink.
кафе kahFYEH - cafe.
кафедра KAHfeedrah - department.
качество KAHchehstvah -

149

quality.
ка́шель KAHSHehl' - cough.
квадра́тный kvahdRAHT-nihy - square (adj).
кварта́л kvahrTAHL - block (in a city).
кварти́ра kvahrTEERah - apartment.
квас kvahs - kvass (fermented drink).
ке́ды KYEHdih - sneakers.
ке́мпинг KYEHMpeeng - camping.
кефи́р keeFEER - a yogurt-like drink.
килогра́мм keelahgRAHM - kilogram.
киломе́тр keelahMYEHTR - kilometer.
кино́ keeNOH - movie; the cinema.
кинотеа́тр keenahteeAHTR - movie theater.
кио́ск keeOHSK - kiosk.
кислоро́д keeslahROHT - oxygen.
ки́слый KEESlihy - sour (adj).
кишка́ keeshKAH - intestine.
кла́дбище KLAHTbee-shcheh - cemetary.
класси́ческий klahsSEECH-ehskeey - classical (adj).
клей kley - glue.
кли́мат KLEEmaht - climate.
кли́псы kleepsih - clip-on earrings.
клоп klohp - bedbug.
клуб kloop - club.
клю́ква KLYOOKvah - cranberries.

ключ klyooch - key.
кни́га KNEEgah - book.
кни́жный магази́н KNEEZHnihy mahgahZEEN - book store.
кно́пка KNOHPkah - push button; snap.
ковёр kahVYOHR - rug.
когда́ kahgDAH - when.
ко́жа KOHzhah - skin; leather.
ко́жаный KOHzhahnihy - leather (adj).
колбаса́ kahlbahSAH - sausage.
коле́но kahlYEHnah - knee.
колесо́ kahleeSOH - wheel.
коли́чество kahlEECHehst-vah - quantity.
ко́локол KOHlahkahl - bell.
колхо́з kahlKHOHS - collective farm.
кома́нда kahMAHNdah - sports team.
командиро́вка kahmahn-deeROHFkah - business trip; assignment.
кома́р kahMAHR - mosquito.
комбина́ция kahmbeen-AHTSeeyah - slip.
коме́дия kahMYEHdeeyah - comedy.
коммуна́льный kahmmoon-AHL'nihy - communal (adj).
ко́мната KOHMnahtah - room.
компле́кт kahmpLYEHKT - complete set.
компози́тор kahmpahZEE-tahr - composer.
компью́тер kahmP'YOOteer

150

- computer.
конве́рт kahnVYEHRT -
envelope.
конди́терская kahnDEEteer
-skahyah - confectionery
shop.
кондиционе́р kahndeetsee-
ahNYEHR - air condit-
ioner.
коне́ц kahnYEHTS - end.
коне́чно kahnYEHSHnah - of
course.
ко́нкурс KOHNkoors -
competition; contest.
консе́рвный нож kahn-
SYEHRVnihy nohsh - can
opener.
консе́рвы kahnSYEHRvih -
canned goods.
ко́нсульство KOHNsool'-
stvah - consulate.
конта́ктная ли́нза kahn-
TAHKTnahyah LEENzah -
contact lens.
конто́ра kahnTOHrah -
office.
конфе́ты kahnFYEHtih -
candy.
конце́рт kahnTSEHRT -
concert.
конько́й kahn'KEE - skates.
конья́к kahn'YAK - cognac;
brandy.
кооперати́в kahahpeerah-
TEEF cooperative store.
копе́йка kahPEYkah -
kopeck.
кора́бль kahRAHBL' - ship.
корзи́на kahrZEEnah -
basket.
кори́ца kahREEtsah -
cinnamon.
кори́чневый kahREECH-

neevihy - brown (adj).
коро́бка kahrOHPkah - box.
коро́ткий kahROHTkeey -
short (adj).
косме́тика
kahsMYEHteekah - make
up.
костёр kahsTYOHR -
campfire.
кость kohst' - bone.
костю́м kahsTYOOM - suit.
котле́та kahtLYEHtah -
cutlet.
ко́фе KOHfyeh - coffee.
коше́рный kahshEHRnihy -
kosher (adj).
ко́шка KOHSHkah - cat.
кра́й kray - edge; rim;
country.
кран krahn - faucet.
краси́вый krahsEEVihy -
beautiful; pretty (adj).
кра́сный KRAHSnihy - red
(adj).
красота́ krahsahTAH -
beauty.
крахма́л krahkhMAHL -
starch.
креди́тная ка́рточка kree-
DEETnahyah KAHRtahch-
kah - credit card.
крем kryehm - cream;
lotion.
кре́пкий KRYEHPkeey -
strong; durable (adj).
кре́сло KRYEHSlah - arm
chair.
крест kryehst - cross.
криво́й kreeVOY - crooked
(adj).
кри́зис KREEzees - crisis.
крик kreek - shout; cry.
крова́ть krahVAHT' - bed.

кровоизлияние krahvah-eezleeYAHneeyeh - hemorrhage.

кровоточить krahvah-taCHEET' - to bleed.

кровь krohf' - blood.

кролик KROHleek - rabbit.

кроме KROHmyeh - except for; but; besides.

круг krook - circle.

круглый KROOGlihy - ciruclar; round (adj).

круиз krooEEZ - cruise.

крыша KRIHshah - roof.

крышка KRIHshkah - lid; cover.

кстати KSTAHtee - incidentally; by the way.

кто ktoh - who.

кто-нибудь KTOHneeboot' - anyone; someone.

куда kooDAH - where to.

кукла KOOKlah - doll; puppet.

культура kool'TOOrah - culture.

купальная шапочка kooPAHL'nahyah SHAHP-ahchkah - bathing cap.

купальник koopAHL'neek - bathing suit.

купе koopYEH - train compartment.

купить kooPEET' - to buy.

курить kooREET' - to smoke.

курица KOOreetsah - chicken.

курорт koorOHRT - resort.

кусок kooSOHK - piece.

кухня KOOKHnyah - kitchen.

Л

лавра LAHVrah - monastery.

лагерь LAHgeer' - camp.

ладно LAHDnah - ok.

ладонь lahDOHN' - palm.

лак lahk - polish; lacquer.

лампа LAHMpah - lamp.

лампочка LAHMpahchkah - light bulb.

лапша lahpSHAH - soup noodle.

левый LYEHvihy - left (direction).

легальный leeGAHL'nihy - legal (adj).

лёгкий LYOHKHkeey - easy (adj).

легко leekhKOH - easily.

лёгкое LYOHKHkahyeh - lung.

лёд lyoht - ice.

лезвия LYEHZveeyah - razor blades.

лекарство leeKAHRstvah - medicine.

лекция LYEHKtseeyah - lecture.

лес lyehs - forest.

лестница LYEHSTneetsah - stairs.

летний LYEHTneey - summer (adj).

лето LYEHtah - summer.

лечение leeCHEHneeyeh - medical treatment.

ли lee - if; whether.

либо LEEbah - or.

лимон leeMOHN - lemon.

лимонад leemahnAHT - lemonade.

липкий LEEPkeey - sticky (adj).

152

листок leesTOHK - leaf;
sheet (of paper).
литература leeteerahTOO-
rah - literature.
литр leetr - liter.
лифт leeft - elevator.
лицо leetsOH - face.
личный LEECHnihy -
personal; private (adj).
лишний LEESHneey - spare;
extra (adj).
лоб lohp - forehead.
лодка LOHTkah - boat.
лодыжка lahDIHSHkah -
ankle.
ложа LOHzhah - theater
box.
ложка LOHSHkah - spoon.
ложный LOHZHnihy - false
(adj).
локоть LOHkaht' - elbow.
лососина lahsahSEEnah -
salmon.
лошадь LOHSHaht' - horse.
лужа LOOZHah - puddle.
лук look - onion.
луна looNAH - moon.
лучше LOOCHsheh - better.
лучший LOOCHsheey -
better; the best (adj).
лыжи LIHzhee - skis.
любить lyoobEET' - to love.
любовь lyoobOHF' - love.
любой lyoobOY - any.
любопыный lyoobah-
PIHTnihy - curious (adj).
люди LYOOdee - people.

M
мавзолей mahvzahLEY -
mausoleum.
магазин mahgahZEEN -
store.
магнитофон mahgneetah-
FOHN - tape recorder.
майка MAYkah - t-shirt.
мак mahk - poppy.
малахит mahlahKHEET -
malachite.
маленький MAHLeen'keey -
small (adj).
малина mahLEEnah -
raspberries.
мало MAHlah - a little; not
enough.
мальчик MAHL'cheek -
boy.
мандарин mahndahREEN -
tangerine.
маринованный mahree-
NOHvahnnihy - marinated
(adj).
марка MAHRkah - stamp.
маслина mahsLEEnah -
olives.
масло MAHSlah - butter.
мат maht - check mate.
матрёшка mahtRYOHSHkah
- wooden, nested dolls.
матч mahtch - sports
match.
мать maht' - mother.
мачеха MAHchehkah -
step-mother.
машина mahSHEEnah - car;
machine.
мебель MYEHbeel' -
furniture.
мёд myoht - honey.
медленный MYEHDleen-
nihy - slow (adj).
медсестра meedseesTRAH -
nurse.
между MYEHZHdoo -
between.
международный meezhdoo-

nahROHDnihy - international.

мелочь MYEHlahch - small change.

менструация meenstroo-AHtseeyah - menstruation.

меньше MYEHN'sheh - less.

меню meenYOO - menu.

мера MYEHrah - measure; extent; degree.

мёртвый MYOHRTvihy - dead (adj).

местный MYEHSTnihy - local (adj).

место MYEHStah - place; seat; site.

месяц MYEHSeets - month.

метр myehtr - meter.

метро meeTROH - subway.

мех myehkh - fur.

механизм meekhahnEEZM - mechanism.

меховая шапка meekhah-VAHyah SHAHPkah - fur hat.

меховой meekhahVOY - fur (adj).

мешок meeSHOHK - bag; sack.

миленький MEEleen'keey - dear; sweet (adj).

милиционер meeleetseeah-NYEHR - policeman.

милиция meeLEEtseeyah - the police.

миллион meelleeOHN - million.

милый MEElihy - nice; sweet; dear; darling (adj).

мимо MEEmah - by; past.

миндалина meenDAHlee-nah - tonsil.

минута meenOOTah - minute.

мир meer - world; peace.

миска MEESkah - bowl.

мишка MEESHkah - teddy bear.

младенец mlahDYEHneets - baby; infant.

младший MLAHTsheey - younger (adj).

мнение MNYEHneeyeh - opinion.

много MNOHgah - a lot.

многообразный mnahgah-ahbRAHZnihy - diverse (adj).

многоцветный mnahgah-TSVYEHTnihy - multicolored (adj).

могила mahGEElah - grave.

могучий mahGOOcheey - powerful.

мода MOHdah - fashion; style.

модный MOHDnihy - fashionable; stylish (adj).

может быть MOHZHeht biht' - maybe; perhaps.

можно MOHZHnah - may; can.

мозг mohsk - brain.

мокрый MOHKrihy - wet (adj).

молитва mahLEETvah - prayer book.

молния MOHLneeyah - lightning; zipper.

молодёжь mahlahDYOHSH - young people.

молодой mahlahDOY - young (adj).

молоко mahlahKOH - milk.

молочная mahLOHCH-

nahyah - dairy.
молчание mahlCHAH-
neeyeh - silence.
монастырь mahnahsTIHR' -
monastary.
монета mahNYEHtah - coin.
море MOHRyeh - sea.
морковь mahrKOHF' -
carrot.
мороженое mahROHZH-
ehnahyeh - ice cream.
мороженный mahROHZH-
ehnnihy - frozen (adj).
мороз mahROHS - frost.
московский mahsKOHF-
skeey - Moscow (adj).
мост mohst - bridge.
мотор mahTOHR - motor.
мотоцикл mahtahTSEEKL -
motorcycle.
моча mahCHAH - urine.
мочевой пузырь mahchee-
VOY poozIHR' - bladder.
мощный MOHSHCHnihy -
powerful (adj).
муж moosh - husband.
мужество MOOZHehstvah -
courage.
мужской mooshSKOY -
men's (adj).
мужчина mooshCHEEnah -
man.
музей mooZEY - museum.
музыка MOOZihkah -
music.
мука mooKAH - flour.
мультфильм mool'tFEEL'M
- cartoon.
мускул MOOSkool - muscle.
мусор MOOsahr - trash;
rubbish.
муха MOOkhah - fly.
мы mih - we.

мыло MIHlah - soap.
мысль mihsl' - thought;
idea.
мышь mihsh - mouse.
мягкий MYAHKHkeey - soft
(adj).
мясо MYAHsah - meat.
мяч myahch - ball.

H

на nah - on; in.
набитый nahBEEtihy -
tightly packed (adj).
наверно nahVYEHRnah -
probably.
наверх nahVYEHRKH - up;
upwards (location).
наверху nahveerKHOO -
above (destination).
наводнение nahvahdNYEH-
neeyeh - flood.
наволочка NAHvahlahchkah
- pillowcase.
навсегда nahfseegDAH -
forever.
награда nahGRAHdah -
reward.
над naht - over; above.
надгробный камень nahd-
GROHBnihy KAHmeen' -
tombstone.
надежда nahDYEHZHdah -
hope.
надо NAHdah - must.
надпись nahtPEES' -
inscription.
назад nahzAHT - back;
backwards.
название nahzVAHneeyeh -
name; title.
называть nahzihVAHT' - to
be called, named.
наизусть naheezOOST' - by

155

heart.
найти nayTEE - to find.
наказа́ние nahkahzAHN-
eeyeh - punishment.
наконе́ц nahkahnYEHTS - at
last; finally.
накра́сть nahkRAHST' - to
steal.
нале́во nahLYEHvah - on the
left.
нало́г nahLOHK - tax.
наме́рение nahMYEHree-
neeyeh - intention.
наоборо́т nahahbahROHT -
the other way around; on
the contrary.
напи́ток nahPEEtahk -
drink.
напо́р nahPOHR - pressure.
напра́во nahPRAHvah - on
the right.
напра́сно nahPRAHSnah -
in vain; for nothing.
наприме́р nahpreeMYEHR -
for example; for instance.
напро́тив nahPROHteef -
opposite; facing.
напряже́ние nahpreeZHEH-
neeyeh - tension; stress;
strain.
нарко́з nahrKOHS -
anesthesia.
наро́д nahROHT - a people;
наро́дный nahROHDnihy -
national; folk (adj).
наро́ст nahROHST - growth;
tumor.
наро́чно nahROHCHnah -
deliberately; on purpose.
нары́в nahRIHF - abscess.
насеко́мое nahseeKOHmah-
yeh - insect.
населе́ние nahseeLYEHnee-
yeh - population.
наси́лие nahSEEleeyeh -
violence.
наслажде́ние nahslahzh-
DYEHneeyeh - enjoyment;
pleasure; delight.
на́сморк NAHsmahrk - head
cold.
настоя́щий nahstahYAH-
shcheey - present; real;
true (adj).
настрое́ние nahstrahYEH-
neeyeh - mood.
нау́шник nahOOSHneek -
earmuff; headphone.
находи́ться nahkhahDEET-
sah - to be found, located.
национа́льность nahtseeah-
NAHL'nahst' - nation-
ality.
на́ция NAHtseeyah -
nation.
нача́ло nahCHAHlah -
beginning.
нача́льник nahCHAHL'-
neek - chief; head; boss.
начина́ть nahcheeNAHT' -
to begin, start.
неблагополу́чный neeblah-
gahpahLOOCHnihy - un-
fortunate; unhappy (adj).
не́бо NYEHbah - sky;
heaven.
небоскрёб neebahSKRYOHP
- skyscraper.
небре́жный neeBRYEHZH-
nihy - careless; negligent;
sloppy; slipshod (adj).
нева́жный neeVAHZHnihy -
unimportant (adj).
невероя́тный neeveerah-
YAHTnihy - incredible;
unbelievable (adj).

невеста neeVYEHStah - bride.

невестка neeVYEHSTkah - daughter-in-law; sister-in-law.

невольный neeVOHL'nihy - unintentional; involuntary (adj).

невыгодный neeVIHgahdnihy - unprofitable; unfavorable (adj).

недавно needAHVnah - not long ago; recently.

недалёкий needahLYOHkeey - nearby (adj).

недалеко needahleeKOH - not far; close by.

неделя needYEHlyah - week.

недоброкачественный needahbrahKAHCHehstveennihy - poor-quality (adj).

недовольный needahvOHL'nihy - dissatisfied (adj).

недолго needOHLgah - not long; brief.

недоразумение needahrahzooMYEHneeyeh - misunderstanding.

недостаток needahsTAHtahk - shortage; scarcity; defect; deficiency.

недостаточно needahsTAHtahchnah - insufficient.

недостижимый needahsteeZHEEmihy - unattainable (adj).

неестественный neeeestEHSTveennihy - unnatural (adj).

нежный NYEHZHnihy - tender; gentle (adj).

независимость neezahVEEseemahst' - independence.

незаконный neezahKOHNnihy - illegal (adj).

незаметно neezahMYEHTnah - unnoticable (adj).

незнакомец neeznahKOHMeets - stranger.

незнакомый neeznahKOHmihy - unfamiliar (adj).

незрелый neezRYEHlihy - unripe; not mature (adj).

неизвестный neeeezVYEHSTnihy - unknown (adj).

нейтральный neytRAHL'nihy - neutral (adj).

некрасивый neeKRAHSeevihy - ugly (adj).

неловкий neeLOHFkeey - awkward; clumsy (adj).

нельзя neel'ZYAH - impossible; one can not.

немного neemNOHgah - a little; not much.

необходимый neeahpkhahDEEmihy - necessary; essential (adj).

необыкновенный neeahbihknahVYEHNnihy - unusual; uncommon (adj).

неопределённый neeahpreedeeLYOHNnihy - vague; indefinite (adj).

неопытный neeOHpihtnihy - inexperienced (adj).

неохотно neeahKHOHTnah - reluctantly.

непонятный neepahnYAHTnihy - incomprehensible; unintelligible (adj).

неправда neePRAHVdah - untruth; falsehood; lie.

неправильный neePRAH-

veel'nihy - wrong;
incorrect (adj).
неприли́чный neepree-
LEECHnihy - improper;
indecent (adj).
неприя́тный neepree-
YAHTnihy - unpleasant;
disagreeable (adj).
нерв nyehrf - nerve.
не́рвный NYEHRVnihy -
nervous; irritable (adj).
несгора́емый шкаф nee-
zgahRAHeemihy shkahf -
safe.
несколько neeSKOHL'kah -
a few; some; several.
неслы́шный neeSLIHSHnihy
- inaudible (adj).
несправедли́вый neesprah-
veedLEEvihy - unfair;
injust (adj).
несча́стный neeSHAHST-
nihy - unhappy; unfor-
tunate (adj).
несча́стный слу́чай nee-
SHAHSTnihy SLOOchay -
accident.
не nee - not.
нет nyeht - no.
нетерпе́ние neeteerPYEH-
neeyeh - impatience.
неудо́бный neeooDOHBnihy
- uncomfortable (adj).
неуспе́шный neeoos-
PYEHSHnihy - unsuccess-
ful (adj).
нече́стный neeCHEHSTnihy
- dishonest (adj).
нечи́стый neeCHEEStihy -
unclean; dirty (adj).
нея́сный neeYAHSnihy -
unclear (adj).
ни́жнее бельё NEEZH-

neeyeh beel'YOH -
underwear.
ни́жний NEEZHnihy - lower
(adj).
ника́к neeKAHK - no way.
никогда́ neekahgDAH -
never.
никто́ neekTOH - no one.
ни́тка NEETkah - thread.
ничего́ neecheeVOH -
nothing.
но noh - but; however.
но́вый NOHvihy - new (adj).
Но́вый год NOHvihy goht -
New Year.
нога́ nahGAH - leg; foot.
нож nohsh - knife.
но́жницы NOHZHneetsih -
scissors.
ноль nohl' - zero.
но́мер NOHmeer - hotel
room; number; issue.
номеро́к nahmeeROHK -
(coat check) ticket.
норма́льный nohrMAHL'-
nihy - normal (adj).
нос nohs - nose.
носи́лки nahSEELkee -
stretcher.
носи́льщик nahSEEL'-
shcheek - porter.
носки́ nahsKEE - socks.
ночь nohch - night.
нра́виться NRAHveetsah -
to enjoy.
нра́вы NRAHvih - customs.
ну noo - well; well then.
нужда́ noozhDAH - need.
ну́жно NOOZHnah - (one)
must, has to.

O

о oh - about.

óба OHbah - both.

обéд ahBYEHT - lunch.

обéдать ahBYEHdaht' - to have lunch.

обезбóливание ahbeesBOH-leevahneeyeh - anesthetization.

обещáние ahbeeSHCHAH-neeyeh - promise.

обúда ahBEEdah - offence; insult.

óбласть OHblahst' - region; area; field; domain.

обмáн ahbMAHN - fraud; deception; deceit.

обмéн ahbMYEHN - exchange.

обменя́ть ahbmeenYAHT' - to exchange.

óбраз OHbrahs - image; way; mode; manner.

образéц ahbrahzYEHTS - sample; model; pattern.

образовáние ahbrahzah-VAHneeyeh - education.

обрáтный ahbRAHTnihy - return; opposite (adj).

обстанóвка ahbstahNOHF-kah - situation; setting.

óбувь OHboof - shoes.

обхóд ahpKHOHT - detour.

общежúтие ahpshchehZHEE-teeyeh - dormitory.

óбщество OHPshchehstvah - society; company.

óбщий OHPshcheey - general; common (adj).

объявлéние ahb"eevLYEH-neeyeh - announcement.

объяснéние ahb"eesNYEH-neeyeh - explanation.

обы́чно ahBIHCHnah - usually.

обязáтельный ahbeeZAH-teel'nihy - obligatory; mandatory (adj).

овёс ahVYOHS - oats.

óвощи OHvahshchee - vegetables.

овся́нка ahfSYAHNkah - oatmeal.

огурцы́ ahgoorTSIH - cucumbers.

одéжда ahDYEHZHdah - clothes.

одея́ло ahdeeYAHlah - blanket.

одинáковый ahdeeNAHkah-vihy - identical (adj).

однáжды ahdNAHZHdih - once; one day.

однáко ahdNAHkah - however; but.

одноврéменный ahdnah-VRYEHmeennihy - simultaneous (adj).

ожерéлье ahzheeRYEHL'yeh - necklace.

óзеро OHzeerah - lake.

океáн ahkeeAHN - ocean.

окнó ahkNOH - window.

óколо OHkahlah - around; approximately; about.

окончáние ahkahnCHAH-neeyeh - completion; end.

окрáска ahKRAHSkah - dye; hair coloring.

олéнина ahlYEHneenah - venison.

он ohn - he.

онá ahNAH - she.

онú ahNEE - they.

опаздáть ahpahzDAHT' - to be late.

опасный ahPAHSnihy - dangerous (adj).

опера OHpeerah - opera.

описание ahpeeSAHneeyeh - description.

опоздание ahpahzDAHneeyeh - delay; tardiness.

определённый ahpreedeeLYOHNnihy - definite; set; certain (adj).

оптик OPteek - optician.

опыт OHpiht - experience.

опять ahPYAHT' - again.

оранжевый ahRAHNzhehvihy - orange (adj).

орех ahRYEHKH - nut.

оркестр ahrKYEHSTR - orchestra.

оса ahSAH - wasp.

осень OHseen' - fall.

осложнение ahslahzhNYEHneeyeh - complication.

осмотр ahsMOHTR - examination; checkup.

основа ahsNOHvah - basis.

особенно ahSOHbeennah - especially.

остановка ahstahnOHFkah - bus stop.

остаток ahsTAHtahk - remainder.

осторожно ahstahROHZHnah - beware; careful.

остров OHStrahf - island.

острый OHStrihy - sharp; pungent; keen (adj).

от aht - from.

ответ ahtVYEHT - answer.

отдел ahdDYEHL - section; department.

отдельно ahdDYEHL'nah - separately; individually.

отдых OHDdihkh - rest.

отец ahTYEHTS - father.

отечество ahTYEHCHehstvah - fatherland.

отказ ahtKAHS - refusal.

открытка ahtKRIHTkah - postcard.

открытый ahtKRIHtihy - open (adj).

отлёт ahtLYOHT - departure (airplane).

отношение ahtnahSHEHneeyeh - attitude; relationship; connection.

отопление ahtahpLYEHneeyeh - heating.

отпуск OHTpoosk - vacation from work.

отрава ahtRAHvah - poison.

отрицательный ahtreeTSAHteel'nihy - negative (adj).

отрывок ahtRIHvahk - passage; excerpt; snatch.

отсутствие ahtSOOTSTveeyeh - absence.

отход ahtKHOHT - departure (train).

отчество OHTchehstvah - patronymic.

отчим OHTcheem - stepfather.

отъезд aht"YEHST - detour.

официант ahfeetseeAHNT - waiter.

официантка ahfeetseeAHNTkah - waitress.

оформление ahfahrmLYEHneeyeh - processing (of documents).

охота ahKHOHtah - wish; desire.

очевидный ahchehVEED-

nihy - obvious (adj).
очень OHcheen' - very.
очередь OHCHehreet' - line.
очки ahchKEE - glasses.
ошибка ahshEEPkah - mistake.
ощущение ahshchoo-SHCHEHneeyeh - feeling; sensation.

П

падеж pahDYEHSH - grammatical case.
пакет pahKYEHT - packet; package.
палатка pahLAHTkah - tent.
палец PAHleets - finger.
пальто pahl'TOH - coat.
памятник PAHMeetneek - monument.
память PAHMeet' - memory.
папироса pahpeeROHSah - cigarette.
папиросница pahpeeROHSneetsah - cigarette case.
пара PAHrah - pair.
пареный PAHreenihy - steamed (adj).
парикмахер pahreekMAHkheer - hairdresser; barber.
парилка pahREELkah - steam room.
парк pahrk - park.
паром pahROHM - ferry.
пароход pahrahKHOHT - ship; steamship.
парусная лодка PAHroosnahyah LOHTkah - sail boat.

пасмурный PAHsmoornihy - overcast (adj).
паспорт PAHSpahrt - passport.
пассажир pahssahZHEER - passenger.
Пасха PAHSkhah - Easter; Passover.
паук pahOOK - spider.
пахнуть PAHKHnoot' - to smell.
пациент pahtseeEHNT - patient.
пачка PAHCHkah - pack; bundle.
певец peevYEHTS - singer.
педиатр peedeeAHTR - pediatrician.
пенициллин peeneetseel-LEEN - penicillin.
пепельница PYEHpeel'neetsah - ashtray.
первоначальный peervah-nahCHAHL'nihy - original (adj).
перевести peereeveesTEE - to translate.
перевод peereeVOHT - translation.
переводчик peereeVOHTcheek - translator; interpreter.
перевязка peereeVYAHSkah - bandaging; dressing.
переговоры peereegahVOH-rihy - negotiations.
перед PYEHreet - before; in front of.
передача peereeDAHchah - broadcast; transmission.
передний peeRYEHDneey - front (adj).
переносный peereeNOHS-

nihy - portable (adj).
переписка peereePEESkah - correspondence.
перерыв peereeRIHF - break; recess.
пересадка peereeSAHTkah - change; transfer (on planes, trains, buses etc).
переулок peereeOOLahk - side street.
переход peereeKHOHT - place to cross; crosswalk.
перец PYEHreets - pepper.
перманент peermahn-YEHNT - permanent wave.
персик PYEHRseek - peach.
перцовка peerTSOHFkah - pepper vodka.
перчатки peerCHAHTkee - gloves.
песня PYEHSnyah - song.
песок peeSOHK - sand.
петрушка peeTROOSHkah - parsley.
печальный peeCHAHL'nihy - sad (adj).
печёнка peechOHNkah - liver (the food).
печень PYEHchehn' - liver (anatomy).
печенье peeCHEHN'yeh - cookie; pastry.
печь pyehch - stove.
пешком peeshKOHM - on, by foot.
пиво PEEvah - beer.
пиджак peedZHAHK - man's suit jacket.
пижама peezhAHMah - pyjamas.
пилав peeLAHF - pilaf.
пилюля peeLYOOlyah - pill.

пинцет peenTSEHT - tweezers.
пирог peeROHK - pie.
пирожное peeROHZH-nahyeh - pastry.
писатель peeSAHteel' - writer.
писать peeSAHT' - to write.
письменно PEES'meennah - in writing.
письмо pees'MOH - letter.
пить peet' - to drink.
пишущая машинка PEESH-ooshchahyah mahSHEEN-kah - typewriter.
пища PEEshchah - food.
плавать PLAHvaht' - to swim.
плакат plahKAHT - poster.
план plahn - city map.
пластырь - PLAHStihr' - band-aide.
платить plahTEET' - to pay.
платок plahTOHK - kerchief.
платье PLAHT'yeh - dress.
плацкартный plahts-KAHRTnihy - reserved (on a train) (adj).
плащь plahshch - raincoat.
племянник pleemYAHN-neek - nephew.
племяница pleemYAHNeet-sah - niece.
плёнка PLYOHNkah - film.
плечо pleeCHOH - shoulder.
плитка PLEETkah - (chocolate) bar.
пломба PLOHMbah - (tooth) filling.
плохо PLOHkhah - badly.

плохо́й plahKHOY - bad; poor (adj).

пло́щадь PLOHshchaht' - area; square.

пляж plyahsh - beach.

по pah - along; about; according to.

по кра́йне ме́ре pah KRAYnyeh MYEHreh - at least.

побе́да pahBYEHdah - victory.

по́вар POHvahr - cook.

повтори́ть pahftahREET' - to repeat.

пого́да pahGOHdah - weather.

под poht - under; beneath.

пода́рок pahDAHrahk - present; gift.

подгу́зник pahdGOOZneek - diaper.

подмётка pahdMYOHTkah - sole (of a shoe).

подписа́ть pahtpeeSAHT' - to sign.

по́дпись POHTpees' - signature.

подро́бность pahdROHPnahst' - detail.

подтвержде́ние pahttveerzhDYEHneeyeh - confirmation.

поду́шка pahDOOSHkah - pillow.

по́езд POHeest - train.

пожа́луйста pahZHAHLstah - please.

пожа́р pahZHAHR - fire.

пожа́тие pahZHAHteeyeh - handshake.

пожило́й pahzheeLOY - elderly (adj).

позавчера́ pahzahfcheeRAH - day before yesterday.

позвони́ть pahzvahNEET' - to call (on the phone).

по́здний POHZDneey - late (adj).

поздравля́ть pahzdrahvLYAHT' - to congratulate.

по́зже POHZHzheh - later.

познако́мить pahznahKOHmeet' - to introduce.

пока́ pahKAH - meanwhile; goodbye (coll).

показа́ть pahkahZAHT' - to show.

покупа́тель pahkooPAHteel' - customer.

поку́пка pahKOOPkah - purchase.

по́лдень POHLdeen' - noon.

по́ле POHLyeh - field; area.

поле́зный pahLYEHZnihy - useful; helpful (adj).

полёт pahLYOHT - flight.

поликли́ника pahleeKLEEneekah - clinic.

поли́тика pahLEEteekah - politics.

по́лка POHLkah - berth; shelf.

по́лночь POHLnahch - midnight.

по́лный POHLnihy - full; complete (adj).

полови́на pahlahVEEnah - half.

половы́е о́рганы pahlah-VIHyeh OHRgahnih - genitals.

положе́ние pahlahZHEHneeyeh - situation; condition.

положи́тельный pahlah-

ZHEEteel'nihy - positive; affirmative (adj).

полоте́нце pahlahTYEHN-tseh - towel.

полтора́ pahltahRAH - one and a half.

полчаса́ pahlcheeSAH - half hour.

по́льза POHL'zah - use; benefit.

помидо́р pahmeeDOHR - tomato.

по́мощь POHmahshch - help.

понима́ть pahneeMAHT' - to understand.

поно́с pahNOHS - diarrhea.

по́нчик POHNcheek - doughnut.

поня́тный pahnYAHTnihy - understandable (adj).

попра́вка pahPRAHFkah - correction; adjustment.

пора́ pahRAH - it's time.

по́рох POHrahkh - powder.

порт pohrt - port.

портре́т pahrtRYEHT - portrait.

портфе́ль pahrtFYEHL' - briefcase.

поря́док pahRYAHdahk - order; sequence.

поса́дка pahSAHTkah - landing.

посла́ть pahsLAHT' - to send.

по́сле POHSlee - after.

по́сле обе́да POHSlee ahBYEHdah - afternoon.

после́дний pahsLYEHDneey - last; latest (adj).

послеза́втра pahslee-ZAHFtrah - day after tomorrow.

посло́вица pahsLOHveetsah - proverb.

посове́товать pahsahVYEH-tahvaht' - to recommend.

посо́льство pahSOHL'stvah - embassy.

посте́ль pahsTYEHL' - bed.

постепе́нно pahsteePYEHN-nah - gradually.

постоя́нный pahstahYAHN-nihy - constant; continuous (adj).

посу́да pahSOOdah - dishes.

посы́лка pahSIHLkah - package.

пот poht - sweat.

потеря́ть pahteerYAHT' - to lose (sth.).

потоло́к pahtahLOHK - ceiling.

пото́м pahTOHM - then; next; afterwards.

потому́ что pahtahMOO shtah - because.

похо́жий pahKHOHzheey - similar; like (adj).

поцелу́й pahtseeLOOY - kiss.

почему́ pahcheeMOO - why.

почему́-то pahcheeMOO-tah - for some reason.

по́чка POHCHkah - kidney.

по́чта POHCHtah - mail; post office.

по́чтамт POHCHTahmt - main postoffice.

почти́ pahchTEE - almost.

почто́вый я́щик pahchTOH-vihy YAHshcheek - mailbox.

по́шлина POHSHleenah -

duty (customs).
поэ́зия pahEHzeeyah -
poetry.
поэ́т pahEHT - poet.
поэ́тому pahEHtahmoo -
therefore.
по́яс POHees - belt; waist.
пра́вда PRAHVdah - truth.
пра́вило PRAHveelah - rule.
пра́вильный PRAHVeel'-
nihy - correct; right (adj).
прави́тельство prahVEE-
teel'stvah - government.
правосла́вный prahvah-
SLAHVnihy - orthodox.
пра́вый PRAHvihy - right
(direction).
пра́здник PRAHZneek -
holiday.
пребыва́ние preebihVAH-
neeyeh - stay.
предложе́ние preedlah-
ZHEHneeyeh - offer;
proposal; suggestion.
предме́т preedMYEHT -
subject.
предприя́тие preedpree-
YAHteeyeh - undertaking;
venture.
предупрежде́ние preedoo-
preezhDYEHneeyeh -
warning.
пре́жде PRYEHZHdyeh -
before; formerly.
пре́жний PRYEHZHneey -
former; previous (adj).
презервати́в preezeervah-
TEEF - contraceptive.
прекра́сный preeKRAHS-
nihy - beautfiful (adj).
преподава́тель preepah-
dahVAHteel' - teacher.
преподава́тельница pree-

pahdahVAHteelneetsah-
teacher (f).
препя́тсвие preePYAHTS-
veeyeh - hindrance.
преступле́ние preestoop-
LYEHneeyeh - crime.
преувеличе́ние preeoovee-
leeCHEHneeyeh - exagger-
ation.
при pree - before.
приве́т preeVYEHT - hi.
привы́чка preeVIHCHkah -
habit.
приглаше́ние preeglah-
SHEHneeyeh - invitation.
при́город PREEgahraht -
suburb.
прие́зд preeYEHST -
arrival.
приём preeYOHM -
reception.
прилёт preeLYOHT -
arrival (on a plane).
прили́чный preeLEESHnihy
- proper; civilized (adj).
приме́р preeMYEHR -
example.
принима́ть preeneeMAHT' -
to accept.
приро́да preeROHdah -
nature.
при́стань PREEstahn' -
dock; pier; wharf.
причёска preeCHOHSkah -
hair-do.
причи́на preeCHEEnah -
reason.
прия́тный preeYAHTnihy -
pleasant (adj).
про proh - about.
пробле́ма prahBLYEHmah -
problem.
прогно́з prahgNOHS -

prognosis; forecast.
продаве́ц prahdahVYEHTS -
salesman.
прода́жа prahDAHzhah -
sale.
прода́ть prahDAHT' - to
sell.
продолже́ние prahdahl-
ZHEHneeyeh - continu-
ation.
произноше́ние praheez-
nahSHEHneeyeh - pronun-
ciation.
происхожде́ние praheez-
khahzhDYEHneeyeh -
origin.
проли́в prahLEEF - strait;
channel.
пропи́ска prahPEESkah -
registration.
про́пуск PROHpoosk -
admission; admittance.
прости́те prahsTEEtyeh -
sorry; excuse me.
про́сто PROHstah - simply.
просто́й prahsTOY -
simple; easy (adj).
просту́да prahsTOOdah -
head cold.
простыня́ prahstihnYAH -
sheet.
про́сьба PROZ'bah -
request.
проте́з (зубно́й) prahTYEHS
zoopNOY - denture.
про́тив PROHteef - against.
профе́ссия prahFYEHS-
seeyah - profession.
профе́ссор prahFYEHSsahr -
professor.
прохла́дный prahkhLAHD-
nihy - cool (adj).
про́шлый PROHSHlihy -
past (adj).
проща́й prahSHCHAY -
farewell.
проявле́ние praheevLYEH-
neeyeh - (film) develop-
ment.
пруд proot - pond.
прямо́й preeMOY - straight
(adj).
пти́ца PTEEtsah - bird.
пу́говица POOgahveetsah -
button.
пуло́вер poolOHveer -
sweater.
пульс pool's - pulse.
пу́нкт poonkt - point;
station; center.
пусто́й poosTOY - empty;
vacant (adj).
путеводи́тель pooteevah-
DEEteel' - guidebook.
путеше́ственник pooteesh-
EHSTveenneek - traveler.
путеше́ствие pooteesh-
EHSTveeyeh - travels;
trip.
путь poot' - trip; way; path.
пчела́ pcheeLAH - bee.
пшени́ца pshehNEEtsah -
wheat.
пье́са P'YEHsah - play;
drama.
пья́ный P'YAHnihy -
drunk; intoxicated (adj).
пя́ница PYAHneetsah -
drunkard.
пятно́ peetNOH - spot;
stain.

P
рабо́та rahBOHtah - work.
рабо́тать rahBOHtaht' - to
work.

166

рабочий rahBOHcheey - worker.

раввин rahvVEEN - rabbi.

равнодушный rahvnah-DOOSHnihy - indifferent (adj).

равный RAHVnihy - equal (adj)

рагу rahGOO - stew.

рад raht - glad; pleased.

радио RAHdeeoh - radio.

радиостанция rahdeeah-STAHNtseeyah - radio station.

радостный RAHdahstnihy - joyful; joyous (adj).

раз rahs - time; once; one.

разве RAHZveh - really?; is that so?

развитие rahzVEEteeyeh - development.

развлечение rahzvlee-CHEHneeyeh - amusement; entertainment.

разговор rahzgahVOHR - conversation.

разговорник rahzgahVOHRneek - phrasebook.

разговорный rahzgah-VOHRnihy - conversational; colloquial. (adj).

раздевалка rahzdeeVAHLkah - cloakroom.

раздражение rahzdrah-ZHEHneeyeh - irritation.

раздутый rahzDOOtihy - swollen; puffed up (adj).

размер rahzMYEHR - size.

разница RAHSneetsah - difference; distinction.

разный RAHZnihy - different (adj).

разрешение rahzreeSHEH-neeyeh - permission; permit.

разумно rahzOOMnah - sensibly; rationally (adj).

рак rahk - crayfish; cancer.

раковина RAHkahveenah - (bathroom) sink.

рана RAHnah - wound.

раненый RAHNeenihy - wounded, injured (adj).

ранний RAHNneey - early (adj).

раньше RAHN'sheh - earlier; sooner.

расписание rahspeeSAH-neeyeh - schedule; timetable.

распродано rahsPROH-dahnah - sold out.

рассвет rahsSVYEHT - dawn; daybreak.

рассказ rahsSKAHS - story; tale; account.

рассольник rahsSOHL'neek - salted cucumber soup.

расстояние rahsstahYAH-neeyeh - distance.

расстройство желудка rahsSTROYstvah zheh-LOOTkah - indigestion.

растение rahsTYEHneeyeh - plant.

растяжение rahsteeZHEH-neeyeh - strain; sprain.

расходы rahsKHOHdih - expenses.

рваный RVAHnihy - torn; ripped (adj).

ребёнок reeBYOHnahk - child.

ребро reebROH - rib.

ревматизм reevmahTEEZM - rheumatism.

редиска reeDEESkah -
radish.
редкий RYEHTkeey - rare;
infrequent (adj).
редко RYEHTkah - rarely.
режиссёр reezheesSYOHR -
(theater) director.
резаный RYEHZahnihy -
cut; sliced (adj).
резиновый reeZEEnahvihy -
rubber (adj).
рейс reys - trip; flight.
река reeKAH - river.
реклама reeKLAHmah -
advertising; sign.
рельс ryehl's - rail; track.
ремонт reeMOHNT - repair.
ремонт обуви reeMOHNT
OHboovee - shoemaker.
рентген reentGYEHN - x-
ray.
репа RYEHpah - turnip.
ресница reesNEEtsah -
eyelash.
республика reesPOO-
bleekah - republic.
ресторан reestahRAHN -
restaurant.
рецепт reeTSEHPT -
prescription.
речь ryehch - speech.
решение reeSHEHneeyeh -
decision.
рис rees - rice.
рисование reesahVAH-
neeyeh - drawing.
рифма REEFmah - ryhme.
робкий ROHPkeey - timid;
shy (adj).
родина ROHdeenah -
homeland.
родители rahDEEteelee -
parents.

родной rahdNOY - native
(adj).
родственник ROHTST-
veenneekee - relatives.
рождение rahzhDYEH-
neeyeh - birth.
Рождество rahzheestVOH -
Christmas.
рожь rohsh - rye.
роза ROHzah - rose.
розетка rahzYEHTkah -
electrical socket.
роль rohl' - role; part.
роман rahMAHN - novel.
роса rahSAH - dew.
роскошный rahsKOHSH-
nihy - luxurious (adj).
российский rahsSEEY-
skeey - Russian (adj).
рост rohst - growth; height.
ростбиф ROHSTbeef - roast
beef.
рот roht - mouth.
рубашка rooBAHSHkah -
shirt.
рубин rooBEEN - ruby.
рубль roobl' - ruble.
рука rooKAH - hand; arm.
рукав rooKAHF - sleeve.
рукавица rookahVEEtsah -
mitten.
руководство rookahVOHT-
stvah - leadership.
рукопись ROOkahpees' -
manuscript.
рукоплескание rookah-
pleesKAHneeyeh -
applause.
рулет rooLYEHT - meat
loaf.
русский ROOSskeey -
Russian (noun & adj).
русская ROOSskahyah -

168

Russian (f).
ручка ROOCHkah - pen.
рыба RIHBah - fish.
рынок RIHNahk - market.
рюкзак ryookZAHK -
backpack.
рябчик RYAHPcheek -
hazel grouse.
ряд ryaht - row; file.
рядом RYAHdahm -
alongside; beside; next to.

С

с se - with; off; since.
сад saht - garden.
салат sahLAHT - salad.
салфётка sahlFYEHTkah -
napkin.
самовар sahmahVAHR -
samovar.
самолёт sahmahLYOHT -
airplane.
самообслуживание sah-
mahahpSLOOzheevahnee-
yeh - self-service (adj).
самостоятельный sahmah-
stahYAHteel'nihy - inde-
pendent (adj).
самоубийство sahmahoo-
BEEYSTvah - suicide.
самоуверенный sahmah-
ooVYEHreennihy - self
confident (adj).
сандалии sahnDAHleeee -
sandals.
санитарный день sahnee-
TAHRnihy dyehn' - one
day a month when stores
are closed for cleaning.
санки SAHNkee - sleigh;
sled.
сапоги sahpahGEE - boots.
сапфир sahpFEER - saphire.

сарказм sahrKAHZM -
sarcasm.
сатира sahTEErah - satire.
сахар SAHkhahr - sugar.
сахарин sahkhahREEN -
saccharin.
сбор zbohr - collection;
gathering.
сборник ZBOHRneek -
anthology; collection.
свадьба SVAHT'bah -
wedding.
свежий SVYEHzheey - fresh
(adj).
свёкла SVYOHKlah - beets.
свекольник sveeKOHL'neek
- beet soup.
сверх svyehrkh - over and
above; in access of.
свет svyeht - light.
светло- SVYEHTlah- -
light-(color).
светлый SVYEHTlihy -
light; bright (adj).
светофор sveetahFOHR -
traffic light.
свеча sveeCHAH - candle.
свидание sveeDAHneeyeh -
appointment; meeting.
свинина sveeNEEnah -
pork.
свинья sveen'YAH - pig.
свобода svahBOHdah -
freedom.
свободный svahBOHDnihy -
free; vacant (adj).
святой sveeTOY - holy;
sacred (adj).
священник sveeshchEHN-
neek - priest; clergyman.
сдача ZDAHchah - change.
север SYEHveer - north.
северный SYEHveernihy -

northern (adj).
сегодня seeVOHdnyah -
today.
сегодняшний seeVOH-
dnyahshneey - today's
(adj).
сейчас seeCHAHS - now.
секретарь seekreeTAHR' -
secretary.
секунда seekOONdah -
second (time measure).
секция SYEHKtseeyah -
section.
село seeLOH - village.
сельдь syehl't' - herring.
сёмга SYOHMgah - lox.
семья seem'YAH - family.
сервиз seerVEES - set (of
dishes or silverware).
сердечный припадок
seerDYEHCHnihy pree-
PAHdahk - heart attack.
сердитый seerDEEtihy -
angry (adj).
сердце SYEHRtseh - heart.
серебро seereeBROH -
silver.
серебряный seeRYEHB-
reenihy - silver (adj).
середина seereeDEEnah -
middle.
серёжки seerYOHSHkee-
earrings.
серьги SYEHR'gee -
earrings.
серый SYEHrihy - grey
(adj).
серьёзный seer'YOHZnihy -
serious (adj).
сестра seesTRAH - sister.
сигара seeGAHrah - cigar.
сигарета seegahRYEHtah -
cigarette.

сила SEElah - strength.
сильный SEEL'nihy -
strong (adj).
синагога seenahGOHgah -
synagogue.
синий SEEneey - dark blue
(adj).
синяк seenYAHK - bruise.
сирень seerYEHN' - lilac.
система seesTYEHmah -
system.
ситечко SEEteechkah -
strainer.
сказка SKAHSkah - tale.
скамейка skahMEYkah -
bench.
сквозь skvohs' - through.
скидка SKEETkah - sale.
сковорода skahvahrahDAH
- frying pan.
скользкий SKOHL'skeey -
slippery (adj).
сколько SKOHL'kah - how
much.
скорая помощь SKOHrah-
yah POHmahshch - ambu-
lance.
скорее skahRYEHeh -
quickly!
скорлупа skahrlooPAH -
(egg) shell.
скорость SKOHrahst' -
speed.
скорый SKOHrihy -
quickly; rapidly (adj).
скромный SKROHMnihy -
modest (adj).
скрытый SKRIHtihy -
hidden; secret (adj).
скульптура skool'pTOOrah
- sculpture.
скучный SKOOCHnihy -
boring (adj).

170

слаби́тельное slahBEEteel'-nahyeh - laxative.
сла́бый SLAHbihy - weak (adj).
сла́ва SLAHvah - glory.
сла́дкий SLAHTkeey - sweet (adj).
сла́дкое (на) SLAHTkahyeh (nah) - (for) dessert.
сле́дствие SLYEHTstveeyeh - result; consequence.
сле́дующий SLYEHdooyooshcheey - next (adj).
слёзы SLYOHzih - tears.
сли́ва SLEEvah - plum.
сли́вки SLEEFkee - cream.
сли́шком SLEESHkahm - too.
слова́рь slahVAHR' - dictionary.
сло́во SLOHvah - word.
сло́жный SLOHZHnihy - complex; difficult (adj).
слома́ть slahMAHT' - to break.
слу́жба SLOOSHbah - church service.
слу́чай SLOOchay - incident.
случа́йно slooCHAYnah - accidentally.
слы́шный SLIHSHnihy - audible (adj).
сме́лый SMYEHlihy - brave; courageous (adj).
смерть smyehrt' - death.
смета́на smeeTAHnah - sour cream.
смех smyehkh - laughter.
смешно́й smeeshNOY - funny (adj).
смотре́ть smahTRYEHT' - to look.

смуще́ние smooSHCHEHneeyeh - embarrassment.
снача́ла snahCHAHlah - at first; in the beginning.
снег snyehk - snow.
соба́ка sahBAHkah - dog.
собо́р sahBOHR - cathedral.
собра́ние sahBRAHneeyeh - meeting.
собы́тие sahBIHTeeyeh - event.
сове́т sahVYEHT - advice.
совпаде́ние sahfpahDYEHneeyeh - coincidence.
совреме́нный sahvreem-MYEHNnihy - contemporary (adj).
согла́сный sahGLAHSnihy - in agreement.
сок sohk - juice.
сокраще́ние sahkrah-SHCHEHneeyeh - abbreviation.
солда́т sahlDAHT - soldier.
солёный sahlYOHnihy - salted (adj).
со́лнечный SOHLneechnihy - sunny (adj).
со́лнце SOHNtseh - sun.
соль sohl' - salt.
сомне́ние sahmNYEHneeyeh - doubt.
сон sohn - sleep; dream.
сообща́ть sahahpSHCHAHT' - to notify, inform.
соревнова́ние sahreevnah-VAHneeyeh - competition; sports match.
сорт sohrt - kind; sort.
сосе́д sahSYEHT - neighbor.
со́ска SOHSkah - pacifier.
состоя́ние sahstahYAHneeyeh - condition.

сотый SOHTihy - hundred.
соус SOHoos - sauce; gravy.
сочетание sahchehTAH-
neeyeh - combination.
сочувствие sahCHOOST-
veeyeh - sympathy.
союз sahYOOS - union.
спальня SPAHL'nyah -
bedroom.
спасибо spahSEEbah -
thank you.
спать spaht' - to sleep.
спектакль speekTAHKL' -
performance; play.
специальность speetsee-
AHL'nahst' - specialty.
спешный SPYEHSHnihy -
hurried; rushed (adj).
спина speeNAH - back;
spine.
список SPEEsahk - list.
спичка SPEECHkah - match.
спокойный spahKOYnihy -
calm; tranquil (adj).
спор spohr - argument.
спорный SPOHRnihy -
controversial (adj).
справка SPRAHFkah -
reference; information.
средний SRYEHDneey -
middle; average (adj).
средство от камаров
SRYEHTstvah aht kah-
mahROHF - mosquito
repellent.
срок srohk - (period of)
time; date; deadline.
срочный SROHCHnihy -
urgent; emergency (adj).
стадион stahdeeOHN -
stadium.
стакан stahKAHN -
(drinking) glass.

станция STAHNtseeyah -
station.
старший STAHRsheey -
older; elder (adj); senior.
старый STAHrihy - old
(adj).
стекло steekLOH - glass.
стена steeNAH - wall.
степень STYEHpeen' -
degree; extent.
стирка STEERkah -
washing; laundry.
стол stohl - table.
столетие stahLYEHteeyeh -
century.
столица stahLEEtsah -
capital (of a state).
столовая stahLOHvahyah -
dining hall.
стоп stohp - stop.
сторона stahrahNAH - side.
стоянка stahYAHNkah -
(bus) stop.
стоянка для машин
stahYAHNkah dlyah
mahSHEEN - parking lot.
страна strahNAH -
country.
страница strahNEEtsah -
page.
странный STRAHNnihy -
strange; weird; odd (adj).
страстный STRAHSTnihy -
passionate (adj).
страх strahkh - fear.
страшный STRAHSHnihy -
horrible; terrifying (adj).
стрижка STREESHkah -
haircut; trim.
строгий STROHgeey -
strict; harsh; severe (adj).
студент stooDYEHNT -
student.

студень STOOdyehn' - aspic.
стук stook - knock.
стул stool - chair.
стыд stiht - shame.
стюардéсса styooahrDYEHSsah - stewardess.
сувенир sooveeNEER - souvenir.
судьбá soot'BAH - fate.
сумасшéдший soomahsh-EHTsheey - crazy; mad; insane (adj).
суп soop - soup.
супрýг soopROOK - husband.
супрýга soopROOgah - wife.
сýтки SOOTkee - 24 hour period; day.
сухóй sooKHOY - dry (adj).
сцéна STSEHnah - stage.
счастливый shahstLEEvihy - happy; lucky (adj).
счёт shchoht - check; bill.
съезд s"yehst - convention; congress.
сын sihn - son.
сыр sihr - cheese.
сырóй sihROY - raw (adj).
сытый SIHTihy - full (of food).

T
табáк tahBAHK - tobacco.
таблéтка tahbLYEHTkah - pill; tablet.
так tahk - so; true.
тáкже TAHKzheh - as well.
таксú tahkSEE - taxi.
тáлия TAHleeyah - waist.
талóн tahLOHN - coupon.
тальк tahl'k - talcum
powder.
там tahm - there.
тамóженник tahMOHZHehnneek - customs official.
тамóжня tahMOHZHnyah - customs.
тампóн tahmPOHN - tampon.
тáнец TAHneets - dance.
тáпочки TAHPahchkee - slippers.
таракáн tahrahKAHN - cockroach.
тарéлка tahRYEHLkah - plate.
твёрдый TVYOHRdihy - hard (adj).
творóг tvahROHK - cottage cheese.
твóрчество TVOHRchehstvah - creative work.
теáтр teeAHTR - theater.
телевизор teeleeVEEzahr - television.
телегрáмма teeleeGRAHMmah - telegram.
телегрáф teeleeGRAHF - telegraph office.
телефóн teeleeFOHN - telephone.
телефóн-автомáт teeleeFOHN-ahftahMAHT - pay phone; phone booth.
телефонистка teeleefahn-EESTkah - operator.
тéло TYEHlah - body.
телятина teelYAHteenah - veal.
тёмно- TYOHMnah- - dark- (color).
тёмные очки TYOHMnihyeh ahchKEE - sunglasses.

173

тёмный TYOHMnihy - dark (adj).

температу́ра teempeerah-TOOrah - temperature.

те́ннис TYEHNnees - tennis.

тень tyehn' - shadow.

тепе́рь teePYEHR' - now.

тёплый TYOHPlihy - warm (adj).

те́рмос TYEHRmahs - thermos.

терпели́вый teerpeeLEE-vihy - patient (adj).

те́сный TYEHSnihy - crowded.

тетра́дь teeTRAHT' - notebook.

тётя TYOHtyah - aunt.

те́фтели TYEHFteelee - meatballs.

ти́хий TEEKHeey - quite (adj).

ткань tkahn' - fabric.

това́р tahVAHR - merchandise.

това́рищ tahVAHReeshch - comrade.

тогда́ tahgDAH - then.

то́же TOHzheh - also.

толпа́ tahlPAH - crowd.

то́лстый TOHLstihy - fat (adj).

то́лько TOHL'kah - only.

то́нкий TOHNkeey - thin (adj).

топа́з tahPAHS - topaz.

тормоза́ tahrmahZAH - brakes (car).

торт tohrt - cake.

тот toht - that (one).

то́чно TOHCHnah - exactly.

тошнота́ tashnahTAH - nausea.

трава́ trahVAH - grass.

траге́дия trahGYEHdeeyah - tragedy.

трамва́й trahmVAY - street car.

тра́сса TRAHSsah - highway.

треска́ treesKAH - cod.

тро́гать TROHgaht' - to touch.

тролле́йбус trahlLEYboos - trolley bus.

тротуа́р trahtooAHR - side walk.

тру́бка TROOPkah - pipe.

тру́дный TROODnihy - difficult (adj).

трусы́ trooSIH - underpants.

туале́т tooahLYEHT - toilet.

туале́тная бума́га tooah-LYEHTnahyah booMAHgah - toiletpaper.

туда́ tooDAH - that way.

туда́ и обра́тно tooDAH ee ahbRAHTnah - roundtrip (ticket).

тума́н tooMAHN - fog.

туне́ц tooNYEHTS - tuna.

тури́ст tooREEST - tourist.

тут toot - here.

ту́фли TOOFlee - shoes.

ты́сяча TIHseechah - thousand.

тюрьма́ tyoor'MAH - prison.

тяжёлый teezhOHLihy - difficult (adj).

У

у oo - at.

уби́йство ooBEEYSTvah -

murder.
убийца ooBEEYtsah -
murderer.
уборная ooBOHRnahyah -
bathroom.
убóрщик ooBOHRshcheek -
janitor; yardsman.
убóрщица ooBOHRshchee-
tsah - cleaning woman.
уважáемый oovahZHAH-
eemihy - respected (adj).
увеличéние ooveeleeCHEH-
neeyeh - increase.
уверéние ooveeRYEHneeyeh
- assurance.
увлечённый oovleeCHOHN-
nihy - enthusiastic (adj).
угол OOgahl - corner.
угрóза ooGROHzah - threat.
ударéние oodahRYEHnee-
yeh - grammatical stress.
удáча ooDAHchah -
success.
удивительный oodeeVEE-
teel'nihy - surprising
(adj).
удóбный ooDOHBnihy -
comfortable (adj).
удóбство ooDOHBSTvah -
convenience.
удовлетворéние oodahvlee-
tvahRYEHneeyeh - satis-
faction.
удовóльствие oodahVOHL'-
stveeyeh - pleasure.
удостоверéние oodahstah-
veeRYEHneeyeh - identi-
fication.
удочка OODahchkah -
fishing pole.
ужáсный oozhAHSnihy -
horrible (adj).
ужé oozhEH - already.

ужин OOZHeen - supper.
узкий OOSkeey - narrow
(adj).
уклóн ookLOHN - bias;
incline.
укóл ooKOHL - injection.
украшéние ookrahSHEH-
neeyeh - decoration;
embellishment.
улица OOLeetsah - street.
улыбка ooLIHPkah - smile.
уменьшéние oomeen'SHEH-
neeyeh - decrease.
умный OOMnihy - smart;
intelligent (adj).
универмáг ooneeveerMAHK
- department store.
университéт ooneeveersee-
TYEHT - university.
упóрный ooPOHRnihy -
stubborn (adj).
упражнéние ooprahzh-
NYEHneeyeh - exersise.
упрёк oopRYOHK - rebuke.
уровень OOrahveen' - level.
урóк ooROHK - lesson.
услóвие oosLOHveeyeh -
condition.
успéх oosPYEHKH -
success.
успокойтельное срéдство
oospahKOHeeteel'nahyeh
SRYEHTstvah - sedative.
устáл(а) oosTAHL(ah) -
tired(f) (adj).
устный OOSTnihy - oral;
verbal (adj).
усы oosIH - mustache.
утомлéние ootahmLYEH-
neeyeh - exhaustion.
утренни OOTreeneey -
morning (adj).
утро OOTrah - morning.

175

утюг ooTYOOK - iron.
уха́ ooKHAN - fish soup.
у́хо OOKHah - ear.
уча́стие ooCHAHSTeeyeh - participation.
уче́бник ooCHEHBneek - textbook.
учёный ooCHOHnihy - scholar; scientist.
учи́тель ooCHEEtyehl' - teacher.
учи́тельница ooCHEEtyehl'neetsah - teacher (f).
учи́ться ooCHEET'sah - to study.
учрежде́ние oochreezh-DYEHneeyeh - institution.

Ф
фальши́вый fahl'SHEEvihy - fake; falsified (adj).
фами́лия fahMEEleeyah - last name; sir name.
фа́ры FAHrih - headlights.
фарфо́р fahrFOHR - china.
фарцо́вщик fahrTSOHF-shcheek - blackmarketeer.
фарширо́ванный fahrshee-ROHvahnnihy - stuffed (food) (adj).
фасо́ль fahSOHL' - beans.
фен fyehn - hairdryer.
фе́рма FYEHRmah - farm.
фильм feel'm - movie.
флот floht - navy.
фойе́ fayYEH - lobby.
фонта́н fahnTAHN - fountain.
форе́ль fahRYEHL' - trout.
фотоаппара́т fahtahahp-pahRAHT - camera.
фотогра́фия fahtahGRAH-

feeyah - photograph.
фра́за FRAHzah - phrase; sentence.
фрукт frookt - fruit.
фунт foont - pound.
фут foot - foot (measure).
футбо́л footBOHL - soccer.

Х
хала́т khahLAHT - robe.
харчо́ kharCHOH - mutton soup.
химчи́стка kheemCHEEST-kah - dry cleaning.
хиру́рг kheerOORK - surgeon.
хлеб khlyehp - bread.
хлебосо́льный khleebah-SOHL'nihy - hospitable (adj).
хлопчатобума́жный khlah-pchahtahbooMAHZHnihy - cotten (adj).
хозя́йка khazYAYkah - housewife.
хокке́й khahkKEY - hockey.
холоде́ц khalahDYEHTS - aspic.
холоди́льник khahlah-DEEL'neek - refrigerator.
холо́дный khahLOHDnihy - cold (adj).
хор khohr - choir.
хоро́ший khahROHsheey - good (adj).
хоте́ть khahTYEHT' - to want.
хотя́ khahtYAH - although.
храм khrahm - cathedral; temple.
хрен khryehn - horse-radish.
хромо́й khrahMOY - lame

176

(adj).

хрупкий KROOPkeey - fragile (adj).

худо́жник khooDOHZHneek - artist.

худо́й khooDOY - thin (adj).

ху́же KHOOzheh - worse.

хулига́н khooleeGAH - hooligan.

Ц

царь tsahr' - tsar.

цвет tsvyeht - color.

цвето́к tsveeTOHK - flower.

це́лый TSEHlihy - whole; entire (adj).

цель tsehl' - goal; aim.

цена́ tseeNAH - price.

це́нный TSEHNnihy - valuable.

центр tsehntr - center.

цепь tsehp' - chain.

це́рковь TSEHRkahf' - church.

цирк tseerk - circus.

цита́та tseeTAHtah - quote.

ци́фра TSEEfrah - number; numeral.

цыга́н/ка tsihGAHN/kah - gypsy/f.

Ч

чаевы́е chahehVIHyeh - tip.

чай chay - tea.

ча́йник CHAYneek - tea kettle.

ча́йница CHAYneetsah - tea caddy.

час chahs - time; hour.

ча́сто CHAHStah - often.

частота́ chahstahTAH - frequency.

часть chahst' - part.

часы́ cheesih - watch.

ча́шка CHAHSHkah - cup.

чек chehk - check.

челове́к chehlahVYEHK - person.

чем chehm - than.

чемода́н chehmahDAHN - suitcase.

чепуха́ chehpooKHAH - nonsense.

че́рез CHEHrees - through; within.

чере́шня chehRYEHSHnyah - sweet cherries.

черни́ка chehrNEEkah - blueberries.

черни́ла chehrNEElah - ink.

чёрно-бе́лый CHOHRnah-BYEHlihy - black-and-white (adj).

чёрный CHOHRnihy - black; dark (adj).

чёрный ры́нок CHOHRnihy RIHNahk - black market.

чёрт chohrt - devil.

черта́ chehrTAH - feature; trait; characteristic.

чесно́к chehsNOHK - garlic.

че́стный CHEHSTnihy - honest (adj).

че́тверть CHEHTveert' - quarter.

чёткий CHOHTkeey - clear; distinct (adj).

чино́вник cheeNOHVneek - clerk.

число́ cheesLOH - number.

чи́стый CHEEStihy - clean (adj).

чита́тель cheeTAHteel' - reader.

чита́ть cheeTAHT' - to

177

read.
чихáнье cheeKHAHN'yeh - sneezing.
член chlyehn - member.
что shtoh - what.
чтóбы SHTOHbih - in order to.
чтó-нибудь SHTOHneeboot' - anything; something.
чувствѝтельный choofst-VEEteel'nihy - sensitive (adj).
чýвство CHOOFSTvah - feeling; sensitivity.
чýвствовать CHOOFST-vahvaht' - to feel.
чудéсный chooDYEHSnihy - wonderful; miraculous (adj).
чужóй chooZHOY - not one's own; foreign (adj).
чулкѝ choolKEE - stockings.
чуть choot' - hardly; scarsely; barely.
чýчело CHOOchehlah - stuffed animal.

Ш
шаг shahk - step.
шампáнское shahmPAHN-skahyeh - champagne.
шампýнь shahmPOON' - shampoo.
шáпка SHAHPkah - hat.
шарф shahrf - scarf.
шáхматы SHAHKHmahtih - chess.
шашлы́к shahshLIHK - shish kebob.
швейцáр shveyTSAHR - doorman.
шёпот SHOHpaht - whisper.

шерстянóй shehrsteeNOY - woolen (adj).
шéя SHEHyah - neck.
ширинá sheereeNAH - width.
ширóкий sheeROHkeey - wide; broad (adj).
шкаф shkahf - closet; cabinet.
шкóла SHKOHlah - school.
шкýра SHKOOrah - skin; hide.
шнýрки SHNOORkee - shoe laces.
шоколáд shahkahLAHT - chocolate.
шóрты SHOHRtihy - shorts.
шоссé shahsSYEH - highway.
штат shtaht - state; staff.
штáтский SHTAHTskeey - civilian (adj).
штóпор SHTOHpahr - corkscrew.
штраф shtrahf - fine.
шýба SHOObah - fur coat.
шум shoom - noise.
шýмный SHOOMnihy - noisy (adj).
шýтка SHOOTkah - joke.

Щ
щéдрый SHCHEHDrihy - generous (adj).
щекá shchehKAH - cheek.
щётка SHCHOHTkah - brush.
щи shchee - cabbage soup.
щýка SHCHOOkah - pike.

Э
экземпля́р egzeemPLYAHR - copy; edition.

экра́н ehkRAHN - screen.
экску́рсия
  ehksKOORseeyah - tour;
  excursion.
экскурсово́д ehkskoorsah-
  VOHT - tour guide.
экспре́сс ehksPRYEHSS -
  express.
электри́ческий ehleek-
  TREEchehskeey - elec-
  trical (adj).
электри́чество
  ehleekTREEchehstvah -
  electricity.
эскала́тор ehskahLAHtahr
  - escalator.
эта́ж ehTAHSH - floor;
  story.
э́тот EHtaht - that (one).

Ю
юбиле́й yoobeeLEY -
  anniversary.
ю́бка YOOPkah - skirt.
ювели́рный yooveeLEER-
  nihy - jewelry (adj).
юг yook - south.
ю́жный YOOZHnihy -
  southern (adj).
ю́мор YOOmahr - humor.
ю́ность YOOnahst' - youth.

Я
я yah - I.
я́блоко YAHBlahkah -
  apple.
я́годы YAHgahdih -
  berries.
яд yaht - poison.
я́зва YAHZvah - ulcer.
язы́к yeezIHK - language;
  tonuge.
яи́чница yahEECHneetsah -

fried eggs.
яйцо́ yayTSOH - egg.
я́ркий YAHRkeey - bright
  (adj).
я́рмарка YAHRmahrkah -
  fair.
я́сно YAHSnah - clearly.
я́щик YAHshcheek - box.

179

English-Russian Dictionary

A

abbreviation - сокращéние sahkrahSHCHEHneeyeh.
about - о/про oh/proh.
above - наверхý/над nahveerKHOO/naht.
abscess - нары́в nahRIHF.
absence - отсýтствие ahtSOOTSTveeyeh.
absorbent cotton - вáта VAHtah.
accent - акцéнт ahkTSEHNT.
accept (to) - принимáть preeneeMAHT'.
access - дóступ DOHstoop.
accident - несчáстный слýчай neeSHCHAHSTnihy SLOOchay.
accidentally - случáйно slooCHAYnah.
acquaintance - знакóмство znahKOHMstvah.
acquainted; familiar (adj) - знакóмый znahKOHmihy.
act - акт ahkt.
act, take action (to) - дéйствовать DEYSTvahvaht'.
action - дéйствие DEYSTveeyeh.
actor - актёр ahkTYOHR.
actress - актрúса ahkTREEsah.
address - áдрес AHdrees.
admission pass - прóпуск PROHpoosk.
admission; admittance - впуск fpoosk.
admit, let in (to) - впускáть fpoosKAHT'.

adult - взрóслый VZROHslihy.
advertising; sign - реклáма reeKLAHmah.
advice - совéт sahVYEHT.
after - пóсле POHSlee.
afternoon - пóсле обéда POHSlee ahBYEHdah.
afterwards - потóм pahTOHM.
again - опя́ть/ещё раз ahpYAHT'/yeeSHCHOH rahs.
against - прóтив PROHteef.
age - вóзраст VOHZrahst.
agreement (in) - соглáсный sahGLAHSnihy.
agreement; contract - договóр dahgahVOHR.
air - вóздух VOHZdookh.
air conditioning - кондиционéр kahndeetseeahNYEHR.
airmail - авиапóчта ahveeahPOHCHtah.
airplane - самолёт sahmahLYOHT.
airport - аэропóрт ahehrahPOHRT.
alarm clock - будúльник booDEEL'neek.
alcohol - алкогóль ahlkahGOHL'.
all; the whole - весь vyehs'.
allergy аллергúя ahlleehrGEEyah.
almost - почтú pahchTEE.
along; about; according to - по pah.
alongside; beside; next to - ря́дом RYAHdahm.

aloud - вслух fslookh.
alphabet - áзбука AHS-bookah.
already - ужé oozhEH.
also; as well - тóже TOH-zheh.
although - хотя́ khahtYAH.
always - всегдá fseegDAH.
ambulance - скóрая пóмощь SKOHrahyah POHmahshch.
American (adj) - америкáн-ский ahmeereeKAHN-skeey.
American/(f) - американец /(-кáнка) ahmeereeKAH-neets/(-KAHNkah).
amusement; entertainment - развлечéние rahzvlee-CHEHneeyeh.
ancient (adj) - дрвéвний DRYEHVneey.
and; also - и ee.
anesthesia - наркóз nahr-KOHS.
anesthetization -обезбóли-вание ahbeesBOHleevah-neeyeh.
anger - гнев gnyehf.
angry (adj) - сердúтый seerDEEtihy.
animal - живóтное zheeVOHTnahyeh.
ankle - лодыжка lahDIHSHkah.
anniversary - юбилéй yoobeeLEY.
announcement - объявлéние ahb"eevLYEHneeyeh.
answer - отвéт ahtVYEHT.
anthology; collection - сбóрник ZBOHRneek.
antibiotic - антибиóтик ahnteebeeOHteek.

any - любóй lyooBOY.
anyone - ктó-нибудь KTOHneeboot'.
anything - чтó-нибудь SHTOHneeboot'.
apartment - квартúра kvahrTEERah.
apparently; evidently - вúдимо VEEdeemah.
appearance - вид veet.
appendicitis - аппендицúт appeendeeTSEET.
appendix - аппéндикс ahPYEHNdeeks.
appetite (hearty appetite!) - аппетúт (прия́тного аппетúта!) ahpeeTEET (preeYAHTnahvah ahpee-TEEtah!).
appetizer - закýска zah-KOOSkah.
applause - рукоплескáние rookahpleesKAHneeyeh.
apple - я́блоко YAHBlah-kah.
appointment; date; meeting - свидáние sveeDAHneeyeh.
approximately; about - óколо OHkahlah.
architecht - архитéктор ahrkheeTYEHKtahr.
architechture - архитек-тýра ahrkheeteekTOOrah.
area; square - плóщадь PLOHshchaht'.
argument - спор spohr.
arm; hand - рукá rooKAH.
arm chair - крéсло KRYEHS-lah.
around (location) - вокрýг vahkROOK.
arrival (on a plane) -

181

прилёт preeLYOHT.
arrival (on a train) - приезд
preeYEHST.
art - искусство eesKOOST-
vah.
artery - артерия ahrTYEH-
reeyah.
arthritis - артрит ahrt-
REET.
artificial (adj) -искусст-
венный eesKOOSTveen-
nihy.
artist - художник khoo-
DOHZHneek.
as well; also - также
TAHKzheh.
ashtray - пепельница
PYEHpeel'neetsah.
aspic - студень/холодец
STOOdyehn'/ khalah-
DYEHTS.
aspirin - аспирин ahspee-
REEN.
assurance - уверение
ooveeRYEHneeyeh.
asthma - астма AHSTmah.
at - у oo.
at first; in the beginning -
сначала snahCHAHlah.
atheism - безбожие bees-
BOHzheeyeh.
atheist - безбожник bees-
BOHZHneek.
athletic (adj) -
атлетичский
ahtleeTEECHskeey.
athletics - атлетика aht-
LYEHTeekah.
at least - по крайне мере
pah KRAYnyeh MYEHreh.
attention - внимание vnee-
MAHneeyeh.
attitude; relationship -

отношение ahtnahSHEH-
neeyeh.
attentively - внимательно
vneeMAHteel'nah.
audible (adj) - слышный
SLIHSHnihy.
aunt - тётя TYOHtyah.
author - автор AHFtahr.
autumn - осень OHseen'.
avenue - авеню/проспект
ahveenYOO/prahsPYEHKT.
awkward; clumsy (adj) -
неловкий neeLOHFkeey.

B
baby; infant - младенец
mlahDYEHneets.
back; backwards - назад
nahzAHT.
back; spine - спина spee-
NAH.
backpack - рюкзак ryook-
ZAHK.
bacon - бекон beeKOHN.
bad; poor (adj) - плохой
plahKHOY.
badge - значок znahCHOHK.
badly - плохо PLOHkhah.
bag - сумка SOOMkah.
baggage - багаж bahgAHSH.
baggage room - камера
хранения KAHmeerah
khrahNYEHneeyah.
bakery - булочная BOO-
lahchnahyah.
balalaika - балалайка
bahlahLAYkah.
balcony - балкон bahl-
KOHN.
ball - мяч myahch.
ballet - балет bahLYEHT.
banana - банан bahNAHN.
bandage - бинт beent.

182

bandaging; dressing - перевязка peereeVYAHSkah.
band-aide - пластырь PLAHStihr'.
bank - банк bahnk.
banquet - банкет bahnKYEHT.
bar of chocolate - плитка шоколада PLEETkah shahkahLAHdah.
barber; hairdresser - парикмахер pahreek-MAHKHeer.
basket - корзина kahrZEEnah.
bathing cap - купальная шапочка kooPAHL'nahyah SHAHPahchkah.
bathing suit - купальник koopAHL'neek.
bathroom - уборная/ванная ooBOHRnahyah/VAHNnahyah.
bathtub - ванна VAHNnah.
battery - батарея bahtahREEyah.
bay; gulf - залив. zahLEEF.
bazaar - базар bahZAHR.
beach - пляж plyahsh.
beads - бусы BOOsih.
beans - фасоль fahSOHL'.
beard - борода bahrahDAH.
beat, strike (to) - бить beet'.
beautiful (adj) - красивый KRAHSeevihy.
beauty - красота krahsahTAH.
because - потому что pahtahMOOshtah.
because of - из-за eezzah.
bed - кровать/постель krahVAHT'/pahsTYEHL'.

bedbug - клоп klohp.
bedroom - спальня SPAHL'nyah.
bee - пчела pchehLAH.
beef - говядина gahvYAHDeenah.
beer - пиво PEEvah.
beet soup - свекольник sveeKOHL'neek.
beets - свёкла SVYOHKlah.
before; formerly - прежде PRYEHZHdyeh.
before; in front of - перед/ до PYEHreet/dah.
begin, start (to) - начинать nahcheeNAHT'.
beginning - начало nahCHAHlah.
behind; beyond; past; for; in; after - за zah.
belief; faith - вера VYEHrah.
believe, have faith (to) - верить VYEHreet'.
bell - колокол KOHlahkahl.
belt; waist - пояс POHees.
bench - скамейка skahMEYkah.
berries - ягоды YAHgahdih.
berth; shelf - полка POHLkah.
better - лучше LOOCHsheh.
better; the best - лучший LOOCHsheey.
between - между MYEHZHdoo.
beware - осторожно ahstahROHZHnah.
bias; incline; slant - уклон ookLOHN.
Bible - Библия BEEbleeyah.
bicycle - велосипед veelah-

seePYEHT.

big; large; great (adj) -
большо́й bahl'SHOY.

bill - счёт shchoht.

billion - миллиа́рд meel-
leeAHRT.

binoculars; opera glasses -
бино́кль beeNOHKL'.

birch - берёза beerYOHzah.

bird - пти́ца PTEEtsah.

birth - рожде́ние rahzh-
DYEHneeyeh.

birthday - день рожде́ния
dyehn' rahzhDYEHneeyah.

bitter (adj) - го́рький
GOHR'keey.

black-and-white (adj) -
чёрно-бе́лый CHOHRnah-
BYEHlihy.

black; dark (adj) - чёрный
CHOHRnihy.

blackberries - ежеви́ка
yeezhehVEEkah.

black market - чёрный
ры́нок CHOHRnihy RIHN-
ahk.

blackmarketeer - фарцо́в-
щик fahrTSOHFshcheek.

bladder - мочево́й пузы́рь
mahcheeVOY poozIHR'.

blanket - одея́ло ahdee-
YAHlah.

bleed (to) - кровоточи́ть
krahvahtahCHEET'.

blessing - благослове́ние
blahgahslahVYEHneeyeh.

block (in a city) - кварта́л
kvahrTAHL.

blonde/(f) - блонди́н/(-ка)
blahnDEEN/(-kah).

blood - кровь krohf'.

blood pressure - давле́ние
dahvLYEHneeyeh.

blood type - гру́ппа кро́ви
GROOPpah KROHvee.

blouse - блу́зка BLOOSkah.

blue (adj) - си́ний SEE-
neey.

blue (light) (adj) - голубо́й
gahlooBOY.

blueberries - черни́ка
chehrNEEkah.

boat - ло́дка LOHTkah.

body - те́ло TYEHlah.

boiled (adj) - варёный
vahRYOHnihy.

bone - кость kohst'.

book - кни́га KNEEgah.

book store - кни́жный
магази́н KNEEZHnihy
mahgahZEEN.

booth; cubicle - каби́на
kahBEEnah.

boots - сапоги́ sahpahGEE.

border - грани́ца grahNEE-
tsah.

boring (adj) - ску́чный
SKOOCHnihy.

borsch; beet soup - борщ
bohrshch.

botanical garden - ботан-
и́ческий сад bahtahn-
EECHehskeey saht.

both - о́ба OHbah.

bottle - буты́лка booTIHL-
kah.

bouillon - бульо́н bool'-
OHN.

boulevard бульва́р bool'-
VAHR.

bowl - ми́ска MEEskah.

box - коро́бка/я́щик kahr-
OHPkah/YAHshcheek.

boy - ма́льчик
MAHL'cheek.

bra - бюстга́льтер byooz-

KHAHL'teer.
brain - мозг mohsk.
brakes (car) - тормоза
tahrmahZAH.
brave; courageous (adj) -
смелый SMYEHlihy.
bread - хлеб khlyehp.
break (to) - сломать slah-
MAHT'.
break; recess - перерыв
peereeRIHF.
breakdown (car) - авария
ahVAHreeyah.
breakfast - завтрак ZAHF-
trahk.
breakfast (to eat) - завтра-
кать ZAHFtrahkaht'.
breathe (to) - дышать
dihshAHT'.
breathing; respiration -
дыхание dihKHAH-
neeyeh.
bribe - взятка VZYAHTkah.
bride - невеста neeVYEHS-
tah.
bridge - мост mohst.
brief; not long - недолго
neeDOHLgah.
briefcase - портфель
pahrtFYEHL'.
bright (adj) - яркий YAHR-
keey.
British (adj) - английский
ahngLEEYskeey.
broadcast; transmission -
передача peereeDAH-
chah.
brooch - брошь brohsh'.
brother - брат braht.
brother-in-law - зять
zyaht'.
brown (adj) - коричневый
kahREECHneevihy.

bruise - синяк seenYAHK.
brunette/(f) - брюнет/(-ка)
bryooNYEHT/(-kah).
brush - щётка SHCHOHT-
kah.
bucket - ведро veedROH.
building - здание ZDAH-
neeyeh.
burn (to) - жечь zhehch.
bus - автобус ahfTOHboos.
bus stop - остановка
ahstahnOHFkah.
business (adj) - деловой
deelahVOY.
business trip -
командировка
kahmahndeeROHFkah.
businessman - бизнесмен
beezneesMYEHN.
busy; occupied (adj) - занятый ZAHNyahtihy.
but - но noh.
butter - масло MAHSlah.
button - пуговица POOgah-
veetsah.
buy (to) - купить kooPEET'.
by heart - наизусть nah-
eezOOST'.
by; near - близко BLEES-
kah.

C
cabbage - капуста kahPOO-
stah.
cabbage soup - щи shchee.
cafe - кафе kahFYEH.
cake - торт tohrt.
calendar - календарь kah-
leenDAHR'.
call (to) - позвонить pahzvahNEET'.
called, named (to be) - называть nahzihVAHT'.

calm; tranquil (adj) - спокойный spahKOYnihy.
calorie - калория kahLOH-
reeyah.
camel - верблюд veer-
BLYOOT.
camera - фотоаппарат
fahtahahppahRAHT.
camp - лагерь LAHgeer'.
campfire - костёр kahs-
TYOHR.
camping - кемпинг KYEHM-
peeng.
Canadian (adj) - канадский
kahNAHTskeey.
Canadian/(f) - канадец
(-надка) kahNAHdeets/ (-
NAHTkah).
canal - канал kahNAHL.
candle - свеча sveeCHAH.
candy - конфеты kahn-
FYEHtih.
canned goods - консервы
kahnSYEHRvih.
can opener - консервный
нож kahnSYEHRVnihy
nohsh.
capital (of a state) -
столица stahLEEtsah.
car - автомобиль/машина
ahftahmahBEEL'/mah-
SHEEnah.
carat - карат kahRAHT.
care; concern - забота
zahBOHtah.
careful - осторожно ahs-
tahROHZHnah.
careless; negligent; sloppy;
slipshod (adj) - небреж-
ный neeBRYEHZHnihy.
carnation - гвоздика gvahz-
DEEkah.
carnival - карнавал kahr-

nahVAHL.
carrots - морковь mahr-
KOHF'.
cartoon (film) - мульт-
фильм mool'tFEEL'M.
cashier - кассир kahsSEER.
cassette - кассета kahs-
SYEHtah.
cast - гипс geeps.
cat - кошка KOHSHkah.
cathedral - собор/храм
sahBOHR/khrahm.
caution - берегись beeree-
GEES'.
caviar - икра eekRAH.
cavity - дупло doopLOH.
ceiling - потолок pahtah-
LOHK.
cemetary - кладбище
KLAHTbeeshcheh.
center - центр tsehntr.
century - столетие stah-
LYEHteeyeh.
century; age - век vyehk.
certainly; absolutely
безусловно beez-
oosLOHVnah.
chain - цепь tsehp'.
chair- стул stool.
champagne - шампанское
shahmPAHNskahyeh.
change (coins) - сдача
ZDAHchah.
change; transfer (on planes,
trains, buses etc). -
пересадка peereeSAHT-
kah.
check - счёт/чек shchoht/
chehk.
check mate - мат maht.
cheek щека shchehKAH.
cheerful (adj) - бодрый
BOHdrihy.

cheese - сыр sihr.
cherries (sour) - вишня
VEESHnyah.
cherries (sweet) - черешня
chehRYEHSHnyah.
chess - шахматы SHAHKH-
mahtih.
chest; breast - грудь groot'.
chicken - курица KOOree-
tsah.
chief; boss - начальник
nahCHAHL'neek.
child - ребёнок reeBYOH-
nahk.
children - дети DYEHtee.
children's (adj) - детский
DYEHTskeey.
china - фарфор fahrFOHR.
chocolate - шоколад shah-
kahLAHT.
choice; assortment; selection - выбор VIHbahr.
choir - хор khohr.
Christmas - рождество
rahzheestVOH.
church - церковь TSEHR-
kahf'.
church service - служба
SLOOSHbah.
cigar - сигара seeGAHrah.
cigarette - сигарета/
папироса seegahRYEHtah/
pahpeeROHSah.
cigarette case - папирос-
ница pahpeeROHSneetsah.
cigarette lighter - зажи-
галка zahzheeGAHLkah.
cinnamon - корица kahREE-
tsah.
circle - круг krook.
circus - цирк tseerk.
ciruclar; round (adj) -
круглый KROOGlihy.

citizen/(f) - гражданин/
(-данка) grahzhdah-
NEEN/(-DAHNkah).
citizenship - гражданство
grahzhDAHNSTvah.
city - город GOHraht.
civil; civilian (adj) - граж-
данский grahzhDAHN-
skeey.
classical (adj) - классич-
еский klahsSEECHehs-
keey.
clay - глина GLEEnah.
clean (adj) - чистый
CHEEStihy.
cleaning woman - уборщица
ooBOHRshcheetsah.
clear; distinct (adj) -
чёткий CHOHTkeey.
clearly - ясно YAHSnah.
clerk - чиновник chee-
NOHVneek.
climate - климат KLEE-
maht.
clinic - поликлиника
pahleeKLEEneekah.
clip-on earrings - клипсы
kleepsih.
cloakroom - гардероб/раз-
девалка gahrdeeROHP/
rahzdeeVAHLkah.
cloakroom attendant/(f) -
гардеробшик/(-щица)
gahrdeeROHPsheek/
(-shcheetsah).
close by; not far - недалеко
needahleeKOH.
closed (adj) - закрытый
zahKRIHtihy.
closet; cabinet - шкаф
shkahf.
clothes - одежда
ahDYEHZHdah.

club - клуб kloop.
coast; bank; shore - бéрег BYEHreek.
coat - пальтó pahl'TOH.
coat-check ticket - номерóк nahmeeROHK.
cockroach - тарака́н tahrahKAHN.
cocoa - кака́о kahKAHoh.
cod - треска́ treesKAH.
coffee - кóфе KOHfyeh.
cognac; brandy - конья́к kahn'YAHK.
coin - монéта mahNYEHtah.
coincidence - совпадéние sahfpahDYEHneeyeh.
cold (adj) - холóдный khahLOHDnihy.
cold (head) - просту́да prahsTOOdah.
collection; gathering - сбор zbohr.
collective farm - колхóз kahlKHOHS.
color - цвет tsvyeht.
colorless; dull (adj) - бесцвéтный beesTSVEHTnihy.
comb - гребёнка greebYOHNkah.
combination - сочетáние sahchehTAHneeyeh.
comedy - комéдия kahMYEHdeeyah.
comfortable (adj) - удóбный ooDOHBnihy.
communal (adj) - коммунáльный kahmmooNAHL'nihy.
competition; contest; sports match - кóнкурс/соревновáние KOHNkoors/sahreevnahVAHneeyeh.

complaint - жáлоба ZHAHlahbah.
completion; end - окончáние ahkahnCHAHneeyeh.
completly; absolutely - совершéнно sahveerSHEHNnah.
complex; difficult (adj) - слóжный SLOHZHnihy.
complication - осложнéние ahslahzhNYEHneeyeh.
composer - композитор kahmpahZEEtahr.
computer - компью́тер kahmP'YOOteer.
comrade - товáрищ tahVAHReeshch.
concert - концéрт kahnTSEHRT.
conclusion - заключéние zahklyooCHEHneeyeh.
condition; state - состоя́ние sahstahYAHneeyeh.
conditions - услóвия oosLOHveeyah.
conductor (musical) - дирижёр deereezhOHR.
confectionery shop -кондитерская kahnDEEteerskahyah.
confirmation - подтверждéние pahttveerzhDYEHneeyeh.
congratulate (to) - поздравля́ть pahzdrahvLYAHT'.
consequently - слéдовательно SLYEHdahvahteel'-nah.
considerable; significant (adj) - значительный znahCHEEteel'nihy.
constant; continuous (adj) - постоя́нный pahstah-

YAHNnihy.
constipation - запор
zahPOHR.
consulate - консульство
KOHNsool'stvah.
contact lens - контактная
линза kahnTAHKTnahyah
LEENzah.
contemporary (adj) - совре-
менный sahvreeMYEHN-
nihy.
continuation - продолже-
ние prahdahlZHEHneeyeh.
contraceptive - презерва-
тив preezeervahTEEF.
controversial (adj) - спорный SPOHRnihy.
convenience - удобство
ooDOHBSTvah.
convention; congress -
съезд s"yehst.
conversation - разговор/
беседа rahzgahVOHR/
beeSYEHdah.
conversational; colloquial.
(adj) - разговорный
rahzgahVOHRnihy.
cook - повар POHvahr.
cook, boil (to) - варить
vahrEET'.
cookie; pastry - печенье
peeCHEHN'yeh.
cool (adj) - прохладный
prahkhLAHDnihy.
cooperative store - коо-
ператив kahahpeerah-
TEEF.
copy; edition - экземпляр
egzeemPLYAHR.
corkscrew - штопор
SHTOHpahr.
corner - угол OOgahl.
correct (adj) - правильный

PRAHVeel'nihy.
correction; adjustment -
поправка pahPRAHFkah.
correspondence - переписка
peereePEESkah.
cottage - дача DAHchah.
cotton (adj) - хлопчато-
бумажный khlahpchah-
tahbooMAHZHnihy.
cough - кашель KAHSHehl'.
country - страна
strahNAH.
countryside - деревня dee-
RYEHVnyah.
coupon - талон tahLOHN.
courage - мужество
MOOZHehstvah.
cousin (f) - двоюродная
сестра dvahYOOrahd-
nahyah seesTRAH.
cousin (m) - двоюродный
брат dvahYOOrahdnihy
braht.
cranberries - клюква
KLYOOKvah.
crayfish - рак rahk.
crazy; mad; insane (adj) -
сумасшедший soomahsh-
EHTsheey.
cream (dairy) - сливки
SLEEFkee.
cream; lotion - крем
kryehm.
creative work - творчество
TVOHRchehstvah.
credit card - кредитная
карточка kreeDEETnah-
yah KAHRtahchkah.
crime - преступление
preestoopLYEHneeyeh.
crisis - кризис KREEzees.
crooked (adj) - кривой
kreeVOY.

cross - крест kryehst.
crosswalk - перехо́д pee-
reeKHOHT.
crowd - толпа́ tahlPAH.
crowded (adj) - те́сный
TYEHSnihy.
cruel; brutal (adj) - жесто́-
кий zhehsTOHkeey.
cruise - круи́з krooEEZ.
cucumber soup -
рассо́льник
rahsSOHL'neek.
cucumbers - огурцы́
ahgoorTSIH.
culture - культу́ра kool'-
TOOrah.
cup - ча́шка CHAHSHkah.
curious (adj) - любопы́т-
ный lyoobahPIHTnihy.
current (adj) - актуа́льный
ahktooAHL'nihy.
curtain - за́навес ZAHnahvees.
customer - покупа́тель
pahkooPAHteel'.
customs; habits - нра́вы
NRAHvih.
customs - тамо́жня tah-
MOHZHnyah.
customs official - тамо́-
женник tahMOH-
zheenneek.
customs charge; duty -
по́шлина POHSHleenah.
cut; sliced (adj) - ре́заный
RYEHZahnihy.
cute; sweet; dear - ми́лень-
кий MEEleen'keey.
cutlet - котле́та kaht-
LYEHtah.

D
daily (adj) - ежедне́вный

yeezhehdNYEHVnihy.
dairy - моло́чная mah-
LOHCHnahyah.
dance - та́нец TAHneets.
dangerous (adj) - опа́сный
ahPAHSnihy.
dark (adj) - тёмный
TYOHMnihy.
dark-(color) - тёмно-
TYOHMnah.
daughter - дочь dohch.
daughter-in-law - неве́стка
neeVYEHSTkah.
dawn; daybreak - рассве́т
rahsSVYEHT.
day - день dyehn'.
day after tomorrow - после-
за́втра pahsleeZAHFtrah.
day before yesterday -
позавчера́ pahzahfcheh-
RAH.
day off - выходно́й день
vihkhahdNOY dyehn'.
daytime (adj) - дневно́й
dneevNOY.
dead (adj) - мёртвый
MYOHRTvihy.
deaf (adj) - глухо́й gloo-
KHOY.
death - смерть smyehrt'.
deception; deceit; fraud -
обма́н ahbMAHN.
decision - реше́ние
reeSHEHneeyeh.
decoration; embellishment -
украше́ние ookrahSHEH-
neeyeh.
decrease - уменьше́ние
oomeen'SHEHneeyeh.
deep; in depth (adj) - глу-
бо́кий glooBOHkeey.
deficit - дефици́т deefee-
TSEET.

190

definite; set; certain (adj) - определённый ahpreedeeLYOHNnihy.

degree; extent - сте́пень STYEHpeen'.

delay; tardiness - опозда́ние ahpahzDAHneeyeh.

deliberately; on purpose - наро́чно nahROHCHnah.

demon - бес byehs.

dentist - зубно́й врач zoobNOY vrahch.

denture - проте́з prahTYEHS.

deoderant - дезодора́нт deezahdahRAHNT.

department - отде́л/ ка́федра ahdDYEHL/ KAHfeedrah.

department store - универма́г ooneeveerMAHK.

departure (airplane) - отлёт ahtLYOHT.

departure (train) - отхо́д ahtKHOHT.

description - описа́ние ahpeeSAHneeyeh.

dessert - десе́рт/на сла́дкое deeSYEHRT/nah SLAHTkahyeh.

detail - подро́бность pahdROHBnahst'.

detour - обхо́д/объе́зд ahpKHOHT/ahp"YEHST.

development (film) - проявле́ние praheevLYEHneeyeh.

development; growth - разви́тие rahzVEEteeyeh.

devil - чёрт chohrt.

diabetes - диабе́т deeahBYEHT.

diagnosis - диа́гноз dee-

AHGnahs.

diamond - бриллиа́нт breeleeAHNT.

diaper - подгу́зник pahdGOOZneek.

diarrhea - поно́с pahNOHS.

dictionary - слова́рь slahVAHR'.

diet - дие́та deeYEHtah.

difference; distinction - ра́зница RAHSneetsah.

different (adj) - ра́зный RAHZnihy.

differently; otherwise - ина́че eeNAHcheh.

difficult (adj) - тру́дный TROODnihy.

dining hall - столо́вая stahLOHvahyah.

director (theater) - режиссёр reezhehsSYOHR.

dirt; filth - грязь gryahs'.

dirty; filthy (adj) - гря́зный GRYAHZnihy.

disability - инвали́дность eenvahLEEDnahst'.

disabled person - инвали́д eenvahLEET.

dish; food; course - блю́до BLYOOdah.

dishes - посу́да pahSOOdah.

dishonest (adj) - нече́стный neeCHEHSTnihy.

disinfect (to) - дезинфици́ровать deezeenfeetsEERahvaht'.

dissatisfied (adj) - недово́льный needahVOHL'nihy.

distance - расстоя́ние rahsstahYAHneeyeh.

diverse (adj) - многообра́з-

ный mnahgahahbRAHZ-
nihy.
do (to) - де́лать DYEHlaht'.
dock; pier; wharf - при́-
стань PREEstahn'.
doctor - врач vrahch.
dog - соба́ка sahBAHkah.
doll; puppet - ку́кла
KOOK-lah.
dollar - до́ллар DOHLlahr.
door - дверь dvyehr'.
doorman - швейца́р shvey-
TSAHR.
dormitory - общежи́тие
ahpshchehZHEEteeyeh.
dosage - дозиро́вка dahzee-
ROHFkah.
double occupency (adj) -
двуспа́льный dvoo-
SPAHL'nihy.
doubt - сомне́ние sahm-
NYEHneeyeh.
doughnut - по́нчик POHN-
cheek.
down; below (location) -
внизу́ vneeZOO.
down; downward (destin-
ation) - вниз vnees.
dozen - дю́жина DYOO-
zheenah.
drawing - рисова́ние
reesahVAHneeyeh.
dress - пла́тье PLAHT'yeh.
drink (to) - пить peet'.
drink - напи́ток nahPEE-
tahk.
drive (to) - е́здить/е́хать
YEHZdeet'/YEHkhaht'.
driver - води́тель vahDEE-
teel'.
driver's license - води́тель-
ские права́ vahDEEteel'-
skeeyeh prahVAH.

drop - ка́пля KAHPlyah.
drugstore - апте́ка ahp-
TYEHkah.
drunk (adj) - пья́ный
P'YAHnihy.
drunkard - пя́ница PYAH-
neetsah.
dry (adj) - сухо́й sooKHOY.
dry cleaning - химчи́стка
kheemCHEESTkah.
duty (customs) - по́шлина
POHSHleenah.
duty-free - беспо́шлинный
beesPOHSHleennihy.
dye; hair coloring - окра́ска
ahKRAHSkah.

E
ear - у́хо OOKHah.
earlier; sooner - ра́ньше
RAHN'sheh.
early (adj) - ра́нний RAHN-
neey.
earmuff; headphone - нау́ш-
ник nahOOSHneek.
earrings - се́рьги/серёжки
SYEHR'gee/seerYOHSHkee.
easily - легко́ leekhKOH.
east - восто́к vahsTOHK.
eastern (adj) - восто́чныий
vahsTOHCHnihy.
Easter; Passover - Па́сха
PAHSkhah.
easy (adj) - лёгкий
LYOHKHkeey.
eat (to) - есть yehst'.
edge; rim - кра́й kray.
education - образова́ние
ahbrahzahVAHneeyeh.
egg - яйцо́ yayTSOH.
egg shell - скорлупа́
skahrlooPAH.
eggplant - баклажа́н bahk-

192

lahzhAHN.

elbow - лóкоть LOHkaht'.

elderly (adj) - пожилóй pahzheeLOY.

elections - вы́боры VIHbahrih.

electrical (adj) - электри́ческий ehleekTREEchehskeey.

electrical socket - розéтка rahzYEHTkah.

electricity - электри́чество ehleekTREEchehstvah.

elevator - лифт leeft.

embarrassment - смущéние smooSHCHEHneeyeh.

embassy - посóльство pahSOHL'stvah.

embroidered (adj) - вы́шитый VIHsheetihy.

emerald - изумру́д eezoomROOT.

empty; vacant (adj) - пустóй poosTOY.

end - конéц kahnYEHTS.

enemy - враг vrahk.

engineer - инженéр eenzheeNYEHR.

English, British (adj) -англи́йский ahngLEEYskeey.

Englishman/(f) - англича́нин(-ча́нка) ahngleeCHAHneen (-CHAHNkah).

enjoy (to) - нра́виться NRAHveetsah.

enjoy oneself (to); have fun - веселúться veeseeLEEtsah.

enough; sufficiently -достáточно dahsTAHtahchnah.

enter (to) - входи́ть fkhahDEET'.

enthusiastic (adj) - увле-чённый oovleeCHOHNnihy.

entrance - вход fkhoht.

envelope - конвéрт kahnVYEHRT.

equal (adj) - рáвный RAHVnihy.

escalator - эскалáтор ehskahLAHtahr.

especially - осóбенно ahSOHbeennah.

eternally - вéчно VYEHCHnah.

European (adj) - европéйский yeevrahPEYskeey.

European - европéец yeevrahPYEHeets.

evening (adj) - вечéрний veeCHEHRneey.

evening - вéчер VYEHchehr.

event - собы́тие sahBIHTeeyeh.

every (adj) - кáждый KAHZHdihy.

everything - всё fsyoh.

everywhere - вездé veezDYEH.

evil; mean; malicious (adj) - злой zloy.

exactly - тóчно/и́менно TOHCHnah/EEMeennah.

exaggeration - преувели-чéние preeooveeleeCHEHneeyeh.

examination; checkup - осмóтр ahsMOHTR.

example - примéр preeMYEHR.

except for; but; besides - крóме KROHmyeh.

excessive; superfluous (adj) - изли́шни eezLEESHneey.

exchange - обмéн ahb-
MYEHN.
exchange (to) - обменять
ahbmeenYAHT'.
excited (adj) - возбуждённый vahzboozhDYOHN-
nihy.
excursion - экскýрсия
ehksKOORseeyah.
excuse, pardon (to) - изви-
нять eezveeNYAHT'.
exersise - упражнéние
ooprahzhNYEHneeyeh.
exhaustion - утомлéние
ootahmLYEHneeyeh.
exhibtion; display - вы́-
ставка VIHstahfkah.
exit - вы́ход VIHkhaht.
expenses - расхóды rahs-
KHOHdih.
expensive; valuable; dear
(adj) - дорогóй dahrah-
GOY.
experience - óпыт OHpiht.
explanation - объяснéние
ahb"eesNYEHneeyeh.
express - экспрéсс ehks-
PRYEHSS.
eye - глаз glahs.
eyebrow - бровь brohf'.
eyelash - ресни́ца reesNEE-
tsah.
eyesight - зрéние ZRYEH-
neeyeh.

F
fabric - ткань tkahn'.
face - лицó leeTSOH.
factory - завóд zahVOHT.
fair - ярмарка YAHRmahr-
kah.
fake; falsified (adj) - фаль-
шивый fahl'SHEEvihy.

fall; autumn - óсень
OHseen'.
false (adj) - лóжный
LOHZHnihy.
family - семья́ seem'YAH.
famous (adj) - знамени́тый
znahmeeNEEtihy.
fan - вéер VYEHeer.
far away - далекó dahlee-
KOH.
farewell - проща́й prah-
SHCHAY.
farm - фéрма FYEHRmah.
farther; continue - дáльше
DAHL'sheh.
fashion; style - мóда MOH-
dah.
fashionable; stylish (adj) -
мóдный MOHDnihy.
fast; quickly; rapidly -
бы́стро BIHStrah.
fat (adj) - тóлстый TOHL-
stihy.
fat; grease - жир zheer.
fate - судьба́ soot'VAH.
father - отéц ahTYEHTS.
fatherland - отéчество
ahtYEHCHehstvah
faucet - кран krahn.
fear, be afraid (to) -
бо́ться bahYAHTsah.
fear - страх strahkh.
feature; trait; characteristic
- черта́ chehrTAH.
feel (to) - чýвствовать себя́
CHOOFSTvahvaht' see-
BYAH.
feel sorry for, pity (to) -
жалéть zhahLYEHT'.
feeling; sensation - ощущ-
éние ahshchooSHCHEH-
neeyeh.
feeling; sensitivity - чýвст-

во CHOOFSTvah.
feminine; woman's (adj) -
женский ZHEHNskeey.
ferry - паром pahROHM.
fever - жар zhahr.
few; some; several - не-
сколько NEEskahl'kah.
field; area - поле POHLyeh.
fight (to) - биться BEETsah.
fight, struggle - борьба
bahr'BAH.
filled dumpling - вареник
vahRYEHneek.
filling (tooth) - пломба
PLOHMbah.
film - плёнка PLYOHNkah.
finally; at last - наконец
nahkahnYEHTS.
find (to) - найти nayTEE.
fine - штраф shtrahf.
finger - палец PAHleets.
fire - пожар pahZHAHR.
first-aid kit - аптечка
ahpTYEHCHkah.
fish - рыба RIHBah.
fish soup - уха ooKHAH.
fishing pole - удочка
OODahchkah.
flashlight - карманный
фонарь kahrMAHNnihy
fahNAHR'.
flexible (adj) - гибкий
GEEPkeey.
flight - полёт pahLYOHT.
flood - наводнение
nahvahdNYEHneeyeh.
floor; story - этаж eh-
TAHSH.
flounder; sole - камбала
KAHMbahlah.
flour - мука mooKAH.
flower - цветок tsveeTOHK.
flu - грипп greep.

fly - муха MOOkhah.
fog - туман tooMAHN.
food - еда/пища yeeDAH/
PEEshchah.
fool (f) - дура DOOrah.
fool (m) - дурак dooRAHK.
foot (by, on) - пешком
peeshKOHM.
foot (measure) - фут foot.
foot; leg - нога nahGAH.
for - для dlyah.
for example - например
nahpreeMYEHR.
for some reason - почему-то
pahcheeMOOtah.
for the first time; first -
впервые fpeerVIHyeh.
forbid (to) - запрещать
zahpreeshchAHT'.
forbidden (to be) - воспрещаться vahspree-
SHCHAHTsah.
forehead - лоб lohp.
foreign (adj) - иностранный
eenahsTRAHNnihy.
foreign; not one's own (adj)
- чужой chooZHOY.
foreigner/(f) - иностра-
нец/(-транка) eenahs-
TRAHneets/(-TRAHNkah).
forest - лес lyehs.
forever - навсегда nahf-
seegDAH.
forget (to) - забывать
zahbihVAHT'.
forgotten (adj) - забытый
zahBIHTihy.
fork - вилка VEELkah.
form, blank, survey -
анкета ahnKYEHtah.
former; previous (adj) -
прежний/бывший
PRYEHZHneey/BIHFsheey.

195

forward; ahead - вперёд
fpeeRYOHT.
found, located (to be) -
находи́ться nahkhah-
DEETsah.
fountain - фонта́н fahn-
TAHN.
fragile (adj) - хру́пкий
KROOPkeey.
fragrant (adj) - арома́тный
ahrahMAHTnihy.
free of charge (adj) - бес-
пла́тный
beesPLAHTnihy.
free; vacant (adj) - свобо́д-
ный svahBOHDnihy.
freedom - свобо́да/во́ля
svahBOHdah/VOHLyah.
freely; voluntarily - во́льно
VOHL'nah.
frequency - частота́ chahstahTAH.
fresh (adj) - све́жий
SVYEHzheey.
fried eggs - яи́чница
yahEECHneetsah.
friend - друг drook.
friendly; amicable (adj) -
дру́жный DROOZHnihy.
friendship - дру́жба
DROOSHbah.
from - от aht.
front (adj) - пере́дний pee-
RYEHDneey.
frost - моро́з mahROHS.
frozen (adj) - заморо́-
женный zahmahROH-
zhehnnihy.
fruit - фрукт frookt.
fry, roast, broil - жа́рить
ZHAHReet'.
frying pan - сковорода́
skahvahrahDAH.

full (of food); satiated (adj)
- сы́тый SIHTihy.
full; complete (adj) -
по́лный POHLnihy.
fully; completely; quite -
вполне́ fpahlNYEH.
funny (adj) - смешно́й
smeeshNOY.
fur (adj) - мехово́й meekhahVOY.
fur - мех myehkh.
fur coat - шу́ба SHOObah.
fur hat - мехова́я ша́пка
meekhahVAHyah SHAHP-
kah.
furniture - ме́бель MYEH-
beel'.
further; farther - да́лее
DAHleeyeh.
future - бу́дущий BOOdoo-
shcheey.

G
game - игра́ eegRAH.
garage - гара́ж gahRAHSH.
garden - сад saht.
garlic - чесно́к chehsNOHK.
garnet - грана́т grahNAHT.
gas - бензи́н beenZEEN.
gas meter - газоме́р gah-
zahMYEHR.
gas station - бензозапра́-
вочная ста́нция beenzah-
zahPRAHvahchnahyah
STAHNtseeyah.
gas tank - бензоба́к beenzahBAHK.
gastritis - гастри́т gahs-
TREET.
gate - воро́та vahROHtah.
general; common; total (adj)
- о́бщий OHPshcheey.
generous (adj) - ще́дрый

SHCHEHDrihy.
genitals - половы́е о́рганы
pahlahVIHyeh OHRgahnih.
geriatric (adj) - гериатри́-
ческий geereeahtREE-
cheeskeey.
German (adj) - герма́нский
geerMAHNskeey.
German - герма́нец
geerMAHNeets.
get, stand up (to) - встава́ть
fstahVAHT'.
gift; souvenir - пода́рок
pahDAHrahk.
gilded (adj) - позоло́чен-
ный pahzahLOCHehn-
nihy.
girl - де́вочка DYEH-
vahchkah.
give (to) - дава́ть dah-
VAHT'.
give as a gift (to) - дари́ть
dahREET'.
glad; pleased - рад raht.
gland - железа́ zhehlee-
ZAH.
glass (drinking) - стака́н
stahKAHN.
glass - стекло́ steekLOH.
glasses - очки́ ahchKEE.
glory - сла́ва SLAHvah.
gloves - перча́тки peer-
CHAHTkee.
glue - клей kley.
go by, past - ми́мо MEEmah.
go, walk (to) - ходи́ть/йдти
khahDEET'/EETtee.
goal; aim - цель tsehl'.
God - Бог bohkh.
gold (adj) - золото́й zahlahTOY.
gold - зо́лото ZOHlahtah.
good (adj) - хоро́ший khah-

ROHsheey.
goodbye - до свида́ния
dahsveeDAHneeyah.
goodbye (coll) - пока́
pahKAH.
goose - гусь goos'.
goulash - гуля́ш gool-
YAHSH.
government -
прави́тельство
prahVEEteel'stvah.
gradually - постепе́нно
pahsteePYEHNnah.
graduate student/(f) -
аспира́нт/(-ка) ahspee-
RAHNT/(-kah).
grain - зерно́ zeerNOH.
gram - грамм grahm.
grammar - грамма́тика
grahmMAHteekah.
grammatical case - паде́ж
pahDYEHSH.
granddaughter - вну́чка
VNOOCHkah.
grandfather - де́душка
DYEHdooshkah.
grandmother - ба́бушка
BAHbooshkah.
grandson - вну́к vnook.
grapes - виногра́д veenahg-
RAHT.
grapefruit - гре́йпфрут
GREYPfroot.
grass - трава́ trahVAH.
grave - моги́ла mahGEElah.
greasy; oily; fatty (adj) -
жи́рный ZHEERnihy.
great (adj) - вели́кий
veeLEEkeey.
greedy (adj) - жа́дный
ZHAHDnihy.
green (adj) - зелёный zee-
LYOHnihy.

greengrocer - зеленщик zeeleenSHCHEEK.

grey (adj) - серый SYEHrihy.

grief - горе GOHRyeh.

grocery store - гастроном gahstrahNOHM.

ground; dirt; earth - земля zeemLYAH.

group - группа GROOPpah.

growth; height - рост rohst.

growth; tumor - нарост nahROHST.

guard; sentry - караул kahrahOOL.

guest - гость gohst'.

guide - гид geet.

guidebook - путеводитель pooteevahDEEteel'.

guilt - вина veeNAH.

guilty (adj) - виноватый veenahVAHtihy.

guitar - гитара geeTAHrah.

gynecologist - гинеколог geeneeKOHlahk.

gypsy/(f) - цыган/ка tsihGAHN/kah.

H

habit - привычка preeVIHCHkah.

hair - волосы VOHlahsih.

haircut; trim - стрижка STREESHkah.

hair-do - причёска preeCHOHSkah.

hairdresser; barber - парикмахер pahreekMAHKHeer.

hairdryer - фен fyehn.

half - половина pahlahVEEnah.

half hour - полчаса pahl-

cheeSAH.

hall; room - зал zahl.

hall monitor - дежурная deezhOORnahyah.

ham - ветчина veetcheeNAH.

hand; arm - рука rooKAH.

handshake - пожатие pahZHAHteeyeh.

hanger - вешалка VYEHshahlkah.

happy; lucky (adj) - счастливый shahstLEEvihy.

hard (adj) - твёрдый TVYOHRdihy.

hard currency - валюта vahLYOOtah.

hard-currency store - Берёзка beerYOHSkah.

hardly; scarsely; barely - едва yeedVAH.

hare - заяц ZAHeets.

harmful (adj) - вредный VRYEHDnihy.

hat - шапка SHAHPkah.

hazel grouse - рябчик RYAHPcheek.

he - он ohn.

head - голова gahlahVAH.

headache - головная боль gahlahvNAHyah bohl'.

head cold - насморк NAHsmahrk.

headlights - фары FAHrih.

headphone; earmuff - наушник nahOOSHneek.

health - здоровье zdahROHV'yeh.

healthy (adj) - здоровый zdahROHvihy.

heart - сердце SYEHRtseh.

heart attack - сердечный припадок seerDYEHCH-

nihy preePAHdahk.
heavy (adj) - тяжёлый
teezhOHLihy.
hedgehog - ёж yohsh.
heel - каблук kahbLOOK.
height; altitude - высота
vihsahTAH.
hello - здравствуйте
ZDRAHSTvooytyeh.
hello (on the telephone) -
алло ahlLOH.
help - помощь POH-
mahshch.
hemophilia - гемофилия
geemahfeeLEEyah.
hemorrhage - кровоизли-
яние krahvaheezlee-
YAHneeyeh.
hemorrhoids - геморрой
geemahrROY.
hepatitis - гепатит gee-
pahTEET.
her; its - её yeeYOH.
here (is) - вот voht.
here - тут/здесь toot/
zdyehs'.
hernia - грыжа GRIHzhah.
hero - герой geeROY.
herring - сельдь syehl't'.
hi - привет preeVYEHT.
hidden; secret (adj) - скрытый SKRIHtihy.
high blood pressure - ги-
пертония geepeertahNEE-
yah.
high; tall; lofty (adj) -
высокий vihSOHkeey.
highway - трасса/шоссе
TRAHSsah/shahsSYEH.
hindrance - препятствие
preePYAHTSTveeyeh.
hip; thigh - бедро beedROH.
his; its - его yeeVOH.

history; story - история
eesTOHreeyah.
hockey - хоккей khahkKEY.
hold, keep, support (to) -
держать deerZHAHT'.
hole - дыра dihRAH.
holiday - праздник PRAHZ-
neek.
holy; sacred (adj) - святой
sveeTOY.
homeland - родина ROH-
deenah.
homosexuality - гомосек-
суализм gahmahseek-
sooahlEEZM.
honest (adj) - честный
CHEHSTnihy.
honey - мёд myoht.
hooligan - хулиган khoo-
leeGAHN.
hope - надежда nah-
DYEHZHdah.
horn; whistle - гудок goo-
DOHK.
horrible (adj) - ужасный
oozhAHSnihy.
horrible; terrifying (adj) -
страшный STRAHSHnihy.
horse - лошадь LOHSHaht'.
horseradish - хрен
khryehn.
hospitable (adj) - хлебо-
сольный khleebahSOHL'-
nihy.
hospital - больница bahl'-
NEEtsah.
hot; intense (adj) - горячий
gahrYAHcheey.
hot (weather) (adj) - жар-
кий ZHAHRkeey.
hotel - гостиница gahsTEE-
neetsah.
hotel room; issue - номер

NOHmeer.
hour - час chahs.
house; home - дом dohm.
housewife - хозяйка khaz-YAYkah.
how - как kahk.
how far - как далеко kahk dahleeKOH.
how long - как долго kahk DOHLgah.
how much - сколько SKOHL'kah.
however; but - однако ahd-NAHkah.
humid (adj) - влажный VLAHZHnihy.
humidity - влажность VLAHZHnahst'.
humor - юмор YOOmahr.
hundred - сотый SOHTihy.
hunger - голод GOHlaht.
hungry (adj) - голодный gahLOHDnihy.
hurried; rushed (adj) - спешный SPYEHSHnihy.
husband - муж/супруг moosh/soopROOK.

I
I - я yah.
ice - лёд lyoht.
ice cream - мороженое mahROHZHehnahyeh.
icon - икона eekOHnah.
iconostasis - иконостас eekahnahSTAHS.
idea - идея eedYEHyah.
identical (adj) - одинаковый ahdeeNAHkahvihy.
identification - удостоверение oodahstahvee-RYEHneeyeh.
if; when - если YEHSlee.

if; whether ли lee.
ill (to be) - болеть bahl-YEHT'.
ill (to fall) - заболеть zahbahLYEHT'.
illegal (adj) - незаконный neezahKOHNnihy.
illness; disease - болезнь bahLYEHZN'.
image; way; mode; manner - образ OHbrahs.
imagination - воображение vahahbrahZHEHneeyeh.
impatience - нетерпение neeteerPYEHneeyeh.
importance - важность VAHZHnahst'.
important (adj) - важный VAHZHnihy.
impossible; one can not - нельзя neel'ZYAH.
impression - впечатление fpeechahtLYEHneeyeh.
improper; indecent (adj) - неприличный neepreeLEECHnihy.
in advance - заранее zahRAHnehyeh.
in front; ahead - впереди fpeereeDEE.
in general - вообще vah-ahpSHCHEH.
in order to - чтобы SHTOHbih.
in the distance - вдали vdahLEE.
in vain; for nothing - напрасно nahPRAHSnah.
in, at, for, to - в v.
inaudible (adj) - неслышный neeSLIHSHnihy.
inch - дюйм dyooym.
incident - случай SLOO-

200

chay.
incidentally; by the way - кста́ти KSTAHtee.
income - дохо́д dahKHOHT.
incomprehensible (adj) - непоня́тный neepahn-YAHTnihy.
increase - увеличе́ние ooveeleeCHEHneeyeh.
incredible; unbelievable - невероя́тный neeveerah-YAHTnihy.
independence - незави́симость neezahVEEseemahst'.
independent (adj) - самостоя́тельный sahmahstah-YAHteel'nihy.
indifferent (adj) - равноду́шный rahvnahDOOSHnihy.
indigestion - расстро́йство желу́дка rahsSTROYstvah zhehLOOTkah.
inexpensive; cheap - дешёвый deeSHOHvihy.
inexperienced (adj) - нео́пытный neeOHpihtnihy.
infection - зараже́ние zahrahZHEHneeyeh.
inflamation - воспале́ние vahspahLYEHneeyeh.
influence - влия́ние vleeYAHneeyeh.
influential (adj) - влия́тельный vleeYAHteel'nihy.
injection - уко́л ooKOHL.
ink - черни́ла chehrNEElah.
innocent (adj) - безви́нный beezVEENnihy.

inscription - на́дпись NAHTpees'.
insect - насеко́мое nahsee-KOHmahyeh.
insect repellent - сре́дство от комаро́в SRYEHTstvah aht kahmahROHF.
inside - внутри́ vnooTREE.
insomnia - бессо́нница beesSOHNneetsah.
instead of - вме́сто VMYEHstah.
institution - заведе́ние/учрежде́ние zahvee-DYEHneeyeh/oochreezh-DYEHneeyeh.
instructions - инстру́кция eenSTROOKtseeyah.
insufficient - недоста́точно needahsTAHtahchnah.
intention - наме́рение nahMYEHreeneeyeh.
interesting (adj) - интере́сный eenteeRYEHSnihy.
intermission - антра́кт ahnTRAHKT.
internal (adj) inner - вну́тренний VNOOtreenneey.
international (adj) - междунаро́дный meezhdoo-nahROHDnihy.
interpreter - перево́дчик peereeVOHTcheek.
intestine - кишка́ keesh-KAH.
Intourist office - бюро́ Интури́ста byooROH eentooREESTah.
introduction - введе́ние vveeDYEHneeyeh.
invitation - приглаше́ние preeglahSHEHneeyeh.
iodine - йод yoht.

iron (to) - гла́дить GLAH-
deet'.
iron - утю́г ооTYOOK.
irritation - раздраже́ние
rahzdrahZHEHneeyeh.
island - о́стров OHStrahf.
issue; edition; output -
вы́пуск VIHpoosk.
issue; number - но́мер
NOHmeer.

J
jam - варе́нье vah-
RYEHN'yeh.
janitor; yardsman - убо́р-
щик ооBOHRshcheek.
jar; can - ба́нка BAHNkah.
jeans - джи́нсы DZHEENsih.
Jew/(f) - евре́й/(-ка)
yeevREY/(-kah).
jewel - драгоце́нность
drahgahTSEHNnahst'.
jewelry (adj) - ювели́рный
yooveeLEERnihy.
Jewish; Hebrew (adj) -
евре́йский yeevREYskeey.
joke - шу́тка SHOOTkah.
journalist - журнали́ст
zhoornahLEEST.
joyful; joyous (adj) - ра́-
достный RAHdahstnihy.
juice - сок sohk.

K
kerchief - плато́к
plahTOHK.
key - ключ klyooch.
kidney - по́чка POHCHkah.
kilogram - килогра́мм keelahgRAHM.
kilometer - киломе́тр keelahMYEHTR.
kind; good (adj) - до́брый

DOHbrihy.
kind; sort - сорт sohrt.
kindness - доброта́ dah-
brahTAH.
kiosk - кио́ск keeOHSK.
kiss - поцелу́й pahtsee-
LOOY.
kitchen - ку́хня KOOKH-
nyah.
knee - коле́но kahLYEHnah.
knife нож nohsh.
knock - стук stook.
know (to) - знать znaht'.
knowledge - зна́ние ZNAH-
neeyeh.
known (well) (adj) - изве́ст-
ный eezVYEHSTnihy.
kopeck - копе́йка kahPEY-
kah.
kosher (adj) - коше́рный
kahshEHRnihy.
kvass (fermented drink) -
квас kvahs.

L
ladies (adj) - да́мский
DAHMskeey.
lake - о́зеро OHzeerah.
lame (adj) - хромо́й khrah-
MOY.
lamp - ла́мпа LAHMpah.
landing - поса́дка pah-
SAHTkah.
language; tonuge - язы́к
yeezIHK.
larger; bigger; greater -
бо́льше BOHL'sheh.
last; latest (adj) - после́д-
ний pahsLYEHDneey.
last (to) - дли́ться DLEE-
tsah.
last name; sir name - фами́-
лия fahMEEleeyah.

late (adj) - поздний POHZDneey.

late (to be) - опоздáть ahpahzDAHT'.

later - пóзже POHZHzheh.

laughter - смех smyehkh.

laundry; linen - бельё beel'YOH.

law - закóн zahKOHN.

lawyer - адвокáт ahdvahKAHT.

laxitive - слабительное slahBEEteel'nahyeh.

leadership - руковóдство rookahVOHTstvah.

leaf; sheet (of paper) листóк leesTOHK.

leather (adj) - кóжаный KOHzhahnihy.

leave, go out, exit (to) - выходить vihkhahDEET'.

lecture - лéкция LYEHKtseeyah.

left (direction) - лéвый LYEHvihy.

leg - ногá nahGAH.

legal; legitimate (adj) - закóнный zahKOHNnihy.

lemon - лимóн leeMOHN.

lemonade - лимонáд leemahnAHT.

length - длинá dleeNAH.

less - мéньше MYEHN'sheh.

lesson - урóк ooROHK.

let's; go ahead! - давáй dahVAY.

letter - письмó pees'MOH.

letter of the alphabet - бýква BOOKvah.

level - ýровень OOrahveen'.

library - библиотéка beebleeahTYEHkah.

lid; cover - крышка KRIHshkah.

lie, tell lies (to) - врать vraht'.

life - жизнь zheezn'.

light - свет svyeht.

light bulb - лáмпочка LAHMpahchkah.

light-(color) - свéтло- SVYEHTlah-.

light; bright (adj) - свéтлый SVYEHTlihy.

lightning - мóлния MOHLneeyah.

lilac - сирéнь seeRYEHN'.

line - óчередь OHCHehreet'.

lip - губá gooBAH.

list - списoк SPEEsahk.

liter - литр leetr.

literature - литератýра leeteerahTOOrah.

little; not enough - мáло MAHlah.

little; not much - немнóго neemNOHgah.

live (to) - жить zheet'.

liver (anatomy) - пéчень PYEHchehn'.

liver (the food) - печёнка peechOHNkah.

loaf of bread - бухáнка bookhAHNkah.

lobby - фойé fayYEH.

local (adj) - мéстный MYEHSTnihy.

lock - замóк zahMOHK.

long (measure) (adj) - длинный DLEENnihy.

long (time) (adj) - дóлгий DOHLgeey.

long ago - давнó dahvNOH.

long time (for a) - дóлго

DOHLgah.
long underwear - кальсо́ны kahl'SOHnih.
look (to) - смотре́ть smah-TRYEHT'.
look; glance - взгляд vzglyaht.
lose (to) - потеря́ть pah-teerYAHT'.
loud (adj) - гро́мкий GROHMkeey.
love (to) - люби́ть lyoo-BEET'.
love - любо́вь lyooBOHF'.
lower (adj) - ни́жний NEEZHnihy.
lox - сёмга SYOHMgah.
luggage - бага́ж bahGAHSH.
lunch - обе́д ahBYEHT.
lunch (to eat) обе́дать ah-BYEHdaht'.
lungs - лёгкие LYOHKH-keeyeh.
luxurious (adj) - роско́ш-ный rahsKOHSHnihy.

M

magazine - журна́л zhoor-NAHL.
maid - го́рничная GOHR-neechnahyah.
mail; postoffice - по́чта POHCHtah.
mailbox - почто́вый я́щик pahchTOHvihy YAH-shcheek.
main; principle (adj) - гла́вный GLAHVnihy.
majority - большинство́ bahl'sheenstVOH.
make-up - косме́тика kahs-MYEHteekah.
malachite - малахи́т mah-

lahKHEET.
malicious; spiteful (adj) - зло́бный ZLOHBnihy.
man - мужчи́на moosh-CHEEnah.
manager - администра́тор/ дире́ктор ahdmeenees-TRAHtahr/deeRYEHKtahr.
manager - заве́дующий zahVYEHdooyooshcheey.
manuscript - ру́копись ROOkahpees'.
map (of the city) - план plahn.
map - ка́рта KAHRtah.
marinated (adj) - марино́-ванный mahreeNOHvahn-nihy.
market - ры́нок RIHNahk.
marriage - брак brahk.
married (for women) - за́-мужем ZAHmoozhehm.
married (for men) - жена́т zhehNAHT.
match - спи́чка SPEECHkah.
matroshka dolls (wooden, nested dolls) - матрёшка mahtRYOHSHkah.
matter; affair; business - де́ло DYEHlah.
mausoleum - мавзоле́й mahvzahLEY.
may; can - мо́жно MOHZH-nah.
mean (to) - зна́чить ZNAH-cheet'.
meaning; sense - значе́ние znahCHEHneeyeh.
meanwhile - пока́ pahKAH.
measure; extent; degree - ме́ра MYEHrah.
meat - мя́со MYAHsah.
meat loaf - руле́т roo-

LYEHT.
meatballs - тефтéли
teefTYEHlee.
mechanism - механи́зм
meekhahnEEZM.
medical treatment - лечé-
ние leeCHEHneeyeh.
medicine - лекáрство
leeKAHRstvah.
meet (to) - встречáть
fstreechAHT'.
meeting - собрáние sah-
BRAHneeyeh.
meeting; encounter -
встрéча FSTRYEHchah.
melon - ды́ня DIHNyah.
member - член chlyehn.
memory - пáмять PAHM-
eet'.
memory; recollection - вос-
поминáние vahspahmee-
NAHneeyeh.
men's (adj) - мужскóй
mooshSKOY.
menstruation - менстру-
áция meenstrooAHtsee-
yah.
mental; emotional (adj) -
душéвный dooshEHV-
nihy.
menu - менló meenYOO.
merchandise - товáр tah-
VAHR.
meter - метр myehtr.
middle - середи́на
seereeDEEnah.
middle; average (adj) -
срéдний SRYEHDneey.
midnight - пóлночь POHL-
nahch.
military (adj) - воéнный
vahYEHNnihy.
milk - молокó mahlahKOH.

million - миллиóн meellee-
OHN.
minute - мину́та meenOOT-
ah.
mirror - зéркало ZYEHR-
kahlah.
misfortune - бедá beeDAH.
mistake - оши́бка ahshEEP-
kah.
misunderstanding - недо-
разумéние needah-
rahzooMYEHneeyeh.
mitten - рукави́ца rookah-
VEEtsah.
modest (adj) - скрóмный
SKROHMnihy.
monastary - монасты́рь/
лáвра mahnahsTIHR'/
LAHVrah.
money - дéньги DYEHN'gee.
money order - дéнежный
перевóд DYEHneezhnihy
peereeVOHT.
month - мéсяц MYEHSeets.
monthly (adj) -ежемéсяч-
ный yeezhehMYEHseech-
nihy.
monument - пáмятник
PAHMeetneek.
mood - настроéние nahs-
trahYEHneeyeh.
moon - лунá looNAH.
more - бóлее BOHleeyeh.
morning (adj) - у́тренни
OOTreeneey.
morning - у́тро OOTrah.
Moscow (adj) - москóвский
mahsKOHFskeey.
mosquito - комáр kah-
MAHR.
mother - мать maht'.
motor - мотóр mahTOHR.
motorcycle - мотоци́кл

205

mahtahTSEEKL.
motorist - автомобилист
ahftahmahbeeLEEST.
mountain - гора́ gahRAH.
mouse - мышь mihsh.
mouth - рот roht.
movement; traffic - движе́ние dveeZHEHneeyeh.
movie - фильм feel'm.
movie theater - кинотеа́тр keenahteeAHTR.
movie; the cinema - кино́ keeNOH.
Mr. (pre-revolutionary) - господи́н gahspahDEEN.
Mrs. (pre-revolutionary) - госпожа́ gahspahZHAH.
much; a lot - мно́го MNOHgah.
much, far - гора́здо gahRAHZdah.
multicolored (adj) - многоцве́тный mnahgahTSVYEHTnihy.
murder - уби́йство ooBEEYSTvah.
murderer - уби́йца ooBEEYtsah.
muscle - му́скул MOOSkool.
museum - музе́й mooZEY.
mushrooms - грибы́ greeBIH.
music - му́зыка MOOZihkah.
must - на́до/ну́жно NAHdah/NOOZHnah.
mustache - усы́ oosIH.
mustard - горчи́ца gahrCHEEtsah.
mutton; lamb - бара́нина bahRAHneenah.
mutton soup - харчо́ kharCHOH.

mutual understanding - взаимопонима́ние vzaheemahpahneeMAHneeyeh.
mystery (story/movie) - детекти́в deeteekTEEF.

N

nail, tack - гвоздь gvohst'.
naked (adj) - го́лый GOHlihy.
name (first) - и́мя EEMyah.
name (last); sir name - фами́лия fahMEEleeyah.
name; title - назва́ние nahzVAHneeyeh.
napkin - салфе́тка sahlFYEHTkah.
narrow (adj) - у́зкий OOSkeey.
nasty; foul; vile (adj) - га́дкий GAHTkeey.
nation - на́ция NAHtseeyah.
national; folk (adj) - наро́дный nahROHDnihy.
nationality - национа́льность nahtseeahNAHL'nahst'.
native (adj) - родно́й rahdNOY.
naturally - есте́ственно yeestYEHSTveennah.
nature - приро́да preeROHdah.
nausea - тошнота́ tashnahTAN.
navy - флот floht.
near; nearby - бли́зко BLEESkah.
nearby; not far off (adj) - недалёкий needahLYOHkeey.
nearest; next (adj) - бли-

жа́йший bleeZHAYsheey.
neat, punctual (adj) - акку-
ра́тный
ahkooRAHTnihy.
necessary; essential (adj) -
необходи́мый neeahp-
khahDEEmihy.
neck - ше́я SHEHyah.
necklace - ожере́лье
ahzheeRYEHL'yeh.
need - нужда́ noozhDAH.
needle - иго́лка
eeGOHLkah.
negative (adj) - отрица́т-
ельный ahtreeTSAHteel'-
nihy.
negotiations - перегово́ры
peereegahVOHrihy.
neighbor - сосе́д sahSYEHT.
nephew - племя́нник pleem
-YAHNneek.
nerve - нерв nyehrf.
nervous; irritable (adj) -
не́рвный NYEHRVnihy.
neutral (adj) -
нейтра́льный
neytRAHL'nihy.
never - никогда́ neekahg-
DAH.
new (adj) - но́вый NOHvihy.
New Year - Но́вый год
NOHvihy goht.
news - изве́стие eez-
VYEHSTeeyeh.
newspaper - газе́та gah-
ZYEHtah.
next (adj) - сле́дующий
SLYEHdooyooshcheey.
nice; sweet; dear; darling
(adj) - ми́лый MEElihy.
niece - племя́ница pleem-
YAHNeetsah.
night - ночь nohch.

no - нет nyeht.
no one - никто́ neekTOH.
no way - ника́к neeKAHK.
noise - шум shoom.
noisy (adj) - шу́мный
SHOOMnihy.
nonalcoholic - безалко-
го́льный beezahlkah-
GOHL'nihy.
nonsense - чепуха́/вздор
chehpooKHAH/vzdohr.
nonstop (of a flight) (adj) -
беспоса́дочный beespah-
SAHdahchnihy.
noon - по́лдень POHLdeen'.
normal (adj) - норма́льный
nahrMAHL'nihy.
north - се́вер SYEHveer.
northern (adj) - се́верный
SYEHveernihy.
nose - нос nohs.
not - не nee.
not long ago; recently -
неда́вно neeDAHVnah.
notebook - тетра́дь
teetRAHT'.
nothing - ничего́ neechee-
VOH.
noticably; visibly - заме́т-
но zahMYEHTnah.
notify (to) - сообща́ть sahahpSHCHAHT'.
novel - рома́н rahMAHN.
now - сейча́с/тепе́рь
seeCHAHS/teePYEHR'.
number - число́ cheesLOH.
numeral - ци́фра tseefRAH.
nurse - медсестра́ meed-
seesTRAH.
nut - оре́х ahrYEHKH.

O

oatmeal - овся́нка ahf-

SYAHNkah.
oats - овёс ahVYOHS.
objection - возражение
vahzrahZHEHneeyeh.
obligatory; mandatory (adj)
- обязательный ahbee-
ZAHteel'nihy.
obstetrician - акушер
ahkooSHYEHR.
obvious (adj) - очевидный
ahchehVEEDnihy.
occupation; work; studies -
занятие zahnYAHteeyeh.
ocean - океан ahkeeAHN.
of course - конечно kahn-
YEHSHnah.
offence; insult - обида
ahBEEdah.
offer; proposal; suggestion -
предложение preedlah-
ZHEHneeyeh.
office - контора kahnTOH-
rah.
office; bureau - бюро
byooROH.
often - часто CHAHStah.
ok - ладно LAHDnah.
old (adj) - старый STAH-
rihy.
older; elder (adj) - старший
STAHRsheey.
olives - маслина mahsLEE-
nah.
on; in - на nah.
on the contrary; the other
way around - наоборот
nahahbahROHT.
on the left - налево nah-
LYEHvah.
on the right - направо
nahPRAHvah.
on time - вовремя VOH-
vreemyah.

once; one day - однажды
ahdNAHZHdih.
one and a half - полтора
pahltahRAH.
one-way (ticket) - в один
конец vahdEEN kahn-
YEHTS.
onion - лук look.
only - только TOHL'kah.
open (adj) - открытый aht-
KRIHtihy.
opera - опера OHpeerah.
opera glasses - бинокль
beeNOHKL'.
operator - телефонистка
teeleefahNEESTkah.
opinion - мнение MNYEH-
neeyeh.
opportunity - возможность
vahzMOHZHnahst'.
opposite; facing - напротив
nahPROHteef.
optician - оптик OPteek.
or - или/либо EElee/
LEEbah.
oral; verbal (adj) - устный
OOSTnihy.
orange (adj) - оранжевый
ahRAHNzhehvihy.
orange (fruit) - апельсин
ahpeel'SEEN.
orchestra - оркестр ahr-
KYEHSTR.
order; sequence - порядок
pahRYAHdahk.
order (to) - заказать zahkahzAHT'.
origin - происхождение
praheeskhahzhDYEH-
neeyeh.
original (adj) - первона-
чальный peervahnah-
CHAHL'nihy.

orthodox (adj) - правосла́в-
ный prahvahSLAHVnihy.
other; another; the other -
друго́й drooGOY.
out-raged (adj) - возмущ-
ённый vahzmooshch-
OHNnihy.
outpatient clinic - амбула-
то́рия ahmboolahTOH-
reeyah.
outside; out of - вне vnyeh.
outward; external (adj) -
вне́шний VNYEHSHneey.
over and above; in access of
- сверх svyehrkh.
overcast (adj) - па́смурный
PAHsmoornihy.
oxygen - кислоро́д
keeslahROHT.

P

pacifier - со́ска SOHSkah.
pack; bundle - па́чка
PAHCHkah.
package - посы́лка
pahSIHLkah.
packet; package -
паке́т pahKYEHT.
page - страни́ца
strahNEEtsah.
pain - боль bohl'.
painkiller -
болеутоля́ющее сре́дство
bahleeootahl-
YAHyooshchehyeh
SRYEHTstvah.
painting - жи́вопись ZHEE-
vahpees'.
pair - па́ра PAHrah.
palace - дворе́ц dvahr-
YEHTS.
pale (adj) - бле́дный
BLYEHDnihy.

palm (anatomy) - ладо́нь
lahDOHN'.
pancake - блин bleen.
pants - брю́ки BRYOOkee.
paper - бума́га booMAHgah.
parents - роди́тели rah-
DEEteelee.
park - парк pahrk.
parking lot - стоя́нка для
маши́н stahYAHNkah
dlyah mahshEEN.
parsley - петру́шка pee-
TROOSHkah.
part - часть chahst'.
participation - уча́стие
ooCHAHSTeeyeh.
passage; excerpt; snatch -
отры́вок ahtRIHvahk.
passenger - пассажи́р
pahssahZHEER.
passionate (adj) - стра́ст-
ный STRAHSTnihy.
passport - па́спорт PAHS-
pahrt.
past (adj) - про́шлый
PROHSHlihy.
pastry - пиро́жное pee-
ROHZHnahyeh.
patient (adj) - терпели́вый
teerpeeLEEvihy.
patient - пацие́нт pahtsee-
EHNT.
patronymic - о́тчество
OHTchehstvah.
pay (to) - плати́ть plah-
TEET'.
pay phone - телефо́н-
автома́т teeleeFOHN-
ahftahMAHT.
peace - мир meer.
peach - пе́рсик PYEHRseek.
pear - гру́ша GROOshah.
pearl - жёмчуг ZHEHM-

chook.
peas - горо́х gahROHKH.
peasant's hut; cabin - изба́
eesBAH.
pediatrician - педиа́тр
peedeeAHTR.
pen - ру́чка ROOCHkah.
pencil - каранда́ш kah-
rahnDAHSH.
penicillin - пеницилли́н
peeneetseeILEEN.
people (a) - наро́д
nahROHT.
people - лю́ди LYOOdee.
pepper - пе́рец PYEHreets.
pepper vodka - перцо́вка
peerTSOHFkah.
performance; play - спек-
та́кль speekTAHKL'.
performer - арти́ст ahr-
TEEST.
perfume - духи́ dooKHEE.
perhaps - мо́жет быть
MOHZHeht biht'.
period of twenty-four
hours; day - су́тки
SOOTkee.
permanent wave - перма-
не́нт peermahNYEHNT.
permission; permit - разре-
ше́ние rahzreeSHEHnee-
yeh.
person - челове́к chehlah-
VYEHK.
personal; private (adj) -
ли́чный LEECHnihy.
photograph - фотогра́фия
fahtahGRAHfeeyah.
phrasebook - разгово́рник
rahzgahVOHRneek.
phrase; sentence - фра́за
FRAHzah.
picture; drawing - карти́на

kahrTEEnah.
pie - пиро́г peeROHK.
piece - кусо́к kooSOHK.
pig - свинья́ sveen'YAH.
pigeon; dove - го́лубь GOH-
loop'.
pike - щу́ка SHCHOOkah.
pilaf - пила́в peeLAHF.
pill - пилю́ля peeLYOO-
lyah.
pill; tablet - табле́тка
tahbLYEHTkah.
pillow - поду́шка
pahDOOSHkah.
pillowcase - на́волочка
NAHvahlahchkah.
pin - була́вка booLAHFkah.
pineapple - анана́с ahnah-
NAHS.
pipe - тру́бка TROOPkah.
pity - жаль zhahl'.
place; seat; site - ме́сто
MYEHStah.
plant - расте́ние rahs-
TYEHneeyeh.
plate - таре́лка tahRYEHL-
kah.
play (to) - игра́ть eeg-
RAHT'.
play; drama - пье́са P'YEH-
sah.
playwright - драмату́рг
drahmahTOORK.
pleasant (adj) - прия́тный
preeYAHTnihy.
please - пожа́луйста
pahZHAHLstah.
pleasure - удово́льствие
oodahVOHL'stveeyeh.
plum - сли́ва SLEEvah.
plumber - водопрово́дчик
vahdahprahVOHTcheek.
pneumonia - воспале́ние

лёгких vahspahLYEHneeyeh LYOHKHkeekh.

pocket - карма́н kahrMAHN.

poet - поэ́т pahEHT.

poetry - поэ́зия pahEHzeeyah.

point; station; center - пу́нкт poonkt.

poison - отра́ва/яд ahtRAHvah/yaht.

police - мили́ция meeLEEtseeyah.

policeman - милиционе́р meeleetseeahNYEHR.

polish; lacquer - лак lahk.

polite; courteous (adj) - ве́жливый VYEHZHleevihy.

politics - поли́тика pahLEEteekah.

pond - пруд proot.

pool - бассе́йн bahsSEYN.

poor (adj) - бе́дный BYEHDnihy.

poor-quality (adj) - недоброка́чественный needahbrahKAHCHehstveennihy.

poppy - мак mahk.

population - населе́ние nahseeLYEHneeyeh.

pork - свини́на sveeNEEnah.

port - порт pohrt.

portable (adj) - перено́сный peereeNOHSnihy.

porter - носи́льщик nahSEEL'shcheek.

portrait - портре́т pahrtRYEHT.

positive; affirmative (adj) - положи́тельный pahlah

ZHEEteel'nihy.

postcard - откры́тка ahtKRIHTkah.

poster - плака́т plahKAHT.

poster; play bill - афи́ша ahFEEshah.

post office (main branch) - по́чтамт POHCHTahmt.

post office - по́чта POHCHtah.

pot; saucepan - кастрю́ля kahstRYOOLyah.

pot cheese - творо́г tvahROHK.

potato - карто́фель kahrTOHfeel'.

pound - фунт foont.

powder - по́рох POHrahkh.

powerful (adj) - мо́щный/ могу́чий MOHSHCHnihy/ mahGOOcheey.

prayer book - моли́тва mahLEETvah.

pregnant (adj) - бере́менная beeRYEHmeennahyah.

prepare (to) - гото́вить gahTOHveet'.

prescription - реце́пт reetsEHPT.

present - пода́рок pahDAHrahk.

present; real; true (adj) - настоя́щий nahstahYAHshcheey.

pressure - давле́ние dahvLYEHneeyeh.

pressure (physical) - напо́р nahPOHR.

pretty (adj) - краси́вый krahsEEVihy.

price - цена́ tseeNAH.

priest; clergyman - свяще́нник sveeshCHEHN

neek.
prison - тюрьма́ tyoor'-MAH.
probably - наве́рно/вероя́тно nahVYEHRnah/veerahYAHTnah.
problem - пробле́ма prahBLYEHmah.
processing - оформле́ние ahfahrmLYEHneeyeh.
profession - профе́ссия prahFYEHSseeyah.
professor - профе́ссор prahFYEHSsahr.
profitable; favorable (adj) - вы́годный VIHgahdnihy.
prognosis; forecast - прогно́з prahgNOHS.
promise - обеща́ние ahbeeSHCHAHneeyeh.
pronunciation - произноше́ние praheeznahSHEHneeyeh.
proper (adj) - прили́чный preeLEESHnihy.
property - иму́щество eemOOSHCHehstvah.
proud (adj) - го́рдый GOHR-dihy.
proverb - посло́вица pahsLOHveetsah.
public bath - ба́ня BAHNyah.
puddle - лу́жа LOOZHah.
pulse - пульс pool's.
punishment - наказа́ние nahkahZAHneeyeh.
purchase - поку́пка pahKOOPkah.
push button; snap - кно́пка KNOHPkah.
pyjamas - пижа́ма peezhAHMah.

Q
quality - ка́чество KAHchehstvah.
quantity - коли́чество kahlEECHehstvah.
quarter - че́тверть CHEHTveert'.
question - вопро́с vahpROHS.
quickly! - скоре́е! skahRYEHeh.
quickly; rapidly (adj) - ско́рый SKOHrihy.
quiet (adj) - ти́хий TEEKHeey.
quote - цита́та tseeTAHtah.

R
rabbi - равви́н rahvVEEN.
rabbit - кро́лик KROHleek.
radio - ра́дио RAHdeeoh.
radio station - радиоста́нция rahdeeahSTAHNtseeyah.
radish - реди́ска reeDEESkah.
rail; track - рельс ryehl's.
railroad car - ваго́н vahGOHN.
rain - дождь dohsht'.
raincoat - плащ plahshch.
raisins - изю́м eezYOOM.
rare; infrequent (adj) - ре́дкий RYEHTkeey.
rarely - ре́дко RYEHTkah.
raspberries - мали́на mahLEEnah.
rate of exchange - валю́тный курс vahLYOOtnihy koors.
rather; fairly - дово́льно dahVOHL'nah.

raw (adj) - сырóй sihROY.
razor - брúтва BREETvah.
razor blades - лéзвия
LYEHZveeyah.
read (to) - читáть chee-
TAHT'.
reader - читáтель chee-
TAHteel'.
ready (adj) - готóвый
gahTOHvihy.
real; actual; effective - (adj)
действúтельный deyst-
VEEteel'nihy.
really; truly - действú-
тельно deystVEEteel'nah.
really?; is that so? - рáзве?
RAHZveh.
rear; back; hind (adj) -
зáдний ZAHDneey.
reason - причúна
preeCHEEnah.
reception - приём
preeYOHM.
recommend (to) - посовéт-
овать pahsahVYEH-
tahvaht'.
record - грампластúнка
grahmplahsTEENkah.
recording (record/tape) -
зáпись ZAHpees'.
red (adj) - крáсный
KRAHSnihy.
reference; information -
спрáвка SPRAHFkah.
refrigerator - холодúльник
khahlahDEEL'neek.
refusal - откáз ahtKAHS.
region; area; field; domain -
óбласть OHblahst'.
registration - регистрáция
reegeesTRAHtseeyah.
relationship; connection -
отношéние ahtnahSHEH-
neeyeh.
relatives - рóдственник
ROHTSTveenneekee.
reluctantly - неохóтно
neeahKHOHTnah.
remainder - остáток ahs-
TAHtahk.
rent (to) - взять напрокáт
vzyaht' nahprahKAHT.
repair - ремóнт reeMOHNT.
repeat (to) - повторúть
pahftahREET'.
republic - респýблика
reesPOObleekah.
request - прóсьба PROZ'-
bah.
research - исслéдование
eesSLYEHdahvahneeyeh.
reserved (on a train) (adj) -
плацкáртный plahts-
KAHRTnihy.
resident - жúтель ZHEE-
teel'.
resort - курóрт koorOHRT.
respected (adj) - уважáе-
мый oovahZHAHeemihy.
rest - óтдых OHDdihkh.
restaurant - ресторáн reestahRAHN.
return (to) - возвращáть
vahzvrahSHCHAHT'.
return; reverse; opposite
(adj) - обрáтный ahb-
RAHTnihy.
reward - награ́да nah-
GRAHdah.
rheumatism - ревматúзм
reevmahTEEZM.
rib - ребрó reebROH.
rice - рис rees.
rich (adj) - богáтый bah-
GAHtihy.
ride; drive - езда́ yeezDAH.

213

right; correct (adj) - правильный PRAHveel'nihy.
right (direction) - правый
PRAHvihy.
ripe; mature (adj) - зрелый
ZRYEHlihy.
river - река reeKAH.
road - дорога dahROHgah.
roast beef - ростбиф
ROHSTbeef.
robe - халат khahLAHT.
rock - камень KAHmeen'.
role; part - роль rohl'.
roll; bun - булка BOOLkah.
roof - крыша KRIHshah.
room - комната KOHM-
nahtah.
rope; string; cord - верёвка
veeRYOHFkah.
rose - роза ROHzah.
roundtrip (ticket) - туда и
обратно tooDAH ee ahb-
RAHTnah.
row - ряд ryaht.
rubber (adj) - резиновый
reeZEEnahvihy.
rubbers; galoshes - галоши
gahLOHshee.
ruble - рубль roobl'.
ruby - рубин rooBEEN.
rude; course (adj) - грубый
GROObihy.
rug - ковёр kahVYOHR.
rule - правило PRAHveelah.
run (to) - бегать BYEHgaht'.
run; race - бег byehk.
Russian (adj) - российский
rahsSEEYskeey.
Russian/(f) - русский/
(русская) ROOSskeey/
(ROOSskahyah).
rye - рожь rohsh.
ryhme - рифма REEFmah.

S
saccharin - сахарин
sahkhahREEN.
sad; melancholy (adj) -
грустный/печальный
GROOSTnihy/peeCHAHL'-
nihy.
safe - несгораемый шкаф
neezgahRAHeemihy
shkahf.
safe (adj) - безопасный
beezahPAHSnihy.
safely; without mishap -
благополучно blah-
gahpahLOOCHnah.
safety pin - английская
булавка ahngLEEYskah-
yah booLAHFkah.
sail boat - парусная лодка
PAHroosnahyah LOHTkah.
salad - салат sahLAHT.
sale - продажа/скидка
prahDAHzhah/SKEETkah.
salesman - продавец prah-
dahVYEHTS.
salmon - лососина lahsah-
SEEnah.
salt - соль sohl'.
salty (adj) - солёный sahl-
YOHnihy.
samovar - самовар sahmah-
VAHR.
sample; model; pattern -
образец ahbrahzYEHTS.
sand - песок peeSOHK.
sandals - сандалии sahn-
DAHleeee.
sandwich - бутерброд
booteerBROHT.
sanitary day (one day a
month when stores/
museums are closed for

214

cleaning) - санита́рный день sahneeTAHRnihy dyehn'.

saphire - сапфи́р sahp-FEER.

sarcasm - сарка́зм sahr-KAHZM.

satire - сати́ра sahTEErah.

satisfaction - удовлетворе́ние oodahvleetvah-RYEHneeyeh.

sauce; gravy - со́ус sahOOS.

sausage - колбаса́ kahlbah-SAH.

save, keep (to); to guard - бере́чь beeRYEHCH.

scarf - шарф shahrf.

schedule; timetable - расписа́ние rahspeeSAH-neeyeh.

scholar; scientist - учёный ooCHOHnihy.

school - шко́ла SHKOHlah.

school vacation - кани́кулы kahNEEkoolih.

scissors - но́жницы NOHZHneetsih.

screen - экра́н ehkRAHN.

sculpture - скульпту́ра skool'pTOOrah.

sea - мо́ре MOHRyeh.

sea food - да́ры мо́ря DAHrih MOHRyah.

seat - ме́сто MYEHStah.

second (time measure) - секу́нда seekOONdah.

secondhand book dealer - букини́ст bookeenEEST.

secretary - секрета́рь seek-reeTAHR'.

section - се́кция SYEHK-tseeyah.

sedative - успокои́тельное средство oospahkahEET-eel'nahyeh SRYEHTstvah.

see (to) - ви́деть VEEdeet'.

self confident (adj) - самоуве́ренный sahmahoo-VYEHreennihy.

self-service - самообслу́живание sahmahahpSLOO-zheevahneeyeh.

sell (to) - прода́ть prah-DAHT'.

send (to) - посла́ть pahs-LAHT'.

sensibly; rationally (adj) - разу́мно rahzOOMnah.

sensitive (adj) чувстви́тельный choofstVEE-teel'nihy.

separately; individually - отде́льно ahdDYEHL'nah.

serious (adj) - серьёзный seer'YOHZnihy.

service station - автозапра́вочная ста́нция ahftah-zahPRAHvahchnahyah STAHNtseeyah.

set (of dishes or silverware) - серви́з seerVEES.

set - компле́кт kahm-PLYEHKT.

shadow - тень tyehn'.

shame - стыд stiht.

shampoo - шампу́нь shahm-POON'.

share, divide (to) - дели́ть deelEET'.

share; lot - до́ля DOHLyah.

sharp; pungent; keen (adj) - о́стрый OHStrihy.

shave (to); get a shave - бри́ться BREETsah.

she - она́ ahNAH.

sheet - простыня́ prahs-

215

tihnYAH.
ship - корабль kahRAHBL'.
ship; steamship - пароход
pahrahKHOHT.
shirt - рубашка rooBAHSH-
kah.
shish kebob - шашлык
shahshLIHK.
shoe laces - шнурки
shnoorKEE.
shoemaker - ремонт обуви
reeMOHNT OHboovee.
shoes - обувь/туфли
OHboof/TOOFlee.
short (adj) - короткий
kahROHTkeey.
shortage; scarcity; defect;
deficiency - недостаток
needahsTAHtahk.
shorts - шорты SHOHRtihy.
should; must; ought to -
должен DOHLzhehn.
shoulder - плечо pleh-
CHOH.
shout; cry - крик kreek.
show (to) - показать pah-
kahZAHT'.
shower - душ doosh.
sick (adj) - больной
bahl'NOY.
side - сторона/бок
stahrahNAH/bohk.
side street - переулок
peereeOOLahk.
side walk - тротуар
trahtooAHR.
sideways - боком BOH-
kahm.
sight; vision - видение
VEEdeeneeyeh.
sign (to) - подписать
pahtpeeSAHT'.
sign; signal - знак znahk.

sign up (to) - записаться
zahpeeSAHTsah.
signature - подпись
POHTpees'.
silence - молчание mahl-
CHAHneeyeh.
silver (adj) - серебряный
seeRYEHBreenihy.
silver - серебро seeree-
BROH.
similar; like (adj) - похо-
жий pahKHOHzheey.
simple; easy (adj) - простой
prahsTOY.
simply - просто PROHstah.
simultaneous (adj) - одно-
временный ahdnah-
VRYEHmeennihy.
sin - грех gryehkh.
since - с seh.
sincere (adj) - искренний
EESkreenneey.
singer - певец peevYEHTS.
sink (bathroom) - раковина
RAHkahveenah.
sister - сестра seesTRAH.
sister-in-law - невестка
neeVYEHSTkah.
situation; condition - поло-
жение pahlahZHEHnee-
yeh.
situation; setting - обста-
новка ahpstahNOHFkah.
size - размер rahzMYEHR.
skates - коньки kahn'KEE.
skating rink - каток
kahTOHK.
skis - лыжи LIHzhee.
skin; hide - шкура SHKOO-
rah.
skin; leather - кожа KOH-
zhah.
skirt - юбка YOOPkah.

216

skullcap - ермо́лка yeer-MOHLkah.

sky; heaven - не́бо NYEHbah.

skyscraper - небоскрёб neebahsKRYOHP.

sleep; dream - сон sohn.

sleep (to) - спать spaht'.

sleeve - рука́в rooKAHF.

sleigh; sled - са́нки SAHNkee.

slip - комбина́ция kahmbeenAHTseeyah.

slippers - та́почки TAHPahchkee.

slippery (adj) - ско́льзкий SKOHL'skeey.

slow (adj) - ме́дленный MYEHDleennihy.

small (adj) - ма́ленький MAHLeen'keey.

small change - ме́лочь MYEHlahch.

smart; intelligent (adj) - у́мный OOMnihy.

smell (to) - па́хнуть PAHKHnoot'.

smell - за́пах ZAHpahkh.

smile - улы́бка ooLIHPkah.

smoke (to) - кури́ть kooREET'.

smoke - дым dihm.

smokey (adj) - ды́мный DIHMnihy.

smooth (adj) - гла́дкий GLAHTkeey.

snack bar - буфе́т boofYEHT.

snack; appetizer - заку́ска zahKOOSkah.

snackbar - заку́сочная zahKOOsahchnahyah.

sneakers - ке́ды KYEHdih.

sneezing - чиха́нье cheeKHAHN'yeh.

snow - снег snyehk.

so; true - так tahk.

soap - мы́ло MIHlah.

soccer - футбо́л footBOHL.

society; company - о́бщество OHPshchehstvah.

socks - носки́ nahsKEE.

sofa - дива́н deeVAHN.

soft (adj) - мя́гкий MYAHKHkeey.

sold out - распро́дано rahsPROHdahnah.

soldier - солда́т sahlDAHT.

sole (of a shoe) - подмётка pahdMYOHTkah.

somehow - ка́к-то KAHKtah.

someone - кто́-нибудь KTOHneeboot'.

something - что́-нибудь SHTOHneeboot'.

sometimes - иногда́ eenahgDAH.

somewhere - где́-нибудь GDYEHneeboot'.

son - сын sihn.

son-in-law - зять zyaht'.

song - пе́сня PYEHSnyah.

sorry - прости́те/извини́те prahsTEEtyeh/eezveeNEEtyeh.

sort; kind; type - род roht.

soul - душа́ dooSHAH.

sound; noise - звук zvook.

soup - суп soop.

soup noodle - лапша́ lahpSHAH.

sour (adj) - ки́слый KEESlihy.

sour cream - смета́на smeeTAHnah.

217

south - юг yook.
southern (adj) - ю́жный YOOZHnihy.
souvenir - сувени́р soovee-NEER.
spare; extra - ли́шний LEESHneey.
speak (to); talk (about) - говори́ть gahvahrEET'.
specialty - специа́льность speetseeAHL'nahst'.
spectator - зри́тель ZREEteel'.
speech - речь ryehch.
speed - ско́рость SKOHrahst'.
spider - пау́к pahOOK.
spoiled; rotten; tainted (adj) - испо́рченный eesPOHRchehnnihy.
spoon - ло́жка LOHSHkah.
sports fan - боле́льщик bahlYEHL'shcheek.
sports match - матч mahtch.
sports team - кома́нда kahMAHNdah.
spot; stain - пятно́ peetNOH.
spring - весна́ veesNAH.
spring (adj) - весе́нний veesYEHNneey.
spruce; Christmas tree - ёлка YOHLkah.
square (adj) - квадра́тный kvahDRAHTnihy.
stadium - стадио́н stahdeeOHN.
stage - сце́на STSEHnah.
stairs - ле́стница LYEHSTneetsah.
stamp - ма́рка MAHRkah.
star - звезда́ zvyehzDAH.

starch - крахма́л krahkhMAHL.
State - госуда́рство gahsooDAHRstvah.
state - штат shtaht.
state; government (adj) - госуда́рственный gahsooDAHRSTveennihy.
station - ста́нция STAHNtseeyah.
station (train) - вокза́л vahkZAHL.
stay - пребыва́ние preebihVAHneeyeh.
steak - бифште́кс beefSHTYEHKS.
steal (to) - накра́сть nahkRAHST'.
steam room - пари́лка pahREELkah.
steamed (adj) - па́реный PAHreenihy.
step - шаг shahk.
step-mother - ма́чеха MAHchehkhah.
stepfather - о́тчим OHTcheem.
stew - рагу́ rahGOO.
stewardess - стюарде́сса styooahrDYEHSsah.
sticky (adj) - ли́пкий LEEPkeey.
still; all the same - всё-таки VSYOHtahkee.
still; yet; else; more; another - ещё yeeSHCHOH.
stockings - чулки́ choolKEE.
stomach - живо́т zheeVOHT.
stop - стоп stohp.
store - магази́н mahgah-

storm - бу́ря BOORyah.
stormy; violent (adj) -
бу́рный BOORnihy.
story; floor - эта́ж
ehTAHSH.
story; tale; account -
расска́з rahsSKAHS.
stove - печь pyehch.
straight (adj) - прямо́й
preeMOY.
strain; sprain - растяже́ние
rahsteeZHEHneeyeh.
strainer - си́течко SEE-
teechkah.
strait; channel - проли́в
prahLEEF.
strange; weird; odd (adj) -
стра́нный STRAHNnihy.
stranger - незнако́мец
neeznahKOHMeets.
strawberries - земляни́ка
zeemleeNEEkah.
street - у́лица OOLeetsah.
street car - трамва́й trahm-
VAY.
strength - си́ла SEElah.
stress (grammatical) -
ударе́ние oodahRYEH-
neeyeh.
stretcher - носи́лки nah-
SEELkee.
strict; harsh; severe (adj) -
стро́гий STROHgeey.
stroke - инсу́льт
eenSOOL'T.
stroll, walk (to) - гуля́ть
goolYAHT'.
strong (adj) - си́льный
SEEL'nihy.
strong; durable - кре́пкий
KRYEHPkeey.
stubborn (adj) - упо́рный

ooPOHRnihy.
student/(f) - студе́нт/(-ка)
stooDYEHNT/(-kah).
study (to) - учи́ться
ooCHEETsah.
stuffed (food) (adj) -
фарширо́ванный fahr-
sheeROHvahnnihy.
stuffed animal - чу́чело
CHOOchehlah.
stuffed cabbage - голубцы́
gahloopTSIH.
stuffy - ду́шно DOOSHnah.
stupid; silly (adj) - глу́пый
GLOOpihy.
subject - предме́т preed-
MYEHT.
substitution - заме́на
zahMYEHnah.
suburb - при́город PREE-
gahraht.
subway - метро́ meeTROH.
success - уда́ча/успе́х
ooDAHchah/oosPYEHKH.
suddenly - вдруг vdrook.
suede - за́мша ZAHMshah.
sugar - са́хар SAHkhahr.
suicide - самоуби́йство
sahmahooBEEYSTvah.
suit - костю́м kahsTYOOM.
suit jacket (man's) -
пиджа́к peedZHAHK.
suitcase - чемода́н cheh-
mahDAHN.
summer - ле́то LYEHtah.
summer (adj) - ле́тний
LYEHTneey.
sun - со́лнце SOHNtseh.
sunburn; sun tan - зага́р
zahGAHR.
sunglasses - тёмные очки́
TYOMnihyeh ahchKEE.
sunny (adj) - со́лнечный

SOHLneechnihy.
sunrise - восхо́д vahs-
KHOHT.
supper - у́жин OOZHeen.
supper (to eat) - у́жинать
OOZHeenaht'.
surgeon - хиру́рг kheer-
OORK.
surprising (adj) - удиви́-
тельный oodeeVEEteel'-
nihy.
swallow (to) - глота́ть
glahTAHT'.
sweat - пот poht.
sweater - пуло́вер poolOH-
veer.
sweet (adj) - сла́дкий
SLAHTkeey.
swim (to) - пла́вать PLAH-
vaht'.
swollen; puffed up (adj) -
разду́тый rahzDOOtihy.
sympathy - сочу́вствие
sahCHOOSTveeyeh.
synagogue - синаго́га seenahGOHgah.
system - систе́ма sees-
TYEHmah.

T
t-shirt - ма́йка MAYkah.
table - стол stohl.
take, seize (to) - брать/
взять braht'/vzyaht'.
takeoff (airplane) - взлёт
vzlyoht.
talcum powder - тальк
tahl'k.
tale - ска́зка SKAHSkah.
talk, chat (to) - бесе́довать
beeSYEHdahvaht'.
talkative (adj) - болтли́вый
bahltLEEvihy.

tampon - тампо́н tahm-
POHN.
tangerine - мандари́н
mahndahREEN.
tape recorder - магнитофо́н
mahgneetahFOHN.
tasteless (adj) - безвку́сный
beezVKOOSnihy.
tasty - вку́сный VKOOS-
nihy.
tax - нало́г nahLOHK.
taxi - такси́ tahkSEE.
taxi stop - стоя́нка stah-
YAHNkah.
tea - чай chay.
tea caddy - ча́йница
CHAYneetsah.
tea kettle - ча́йник CHAY-
neek.
teacher (f) - преподава́-
тель/(-ница)//учи́тель/
(-ница) preepahdahVAH-
teel'/(-neetsah) ooCHEE-
teel'/(-neetsah).
tears - слёзы SLYOHzih.
teddy bear - ми́шка
MEESHkah.
telegram - телегра́мма
teeleeGRAHMmah.
telegraph office - телегра́ф
teeleeGRAHF.
telephone - телефо́н teelee-
FOHN.
telephone booth - телефо́н-
автома́т teeleeFOHN-
ahftahMAHT.
television - телеви́зор
teeleeVEEzahr.
temperature - гра́дус
GRAHdoos.
temporarily - вре́менно
VRYEHmeennah.
tender; gentle; delicate

(adj) - нéжный NYEHZH-nihy.
tennis - тéннис TYEHN-nees.
tension; stress; strain - напряжéние nahpree-ZHEHeeyeh.
tent - палáтка pahLAHT-kah.
textbook - учéбник ooCHEHBneek.
than - чем chehm.
thank (to) - благодари́ть blahgahdahREET'.
thank you - спаси́бо spah-SEEbah.
thankful; grateful (adj) - благодáрный blahgah-DAHRnihy.
thanks a lot - большóе спаси́бо bahl'SHOHyeh spahSEEbah
that (one) - э́тот EHtaht.
that way - тудá tooDAH.
theater - теáтр teeAHTR.
theater box - лóжа LOHZH-ah.
then - тогдá tahgDAH.
then; next; afterwards - потóм pahTOHM.
there - там tahm.
therefore - поэ́тому pahEHtahmoo.
thermometer - грáдусник GRAHdoosneek.
thermos - тéрмос TYEHR-mahs.
they - они́ ahNEE.
thick, dense (adj) - густóй goosTOY.
thief - вор vohr.
thin (adj) - тóнкий/худóй TOHNkeey/khooDOY.

thirst - жáжда ZHAHZH-dah.
thought; idea - мысль mihsl'.
thousand - ты́сяча TIHsee-chah.
thread - ни́тка NEETkah.
threat - угрóза ooGROHzah.
threatening (adj) - грóзный GROHZnihy.
throat - гóрло GOHRlah.
through - сквозь skvohs'.
through; within - чéрез CHEHrees.
thumb - большóй пáлец bahl'SHOY PAHleets.
thunder - гром grohm.
thunderstorm - грозá grahZAH.
ticket - билéт beeLYEHT.
ticket office - (билéтная) кácca beeLYEHTnahyah KAHSsah.
tie - гáлстук GAHLstook.
tie; connection - связь svyahs'.
tightly packed (adj) - наби́тый nahBEEtihy.
time (it's) - порá pahRAH.
time (period of); date; deadline - срок srohk.
time - врéмя VRYEHmyah.
time; hour - час chahs.
timetable - расписáние rahspeeSAHneeyeh.
time; once; one - раз rahs.
timid; shy (adj) - рóбкий ROHPkeey.
tip - чаевы́е chahehVIHyeh.
tired (f) (adj) - устáл(а) oosTAHL(ah).
to; toward - к k.
to; up to; before до dah.

221

tobacco - табáк tahBAHK.
today - сегóдня
seeVOHdnyah.
today's (adj) - сегóдняшний
seeVOHdnyahshneey.
together - вмéсте
VMYEHstyeh.
toilet - туалéт tooahLYEHT.
toilet paper - туалéтная
бумáга tooahLYEHT-
nahyah booMAHgah.
tomato - помидóр
pahmeeDOHR.
tombstone - надгрóбный
кáмень nahdGROHBnihy
KAHmeen'.
tomorrow - зáвтра
ZAHFtrah.
tomorrow's (adj) - зáв-
трашний ZAHFtrahsh-
neey.
tongue; language- язы́к
yeezIHK.
tonsil - миндáлина
meenDAHleenah.
tonsils - глáнды GLAHN-
dih.
too (much) - сли́шком
SLEESHkahm.
tooth - зуб zoop.
toothache - зубнáя боль
zoobNAHyah bohl'.
toothbrush - зубнáя щётка
zoobNAHyah SHCHOHT-
kah.
toothpaste - зубнáя пáста
zoobNAHyah PAHStah.
top - верх vyehrkh.
torn; ripped (adj) - рвáный
RVAHnihy.
touch (to) - трóгать TROH-
gaht'.
tour - эксýрсия ehksKOOR-

seeyah.
tour guide - экскурсовóд
ehkskoorsahVOHT.
tourist - тури́ст tooREEST.
towel - полотéнце pahlah-
TYEHNtseh.
tower - бáшня BAHSHnyah.
toy - игрýшка eegROOSH-
kah.
traffic light - светофóр
sveetahFOHR.
tragedy - трагéдия
trahGYEHdeeyah.
train - пóезд POHeest.
train compartment - купé
koopYEH.
transfer; change (planes,
trains, buses etc) - пере-
сáдка peereeSAHTkah.
translate (to) - перевести́
peereeveesTEE.
translation - перевóд
peereeVOHT.
translator - перевóдчик
peereeVOHTcheek.
trash- мýсор MOOsahr.
traveler - путешéственник
pooteeshEHSTveenneek.
travels; trip - путешéствие
pooteeshEHSTveeyeh.
treatment - лечéние
leeCHEHneeyeh.
tree - дéрево DYEHreevah.
trip; flight - рéйс reys.
trip; way; path. - путь
poot'.
trolley bus - троллéйбус
trahlLEYboos.
truck - грузови́к groozah-
VEEK.
true; faithful (adj) - вéрный
VYEHRnihy.
truth - прáвда PRAHVdah.

tsar - царь tsahr'.
tuna - тунец tooNYEHTS.
turkey - индейка eenDEY-
kah.
turn on, switch on (to) -
включать vklyooCHAHT'.
turn out, switch off (to) -
выключать vihklyoo-
CHAHT'.
turnip - репа RYEHpah.
tweezers - пинцет peen-
TSEHT.
typewriter - пишущая
машинка PEESHooshch-
ahyah mahSHEENkah.

U

ugly (adj) - некрасивый
neekrahsEEVihy.
ulcer - язва YAHZvah.
umbrella - зонтик ZOHN-
teek.
unattainable (adj) - недостижимый needahstee-
ZHEEmihy.
uncle - дядя DYAHdyah.
unclean; dirty (adj) - не-
чистый neeCHEEStihy.
unclear (adj) - неясный
neeYAHSnihy.
uncomfortable (adj) - неу-
добный neeooDOHBnihy.
unconscious (adj) - бессоз-
нательный
beessahzNAH-teel'nihy.
under; beneath - под poht.
underpants - трусы troo-
SIH.
undershirt - майка MAY-
kah.
understand (to) - понимать
pahneeMAHT'.
understandable (adj) - по-

нятный pahnYAHTnihy.
undertaking; venture -
предприятие
preetpreeYAHteeyeh.
underwear - нижнее бельё
NEEZHneeyeh beel'YOH.
unfair; injust (adj) - нес-
праведливый neesprah-
veedLEEvihy.
unfamiliar (adj) - незна-
комый neeznahKOHMihy.
unfortunate; unhappy (adj)
неблагополучный nee-
blahgahpahLOOCHnihy.
unhappy; unfortunate (adj)
несчастный neeSHAHST-
nihy.
unimportant (adj) - неваж-
ный neeVAHZHnihy.
unintentional; involuntary
(adj) - невольный nee-
VOHL'nihy.
union - союз sahYOOS.
universal; general (adj) -
всеобщий fseeOHP-
shcheey.
university - университет
ooneeveerseeTYEHT.
unknown (adj) - неизвест-
ный neeeezVYEHSTnihy.
unnatural (adj) - неестественный neeyehstEHST-
veennihy.
unnoticable (adj) - неза-
метно neezahMYEHTnah.
unpleasant; disagreeable
(adj) - неприятный
neepreeYAHTnihy.
unprofitable; unfavorable
(adj) - невыгодный
neeVIHgahdnihy.
unripe; not mature (adj) -
незрелый neezRYEHIihy.

unsuccessful (adj) - безус-
пéшный beezoosPYEHSH-
nihy.
until - до dah.
untruth; falsehood; lie -
непрáвда neePRAHVdah.
unusual; uncommon (adj) -
необыкновéнный neeah-
bihknahVYEHNnihy.
up, upwards - (destination)
вверх vvyehrkh.
up; upwards (location) -
навéрх nahVYEHRKH.
upper; top (adj) - вéрхний
VYEHRKHneey.
uprising; revolt - восстáние
vahsSTAHneeyeh.
urgent; emergency (adj) -
срóчный SROHCHnihy.
urine - мочá mahCHAH.
use; benefit - пóльза
POHL'zah.
useful; helpful (adj) - по-
лéзный pahLYEHZnihy.
useless (adj) - бесполéзный
beespahlYEHZnihy.
usually - обы́чно ahBIHCH-
nah.

V

vacation (from work) -
óтпуск OHTpoosk.
vagina - влагáлище vlah-
GAHleeshcheh.
vaginal infection - воспа-
лéние влагáлища vahs-
pahLYEHneeyeh vlahGAH-
leeshchah.
vague; indefinite; uncertain
(adj) - неопределённый
neeahpreedeeLYOHNnihy.
valley - долúна dahLEEnah.
valuable (adj) - цéнный

TSEHNnihy.
value; worth - достóинство
dahsTOHeenstvah.
vanilla - ванúль vahNEEL'.
vaseline - вазелúн vahzee-
LEEN.
veal - теля́тина teelYAH-
teenah.
vegetable salad - винегрéт
veeneegRYEHT.
vegetables - óвощи OHvah-
shchee.
vegetarian - вегетариáнец
veegeetahreeAHNeets.
vein - жúла ZHEElah.
vein - вéна VYEHnah.
vending machine - автомáт
ahftahMAHT.
venison - олéнина ahLYEH-
neenah.
verb - глагóл glahGOHL.
very - óчень OHcheen'.
vest - жилéт zheeLYEHT.
victory - побéда pahBYEH-
dah.
village - селó seeLOH.
violence - насúлие nahSEE-
leeyeh.
virus - вúрус VEEroos.
visa - вúза VEEzah.
visible; clear; obvious -
вúдно VEEDnah.
vitamins - витамúны
veetahMEEnih.
vodka - вóдка VOHTkah.
voice - гóлос GOHlahs.
voltage - вольтáж vahl'-
TAHSH.
vote (to) - голосовáть
gahlahsahVAHT'.

W

waist - тáлия TAHleeyah.

wait (to) - ждать zhdaht'.
waiter - официант ahfee-
teeAHNT.
waitress - официантка
ahfeetseeAHNTkah.
wall - стена steeNAH.
wallet; billfold - бумажник
booMAHZHneek.
want (to) - хотеть khah-
TYEHT'.
war - война voyNAH.
warm (adj) - тёплый
TYOHPlihy.
warning - предупреждение
preedoopreezhDYEH-
neeyeh.
washing; laundry - стирка
STEERkah.
wasp - оса ahSAH.
watch - часы cheesih.
water - вода vahDAH.
watermelon - арбуз ahr-
BOOZ.
wave - волна vahlNAH.
we - мы mih.
weak (adj) - слабый SLAH-
bihy.
weather - погода pahGOH-
dah.
wedding - свадьба SVAHT'-
bah.
week - неделя neeDYEH-
lyah.
weekday - будний день
BOODneey dyehn'.
weight - вес vyehs.
well; healthy (adj) - здоровый zdahROHvihy.
well; well then - ну noo.
west - запад ZAHpaht.
western (adj) - западный
ZAHpahdnihy.
wet (adj) - мокрый MOHK-

rihy.
what - что shtoh.
wheat - пшеница psheh-
NEEtsah.
wheel - колесо kahleeSOH.
when - когда kahgDAH.
where - где gdyeh.
where to - куда kooDAH.
which - какой kahKOY.
whisper - шёпот SHOHpaht.
white (adj) - белый BYEH-
lihy.
who - кто ktoh.
whole; entire (adj) - целый
TSEHlihy.
why - почему pahcheeMOO.
wide; broad (adj) - широкий
sheeROHkeey.
widow - вдова vdahVAH.
widower - вдовец vdahv-
YEHTS.
width - ширина sheeree-
NAH.
wife - жена/супруга
zhehNAH/soopROOgah.
wild (adj) - дикий
DEEkeey.
wild game - дичь deech.
wind - ветер VYEHteer.
window - окно ahkNOH.
windshield - ветровое
стекло veetrahVOHyeh
steekLOH.
windy (adj) - ветреный
VYEHTreenihy.
wine - вино veeNOH.
winter - зима zeeMAH.
winter (adj) - зимний
ZEEMneey.
wish; desire - желание
zheeLAHneeyeh.
with; off; since - с se.
without - без byehs.

without transfer - беспере-
садочный beespeeree-
SAHdahchnihy.
woman - женщина ZHEHN-
shcheenah.
wonderful; miraculous
(adj) - чудесный
chooDYEHSnihy.
wooden (adj) - деревянный
deereevYAHNnihy.
woolen (adj) - шерстяной
shehrsteeNOY.
word - слово SLOHvah.
work - работа rahBOHtah.
work (to) - работать rah-
BOHtaht'
worker - рабочий rah-
BOHcheey.
workers' cooperative -
артель ahrTYEHL'.
world - мир meer.
worried, agitated (to be) -
волноваться vahlnah-
VAHtsah.
worried; troubled (adj) -
беспокойный bees-
pahKOYnihy.
worry, trouble, bother,
disturb (to) - беспокоить
beespahKOHeet'.
worse - хуже KHOOzheh.
worship service - бого-
служение bahgahsloo-
ZHEHneeyeh.
wound - рана RAHnah.
wounded (adj) - раненый
RAHNeenihy.
wrapping for mailing
printed matter -
бандероль bahndeeROHL'.
write (to) - писать pee-
SAHT'.
writer - писатель peeSAH-

teel'.
writing (in) - письменно
PEES'meennah.
wrong; incorrect (adj) -
неправильный nee-
PRAHveel'nihy.

X
x-ray - рентген
reentGYEHN.

Y
year - год goht.
years - лет lyeht.
yearly; annual (adj) -
ежегодный yeezheh-
GOHDnihy.
yellow (adj) - жёлтый
ZHOHLtihy.
yes - да dah.
yesterday - вчера fcheh-
RAH.
yesterday's (adj) - вчерашний fcheeRAHSHneey.
yogurt-like drink - кефир
keeFEER.
young (adj) - молодой
mahlahDOY.
young lady; waitress - девушка DYEHvooshkah.
young people - молодёжь
mahlahDYOHSH.
younger (adj) - младший
MLAHTsheey.
youth - юность YOOnahst'.

Z
zero - ноль nohl'.
zipper - молния
MOHLneeyah.
zoo - зоопарк zahahPAHRK.

226

The Moscow Subway System

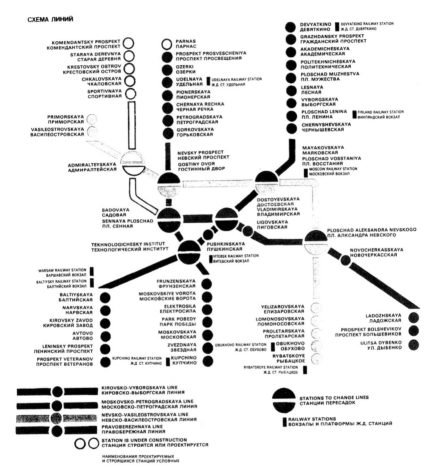

The St. Petersburg Subway System

AUDIO CASSETTES are available for use with this text

Enhance your language education and gain conversational skills with cassettes designed to accompany our *Phrasebook and Dictionary* series. The set of two tapes includes two hours of lessons to improve pronunciation, vocabulary, and grammar.

You can easily turn your phrasebook into a learning aide with these masterful tapes—handy for jogging or walking, the car, or home or classroom use.

UKRAINIAN Phrasebook and Dictionary
Cassettes to accompany:
ISBN 0-7818-0191-5 $12.95

RUSSIAN Phrasebook and Dictionary
Cassettes to accompany:
ISBN 0-7818-0192-3 $12.95

For ordering, contact your local bookstore, or send check or money order for the price of the item plus $4.00 shipping and handling for the first book, $.50 for each additional to Hippocrene Books, Inc., 171 Madison Avenue, New York, NY 10016.

Related Dictionaries from Hippocrene . . .

UKRAINIAN PHRASEBOOK AND DICTIONARY

Olesj Benyuch and Raisa I. Galushko

This invaluable guide to the Ukrainian language, including a 3,000 word mini-dictionary, provides situational phrases and vocabulary that's the most up-to-date available.

More than simply a dictionary, the book offers advice for ordering meals, making long-distance calls, shopping procedures, and countless tips to greatly enhance your visit to the new republic of Ukraine. Accompanying audio cassettes designed to increase vocabulary and pronunciation are also available.

205 pages   5 1/2 x 8 1/2 $9.95 paper   ISBN 0-7818-0188-5
Accompanying Cassettes: $12.95 set of two   ISBN 0-7818-0191-5

MASTERING RUSSIAN

Erica Haber

This imaginative course, designed for both individual and classroom use, assumes no previous knowledge of the language. The unique combination of practical exercises and step-by-step grammar emphasizes a functional approach to new scripts and their vocabularies. Everyday situations and local customs are explored variously through dialogues, drawings and photos. Cassettes are available for accompaniment with the lessons.

320 pages $14.95 paper   0-7818-0270-9

Mastering Russian Audio Cassettes
Set of two: $12.95   0-7818-0271-9

Mastering Russian Book and Cassettes Set
Set of cassettes & book: $27.50   0-7818-0272-5

RUSSIAN-ENGLISH/ENGLISH-RUSSIAN DICTIONARY OF BUSINESS AND LEGAL TERMS

Shane DeBeer

Compiled by a practicing attorney actively engaged in bi-lateral legal and business matters, this dictionary contains approximately 40,000 entries, a pronunciation guide, a table of abbreviations, an extensive bibliography and twelve commercial glossaries specializing in sectors from agriculture to oil to tourism.

800 pages   5 1/2 x 8 1/2 $39.95 cloth   ISBN 0-7818-0163-X